Tommaso Cherubini

INVISIBLE ECOLOGIES

FORMA

EDITORIAL PROJECT
Forma Edizioni srl
Florence, Italy
redazione@formaedizioni.it
www.formaedizioni.it

EDITORIAL DIRECTION
Laura Andreini

EDITORIAL STAFF
Maria Giulia Caliri
Monica Giannini
Arianna Iodice
Ester Menichelli

GRAPHIC DESIGN AND LAYOUT
Deepa Mary Parapatt
Isabella Peruzzi

PHOTOLITHOGRAPHY
Forma Edizioni

PROMOTION AND MARKETING
Stefano Baldassarri
Giulia Di Stefano

SPECIAL PROJECTS
Anna Mainoli

EXTERNAL RELATIONS
Irene Borsotti

TEXTS
© The authors

TRANSLATIONS
Katherine Fay

IMAGE CREDITS
Servizio Idrologico Regionale della Toscana –
Portal of the Directorate for Soil Defense
and Civil Protection
pp. 11, 17, 18

© N. Harth. Courtesy of The Josephine Ulrick
and Win Schubert Charitable Trust Collection
p. 12

Courtesy of Salvatore Iaconesi and Oriana Persico
p. 14

Courtesy of Yin Xiuzhen & Pace Gallery,
London, New York, Beijing
p. 15

© TorriniFotogiornalismo
p. 19

© CC BY-SA 3.0 by Sailko
p. 21

© Google Maps, 2025
p. 22 [B]

© Fototeca dei Musei Civici Fiorentini
p. 22 [C], p. 23

Unless otherwise specified:
© Tommaso Cherubini

INVISIBLE ECOLOGIES
Tommaso Cherubini
17.09-12.10.2025

A PROJECT PROMOTED BY
Forma Edizioni

ARTWORK
Tommaso Cherubini

WITH THE SUPPORT OF MIC
AND SIAE FOR THE PROGRAM
Per Chi Crea

IN COLLABORATION WITH
Association Rifugio Digitale E.T.S.
Publiacqua

ART DIRECTOR
Laura Andreini

PROJECT CURATED BY
Arianna Iodice
Ester Menichelli

SCIENTIFIC COORDINATION
Forma Edizioni

EXTERNAL RELATIONS
Irene Borsotti

TRANSLATIONS
Katherine Fay

TEXTS
© The authors

MUSIC
Corgiat, *Fllllow*, 2025

PRESS OFFICE AND COMMUNICATION
Association Rifugio Digitale E.T.S.
Niccolò Natali
Giulia Guasti

GRAPHIC AND SET-UP PROJECT
Deepa Mary Parapatt
Vitoria Muzi
Mattia Gerardi

VIDEO INSTALLATION
Associazione Rifugio Digitale E.T.S.

With the support of MiC and SIAE
for "Per Chi Crea" program

In collaboration with

With the contribution of

Table of contents

Invisible Ecologies is an artistic and theoretical project that arises out of the need to rediscover the silent presence of water, the element that for centuries has run through, supported and, occasionally, threatened Florence. The book, which accompanies the eponymous installation by Tommaso Cherubini, a visual and digital artist under 35 years old, is the record of that project, developed between generative art, ecology and artificial intelligence. The initiative was sponsored by Forma Edizioni, with the support of the Ministry of Culture and SIAE, as part of the "Per Chi Crea" program, launched to support and showcase young talents and support contemporary artistic research. The work finds its ideal dimension in Rifugio Digitale, the Florentine gallery devoted to artistic experimentation and to the technical processes of contemporary new media.

Using a transdisciplinary approach, and the language of digital art, the artist reproduces a conversation between nature, technology and sensory perception. At the center of the work is the unresolved, variable relationship between Florence and the Arno, a bond going back more than two thousand years that has shaped the urban landscape and the collective memory of the city. The project does not merely narrate the river, but reflects on what it has observed and preserved over the centuries, on the stories, events and changes still to be revealed.

The work develops through two complementary sections, *Decoding Signals* and *Encoding Visions*, weaving the apparently distant languages of scientific measurement and free imagination. The first section starts from a vast collection of hydrometric, pluviometric, and thermometric data provided by the Regional Hydrologic Service of Tuscany, which the artist has converted into visual configurations that are both dynamic and parametric. This process transforms natural phenomena into an emotional and sensory vocabulary, providing the conversation with numerical accuracy as well as the subjectivity of experience. The second section is open, instead, to a speculative exploration, in which artificial intelligence is used to generate alternative images of the landscape and history of the river, combining historical data, texts and archives with generative models. This landscape is not documented, but reinvented, filtered through a non-human perspective to become a realm of possibility.

The study of *Invisible Ecologies* reveals how the memory of the past does not follow a single, linear temporal flow, but is instead a field of fluid possibilities that can be rewritten and reinterpreted through multiple perspectives. Today, the complexity and quantity of data collected by sensors and using algorithmic means require that we develop new modes of reading and understanding them, moving beyond the traditional methods of classification and representation.

In this work, Tommaso Cherubini uses technology to dredge up the deepest, most stratified memories of the Arno River, uniting his study of the river's temperament to imaginary visions that give us a picture of the river as a living, breathing entity. This book delivers the results of that complex operation in editorial form, flanking the pictures, tables of data and algorithms with screenshots of processes and theoretical reflections, technical notes and intense historical narratives. From the earliest geological upheavals to the most recent floods, the Arno reveals its character as a narrator and sentient organism, a living archive of environmental and social tension that has shaped Florence as much as the human actions that have tried to dominate its river.

The tone is polyphonic and faceted, bringing social memory to scientific analysis, critical theory to visual imagination. In this contrast, technology becomes a tool to refine our ability to listen and restore affective depth to phenomena that are often invisible: the fluctuations of the water, the thresholds of risk, the environmental sentiments that the city perceives but that escape official measurement.

Invisible Ecologies does not seek a solution, or even a technical exaltation. Rather, it offers itself as an exercise of attention, a gentle suggestion that we should listen quietly to a river that, for centuries, has been watching us and that remembers us. If we listen carefully enough, it has something precious to tell us about how to live in this world.

Laura Andreini
Editorial Director of Forma Edizioni

Invisible Ecologies

Tommaso Cherubini

As is the case with each of my projects, *Invisible Ecologies* arises out of the ongoing tension between my work of technological research and my artistic sensitivity. Experimentation with visual tools, programming languages and artificial intelligence are inextricably woven into my need to understand the present time, the relationship between human beings and the environment, the pressure I feel to review habits and values and to tell stories that can still generate mutual awareness and possibly lead to change.

In the relationship between human beings and nature, I perceive a deeply rooted tendency to consider everything a tool, something to be used to produce, transport and grow. In a hyperactive system that does not leave itself time to reflect, this logic has become a habit: we seldom ask ourselves what it really means to live in an environment, to share space with other living beings. Nature becomes resource, raw material, functional support to our needs, rather than living space in which we are guests, an entity with which we can establish a relationship. The habit of not asking ourselves questions has encouraged the growth of a system that consumes and exploits carelessly, without providing anything in return. But perhaps it is not enough to seek technical or reparative solutions.

As I see it, what is necessary is a paradigm reversal: we need to feel like guests, rather than owners, and accept that we are only one of the many species that live on this planet. It's not a matter of idolatrizing nature, but of recognizing our limits and restoring value to things that exist for their own sake. It is time to recognize that we are part – not the center – of a finely-balanced system that is much bigger than us and that can exist without us. In that sense, I think we have to start to question much of what we are in the habit of doing, not only to find technical solutions to the problems we have created, but reassessing the actual conditions of our lifestyle. Too often we approach the environmental crisis with the same mental attitude that generated it, attempting to correct the effects without touching the underlying causes. We measure every choice in terms of our own benefit, our comfort, our economy, but only rarely to we ask ourselves if this is the way it is supposed to be, with this absolute human centrality. Perhaps that is where we can start to make a real change, if we can see ourselves not as the pinnacle but as the most fragile element, and at the same time the one with the greatest impact, in a complex system that requires equilibrium, responsibility and the ability to listen.

Invisible Ecologies is built on a dual outlook: on the one hand, profound, sincere respect for those who study and care for the Arno River with scientific skill and devotion. The river is the focus of research in this project, with its stories, its history, the tools and methods of its measurement, the complex scientific models that make its behavior predictable so that we can protect its balance and prevent dangerous situations. On the other hand, there is the urgent desire to abandon – even only for a moment – that anthropocentric vision that for centuries has made us the subject of every narrative, and try to listen to a different, deeper story that recognizes the ecological subjectivity of the river, viewing it as a living thing with its own sensations, intelligence and memories, capable of perceiving and reacting, of describing the world through its structures. I wanted to imagine, in the most radical and open way possible, what the river could see, hear and remember if it could articulate its fluid, multi-layered experience, if it could describe for us the time through which it has flowed and is still flowing.

What I was seeking in this project was a balance between the rigor of scientific analysis and the freedom of the imagination; between the objectivity of measurable data and the subjectivity of emotional and sensorial experience. I studied maps, graphs, hydrological databases, learning the numbers and codes that would guide me in understanding the invisible history of the river, its behavior and the changes it has undergone in time. Then I purposely chose to pause that analytical logic, to set it aside and make room for another type of study: I tried to forget what I knew, to let the river itself emerge as a living, complex personality. The work invites those who see it to do the same: to slow down, look with fresh eyes, listen without haste, and above all, let themselves be carried away on a perceptive current that blurs the line between reason and intuition, questioning our position in the world and the relationship we choose to establish with our surroundings.

A project like this can never take shape as a solitary endeavor. It is the result of a collective, ongoing process operating on many layers and fed daily through meetings, exchanges and shared information.

The world of New Media Art is profoundly interwoven with open-source culture, the universe of data and the physical and digital communities where professionals and enthusiasts exchange information, support and contaminate one another reciprocally. In this ecosystem, every tool, every method, every language becomes part of the commonwealth.

In this spirit, I want to express my gratitude to all those people who, over the years, have been part of my network: friends, colleagues, collaborators with whom I have shared workflows, models, experiments, bugs and solutions. Without their direct or indirect support, this project would never have been able to take shape.

Particular thanks go to those who, during the intense months of development, helped me concretely to overcome the inevitable technical glitches, preventing me from falling into the oblivion of the bugs – an oblivion that would have jeopardized the quality of the work itself: Eduard Tampu, Federica Sorba, Luca Montironi and Riccardo Franco Loiri.

I want to express my warmest thanks to the staff of Forma Edizioni and Rifugio Digitale, whose kindness, attention and professionalism accompanied every minute of the process of creation and realization of the exhibition.

Tommaso Cherubini was born in Macerata in 1995. He is a visual artist whose practice moves between generative AI, data processing, immersive environments and multimedia installations. His artistic research focuses on the translation of archives and historical databases into stratified visual experiences, giving shape to fluid narratives that explore the realms of memory, time and the landscape.

His goal is to highlight contemporary challenges and problems through New Media Art, revisiting historical archives and databases thanks to generative AI, and giving new life to data and pictures. It is clear in his projects that he sees art as an engine capable of arousing awareness and fostering behavioral change, giving rise to a process of advocacy and a new consciousness of social and environmental issues.

In addition to his personal projects, he works as a freelance professional in the sectors of digitalization of the cultural heritage, advertising and set design for live musical events. As a trainer, expert in generative AI, he cooperates with public schools and companies, and has spoken at conferences and webinars sponsored by institutions like ICOM – the International Council of Museums.

He has worked on projects for major cultural institutions like the Egyptian Museum of Turin, and for some of the most influential musical artists on the contemporary scene, including Lazza.

His work has been presented in a wide range of important contexts and places like Milan Design Week 2025, the Natural Science Museum of Turin, the Hunting Lodge of Stupinigi, the Planetarium of Turin and Graphic Days 2024.

Experimenting an Affective Methodology of Observation and Speculation

Arianna Iodice
Ester Menichelli

The project *Invisible Ecologies* took form with the idea of reflecting on the relationship between humans and their environment through an emblematic local case: the interaction between the Arno River and the city of Florence. Taking this historic and environmental bond as its starting point, the project engages in a broader study of the ways in which we observe, depict and interpret the ecosystem in which we live. The project is sponsored jointly by Forma Edizioni and Rifugio Digitale, both of which are active in the area and committed to the valorization of contemporary artistic practices. They are grateful for the contribution of Publiacqua, the company responsible for management of the integrated water service in the central portion of the Arno Valley, which covers the provinces of Florence, Prato, Pistoia and Arezzo. The project thus involves a significant environmental and territorial area of particular importance for Tuscany.

Invisible Ecologies came about, in fact, as an attempt to explore the deeply rooted bond in space between the environmental entity of the river and the material and symbolic extension of the human community that is the city, from the technological, environmental and perceptive viewpoints. This relationship, rich in the sediments of time, becomes the threshold from which to articulate a broader reflection, scalable from local to systemic, on the mode of ecological and technologically mediated perception of reality. In this context, the act of observation is not imagined as a neutral gesture, but as a technical, transformative process, capable of generating functioning abstractions. The act of measurement – number, curve, threshold – has operated through history as the primary active interface between the human and his surroundings, a system of access to reality that, in the very act of quantification, produces a distance, a transcription. The river, observed and interpreted by means of instruments of measurement, is detached from its organic existence and reassembled in a new form: a mental object, a data source, endowed with a life of its own. It is a computed entity that acts on reality, shaping spaces, policies, ideas. But it is just in this detachment that *Invisible Ecologies* chooses to insert itself, restoring to the informative dimension an affective and sensitive component it otherwise risks losing. The subject is extraordinary: thousands of years old and mobile like the Arno River, and the project reflects on how the languages of measurement and those of speculation can coexist, generating new forms of knowledge and relationships. It is no longer just an object to be observed, here the river becomes a surface to be crossed, an organism capable of expression, a vehicle of other possible ecologies. Starting from this deeply probing perception, the project proposes an affective method of observation and speculation. In the meaning which Spinoza gave to the term, "affect" is what moves us, what changes our state of mind: an intensity that binds bodies across space, generating transformations. Restoring affectivity to what has been measured does not mean rejecting technology, but giving it new meaning. It is not a matter of contrasting feelings and data, but of recognizing that every technical device is also a sensor and thus perceptive, and that every image is in itself a narrative. It means allowing the data, once extracted and viewed, to be inhabited by what they measure, restoring molecularity to the objects measured, with all their ability to act beyond the mathematical abstraction.

The structure of the work by Tommaso Cherubini reflects this tension. The two chapters that compose it – *Decoding Signals* and *Encoding Visions* – contrast with each other, using two languages, two explanatory logics. The former moves in the sphere of what the philosopher Yuk Hui defines, in his essay *Recursivity and Contingency* (2019) "*calculating reason*": computation as a method construction of variables, and variables as a method of interpreting reality. In the recursive repetition of measurements, in the comparison between timing, data and levels, there is an excess, a remainder. The river, even when reduced to mere signal, does not let itself run out. It is here that the second way appears: that of "speculative reason", which does not reject the data but exceeds them, bursts through them, bends them to imagine other ways of existing.

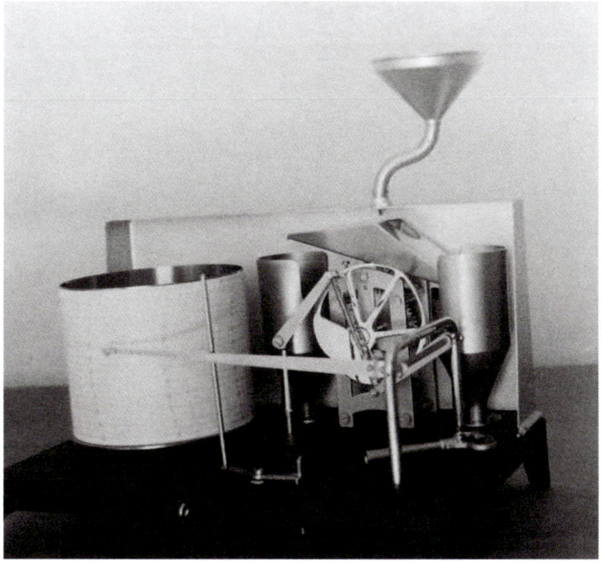

[A] Recording rain gauge from 1946, a historical device that traces atmospheric precipitation

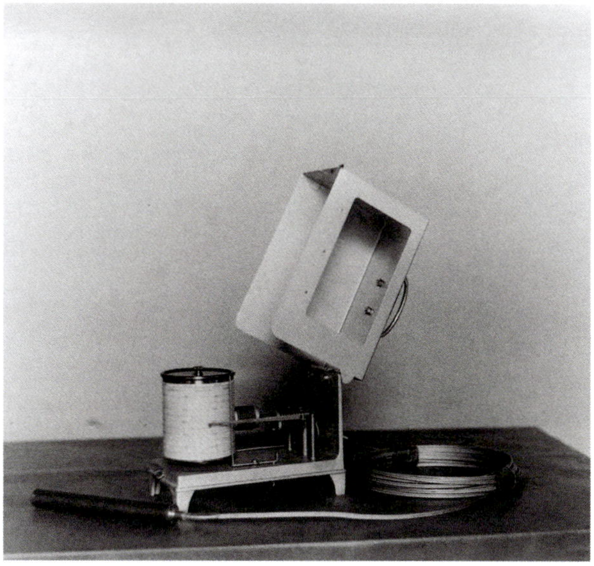

[B] Hydrometric instrument from 1946 for measuring temperature and river flow

Invisible Ecologies does not contrast analyses and imagination, but makes them reinforce one another. It processes data, extracting them from functional opacity and returning them as emotions, visual and perceptive experiences. It uses artificial intelligence not as an oracle but as a tool to disarticulate the anthropocentric view and imagine a different subjectivity of the river, another time, another memory. In this way, technology becomes a vehicle of speculation, not in the sense of abstract thought, but as a concrete exercise of possibility: a practice based on the phenomenon which goes beyond it. The audiovisual work wants to generate a shift in perception, establishing a critical distance between the concepts of appearance and those of possibility. It constructs situations using historical and technical data, playing on the perception of the possible to speculate on our own position within the system observed.

The real subject of this process is not nature, specifically, as a definite entity, but the relationship between it and us, its intensity, the mutual transformation experienced by both. It is view of nature at scale, evanescent, impossible to grasp entirely, a nature that we can only approach, evoke, compose. *Invisible Ecologies* does not claim to grasp it, but only to move toward and with it. It is an attempt to observe it and at the same time to participate in it, using various instruments – artistic, theoretical, scientific, analytic, digital – not to reveal a single truth, but to open the system to its profound instability.

In this sense, the affective method is not a formula, but a gesture, an act of listening. It is a way to build knowledge while remaining in touch with that which passes through it.

Using this new methodological perspective, Tommaso Cherubini produces an audiovisual work that relates visual languages to generative models. *Decoding Signals* re-elaborates the hydrometric, thermometric and pluviometric measurements of the Arno basin, drawn from the public archive of the Regional Hydrologic Service of Tuscany, through parametric displays constructed with TouchDesigner, a digital environment of visual development based on nodes whose form, color and movement follow an affective grammar inspired by Plutchik's Wheel of Emotions. *Encoding Visions* assigns to models of generative AI – including Stable Diffusion, Runway, Luma AI and Sora – the task of shaping non-anthropocentric environmental views, based on the phenomena observes, historical data, pictures and texts drawn from the archives. The generative models do not act here like arbitrary generators, but as devices for transfiguration: they upload the input to open it onto possible trajectories, settings that blur the borders between what has been and what might be. It is here that we see the play between probability and possibility, in which our perception shifts from the data to the relationship, and the river emerges as a subjective entity capable of renegotiating our position within the system observed.

Through this dual articulation, the work creates a tension between measurement and imagination, observation and participation, without eliminating the distance produced by technology, but inhabiting it like transformative space. In this passage, the organic aspect is not excluded: it emerges as an excess, something that escapes computation but that passes through the codes, reactivating the data as relational and perceptive form.

Connection Through Visualization: The Archive as Art Form for the Production of Sensory Memories

Daniela Cotimbo
Founder and curator of Re:humanism

In an essay written in 2019, the philosopher, Timothy Morton, analyzes the prerogatives of an ecological way of thinking, which he introduces by inviting the reader to take the radical step of going beyond the concept of "nature" as a benevolent, faceless agent to be viewed fondly from a nostalgic perspective. According to the author, nature has become a plastic reproduction of the real thing, its mythology buried in a typical worldview of sedentary, agricultural civilizations which contribute to consolidate both the concept of possession and the illusion of an inexhaustible availability of resources. Increasingly extreme climate events are unquestionable evidence of the fallacy of this belief. Morton would have us return, instead, to an ecological way of thinking according to which interconnection unfolds like a fan of demands, touching the borders between human and artificial, questioning the fleeting essence of what we call the individual. In this way, the philosopher opens us up to a series of issues that frame ecology as a set of ecosystemic relationships, including some that have artificial agents. In the same text, the author also refers explicitly to art, showing how it is not the ecological subject that determines the validity of an artistic reflection, so much as the process leading to it and the interconnections that link the environment to its form.

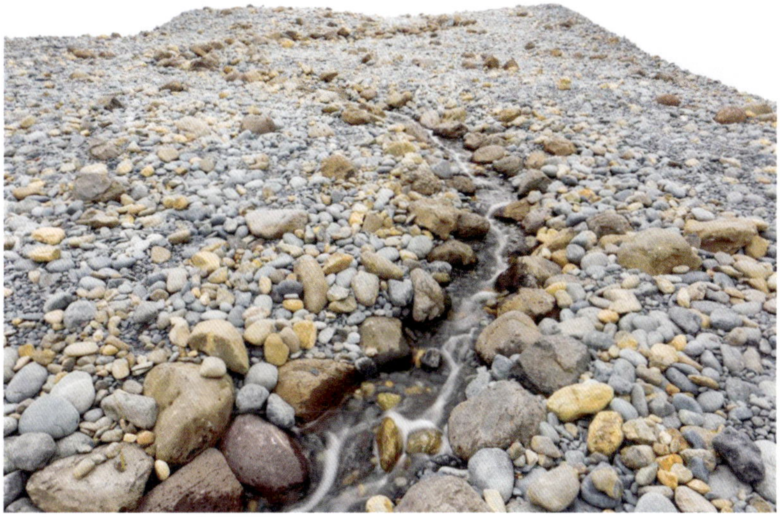

[A] Olafur Eliasson, *Riverbed*, 2014, QAGOMA, Brisbane, Queensland, Australia

More cautious in refuting the concept of nature is the art historian T. J. Demos, who believes that excluding it is not an option, as this would exclude, for example, the crucial role of nature in the rebirth of indigenous and environmentalist activism based on the full integration of human beings into the natural world, of which they are, indeed, an integral part. Demos has the merit of having reviewed the history of environmental art in three significant periods, starting from the Sixties and ending with his current observations, which are an approach to *Political Ecologies* that is based on the development of strategies, actions and claims capable of linking environmental challenges to those of global justice.

There are so many practical examples we could cite in this connection, especially if we focus on those connected to the importance of listening to our fluvial environments. We can certainly point significantly to *Washing River* (1995), by the Chinese artist Yin Xiuzhen, who created the work, consisting of ten cubic meters of blocks of ice, using water drawn from the Funan River at Chengdu, at a time when it was terribly polluted. Passers-by were invited to "wash" those blocks with sponges, while they gradually melted, restoring the water to the river. Another interesting example is the *Water Ekiden-Manosegawa River Art Project* (1999), by the Japanese artist Ichi Ikeda. The project was centered on the Manosegawa, a river that extends for about twenty-six kilometers south of the islands of Kyushu in Japan and that, because of the discharge into it of waste water from industrial plants and hog raising farms, had undergone severe pollution. Faced with this situation, the artist chose to involve the local population actively, developing an approach based on collective responsibility that, after years of community discussion, led to the creation of four settlements distributed along the course of the river, with the goal of creating a network of "water stations" designed to collect and manage different types of water resources: rainfall, spring water and treated water for irrigation.

On a more evocative level, however, we have *Riverbed* (2014–15), a work by the celebrated Danish artist, Olafur Eliasson, who transformed the space of a museum into an artificial fluvial landscape, translating the relationship between bodies of water, climate change and sensory perception into an immediate physical experience.

If ecological thought arises as a form of interdependence between different agents, any attempt to adapt the old ideas of nature to a more contemporary understanding from the cultural standpoint has to approach them from a background of knowledge of the technological infrastructures involved. These consist not only of tangible elements but also of cognitive structures which, today, must occupy a central role in global consideration.

For the American artist and scholar, James Bridle, technology is profoundly interwoven into our environments and our relationships with other living creatures. Bridle rejects the modern idea that it is a neutral extension of human thought, or a means for dominating nature. On the contrary, he supports the idea that every form of technical innovation arises within a world already populated by relationships with the environment and with the other living beings and social systems. This means that, framing an ecological mindset, as stated in the beginning by Morton, involves questioning our role in a complex global system in which human, animal, organic and artificial elements all participate and interact.

In this connection, media theoretician Jussi Parikka develops some particularly interesting ideas about *media ecologies* from a materialistic standpoint. Contrary to more metaphorical interpretation, he insists on the importance of the physical aspect of the media, in particular the fact that digital devices are made using mineral resources, produce waste and have an ecological and geopolitical history. In *A Geology of Media,* the author observes that our technological devices are made of raw materials extracted from the earth, like copper, lithium, coltan. At the end of their useful life they become *e-waste*, electronic waste, and are often exported to the countries of the global south. Following the same path as *media archaeology,* Parikka claims that art does not merely represent, but manipulates, interrogates, dismantles and reassembles the media. In this sense, artists become archeologists of media fossils: they recover, disassemble and reinterpret technological objects and data, bringing to light stratifications of time, geopolitical conflicts, ecological interdependencies. In continuity with the authors we have mentioned thus far, Parikka considers art a form of non-linear, speculative thought that can highlight the profound stories of the media, the extractive chains, the toxic extracts, and also the alternative possibilities of relationships with the world. The author devotes a specific reflection to the subject of archives, suggesting that they could become speculative spaces, capable of triggering critical thought and political imagination by giving shape to significant counter-histories.

The practice of viewing archives as sites of cultural redefinition developed, in particular, in the Seventies, in response to the Fordian model and to the need to explore different genealogies that investigated the limits of a linear time-frame. What grew out of this, according to the curator and art critic Marco Scotini was the idea of the past as a possible space to probe, distort and rewrite depending on different subjectivities and temporal viewpoints.

Today, work on archives is rendered even more stratified by the spread of technologies for the collection and processing of data. Sensors and predictive algorithms draw on a vast quantity of data, the collection and classification of which are no longer exclusive human prerogatives. The projects of algorithmic generation are comparable to ancient cartographic endeavors, that attempted to bring order to a complex reality. They probe these enormous archives in search of a substantial paradigm shift. For the media theoretician Lev Manovich, *Data Visualization* is not based exclusively on the calculation of numerical data but on the analysis of texts, pictures, sounds and other media content and on the networks of relationships among them. In this view, artists who work with data are not interested merely in making them legible, but in activating connections between distant worlds. It has reached a point that we can see the outlines in time of a chain of practices that examine data

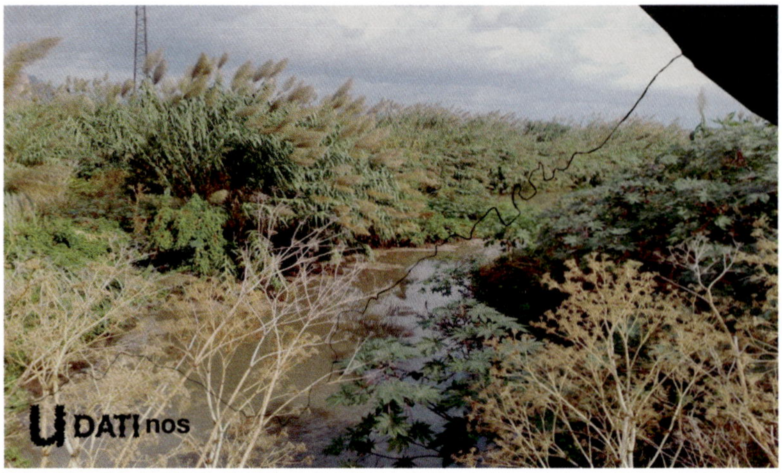

[B] Salvatore Iaconesi and Oriana Persico, U-DATInos, 2020, Mare Memoria Viva Urban Ecomuseum, Palermo

and the complexity of phenomena as a model we can use to rewrite the history of the archives themselves.

The scholar, Saverio Macrì, who, in turn, cites Gilbert Simondon, believes that this type of practice refers back to the idea of activating that process of *identification* whereby the individual characteristics of each of us do not precede our relationships but are the direct consequence of them. Along the lines of this interpretative filter, the artistic process that exploits the visualization of the data appears as a joint presence of objects and events, a critical process of development that, by combining different experiences opens the way to new possibilities, rewriting sentient memories.

We see this, for example in *U-DATInos* (2020), the project by Salvatore Iaconesi and Oriana Persico which has as its focus the Oreto River in Palermo, infamous for its deterioration due to the presence of intensive waste disposal and illegal sewage discharges. *Udàtinos* in Greek means aquatic, made of water, and in some way reminds us of the fluid nature, not only of the river, which is the subject of observation, but also of the data at which the word itself seems to hint.

The artists involved students, citizens and scientists in a collection of data based on the participatory action that they replicated with sounds and lights and the creation of a meditative space in which to listen to the river and hear its needs.

The poetic potential of visualizing data was then added to the still unexplored potential of *latent spatiality*, the dimension implicit in today's generative artificial intelligence, which led to a further leap forward in the transformation of data into perceptible experience. With access to voluminous datasets, the so-called large language models of artificial intelligence process statistical patterns and generate content that is the reflection of the collective electronic unconscious. The repetitive media focus on reality merges with the evocative potential of natural language that, using special prompts – textual commands – re-evokes fragments of collective memories.

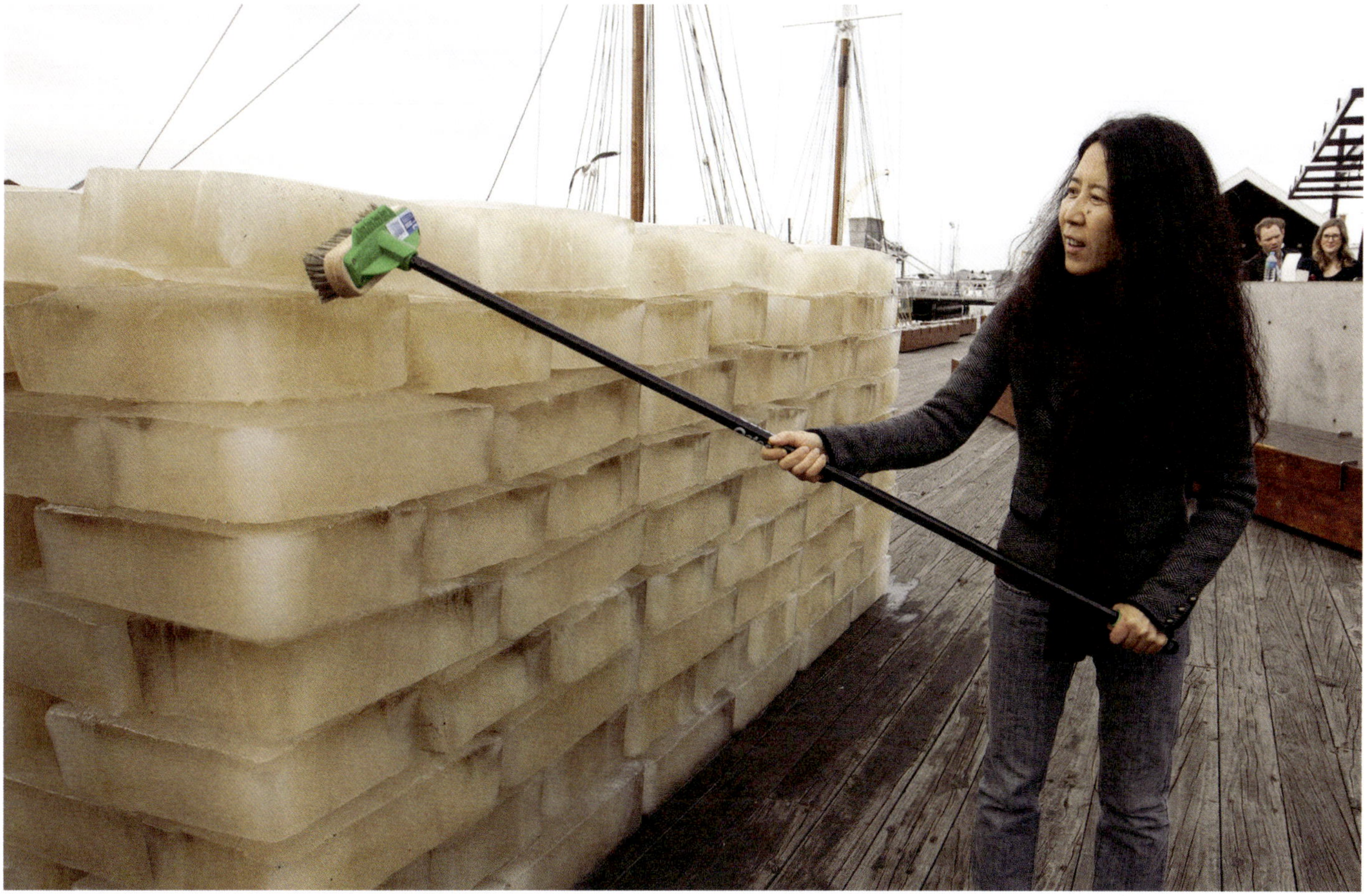

[C] Yin Xiuzhen, *Washing River*, 1995

For Joanna Zylinska, theoretician and artist, the desire to restore vitality and fluidity to data can be seen as a form of animism, an attitude that has always accompanied our relationship with the media (we only need to think of cinema, for example) and that assists us in developing new forms of awareness with regard to the reality of our environment.

Thus, in *Invisible Ecologies*, Tommaso Cherubini explores the memory of the Arno River, whose history is presented as a stratification of personal and collective reminiscences, at times traumatic, that thanks to artificial intelligence rise to the surface and acquire new vitality. On the one hand, the artist involves us in an emotional labor of listening to the river, translating its movements into an emotional language that reaches the deepest levels of consciousness through flows of data, color and sounds. On the other, he exploits the visual archive that feeds the large language models of generative AI pertaining to the river, to offer access to shared visions, attempting to interpret the subjectivity of the river itself. In this reciprocal exchange, the river and those who navigate it find points of contact: they meet on a sensitive border that becomes a common heritage. They may not speak the same language, but even so, they are able to connect, inserting themselves fully in the train of ecological thought and interrogating technology as the perceptible pathway. In this way, the work links us to a constellation of practices born of the need to reawaken new forms of environmental awareness, capable of speaking directly to our sensitivity and filling that gap in sensitivity that seems to distinguish our mode of inhabiting contemporary life, in this hyperconnected world.

BIBLIOGRAPHY

→ Timothy Morton, *Come un'ombra dal futuro. Per un nuovo pensiero ecologico*, Aboca edizioni, Sansepolcro, 2019.
→ T. J. Demos, *Decolonizing Nature: Contemporary Art and the Politics of Ecology*, Sternberg Press, London, 2016.
→ James Bridle, *Modi di essere. Animali, piante e computer: al di là dell'intelligenza umana*, Rizzoli, Milan, 2022.
→ Jussi Parikka, *A Geology of Media*, University of Minnesota Press, Minneapolis, 2015.
→ Marco Scotini, *L'inarchiviabile. L'archivio contro la storia*, Meltemi editore, Sesto San Giovanni, 2022.
→ Lev Manovich, *What is visualisation?*, in *Visual Studies*, vol. 26, 2011.
→ Saverio Macrì, *Feeling Data: New Perspectives for the Aesthetic Experience*, in Antonio Branca, Andrea Mecacci and Francesco Valagussa (edited by), *Kant's Geographies*, "Aisthesis" series, vol. 18, no. 2, Mimesis, Sesto San Giovanni, 2024.
→ Joanna Zylinska, *The Shadow Animism of AI* in Antonio Somaini (edited by), *The world Through AI*, JBE Books, Paris, 2025.

The Arno Renewed, a River to Experience

Erasmo D'Angelis
President of the Foundation
Earth Water Agenda

The birthplace of the legendary river is a little spring on the slopes of Mount Falterona, at an altitude of 1,372 meters (4,500 feet) in the wonderful Foreste Casentinesi National Park, protected by the dense growth of splendid fir and beech trees. The river flows over 241 kilometers (150 miles) until it reaches the Tyrrhenian Sea at Bocca d'Arno in Marina di Pisa. Its first water came burbling down prehistoric cliffs that seem sculptured by Michelangelo, alongside the verses of Dante engraved on a marble plaque:

> Through Tuscan country speeds apace a stream from Falterona issuing, and a hundred miles contenteth not its race. This body from the banks of it I bring. To tell you who I am, since yet hath been but little noised my name, were a vain thing [...].

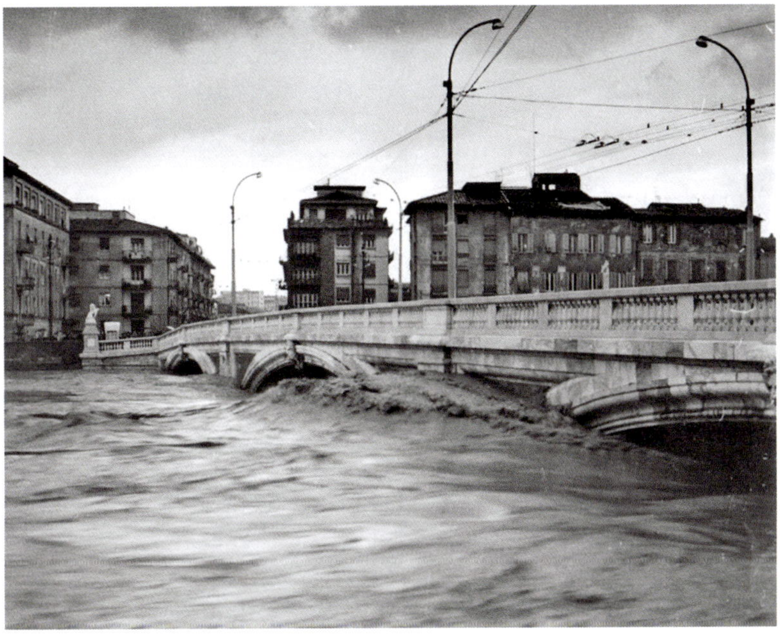

[A] Historical photo of Ponte Solferino (Pisa) during the 1966 Florence flood, documenting the Arno River overflow

> 'If my mind rightly pierce within that screen to thy intention', then to me replied he who spoke first, 'Tis Arno thou dost mean'.

At the time of the Etruscans, the Olympus of Fal Trona, the Throne of the Gods, was located at the source, and was the equivalent of the oracle for the temples dedicated to Zeus Olympus in Athens, or Apollo in Delphi on Mount Parnassus. The Etruscans honored the god of the Arno by leaving small gifts and, in fact, about 600 statuettes of divinities have been dredged out of the nearby lake of Ciliegeta, including representations of Diana, Mars and the demigod Hercules, one of whose proverbial tasks was to sail up the Arno as far as its source. The word Arno itself is very ancient: its origins lie deep in the prehistoric shadows of the early Indo-European colonists and their root word *er/or* meaning "to set in motion", "to shake", and certainly reflected its impetuous nature. But at its source it is a merry little stream sparkling in the shafts of sunlight that penetrate its robust vegetation. As it merges with other little streams, it grows in size and strength, sustained by the steady breeze that blows through the fragrant underbrush.

We don't know exactly when the *Big Bang* of the Arno came about, but we understand its hydrographic profile. We know that for thousands of years it flowed into the paleolake of the Upper Valdarno that covered the vast area with its Jurassic borders south of Florence and all the way to Arezzo, where a tributary flowed into the Lakeland basin of the Val di Chiana, supplying the early Tiber River all the way to the sea. In the Pleistocene era, around 300,000 years ago, after a number of violent earthquakes and years of fluvial sedimentation and erosion, the Arno experienced a change of course and its waters began to flow through the Pontassieve narrows, into the paleolithic lake on the Florentine plane at the Masso della Gonfolina, a rocky cliff now located near Lastra a Signa which acted like a dam on the river. Leonardo understood this evolutionary process and, in his *Atlantic Code*, he described the cliff as follows:

> [...] in the form of a high barrier, it held the river back so that, before it could flow into the sea [...] it formed two great lakes, of which the first is where today we see the end of the city of Florence, with Prato and Pistoia; Mount Albano followed the rest of the riverbank up to where now the town of Serravalle lies.

The mountain's base was cut through by fluvial erosion about five thousand years ago, and as the by then not-so-little stream forced its way through the gravel in search of the sea, it settled into its current bed.

The history of our river is as surprising as its natural environment. In the cities where it passed, history, art and culture flourished, while at the same time, its first waters were home to little brown trout, barbel and chub. The silence of the surrounding forest was broken only by the distant rustle of deer and boar, and the mating calls of the other creatures that reigned supreme in one of the most wild and beautiful parts of the country. Amid the backdrop of mountains and hills, with their towers and castles, fortresses and outposts, charming medieval villages and prosperous little towns, with their farmlands and pastures, the river gathered up 14 major tributaries and countless minor ones until it reached the sea, creating a vast river basin of 8,200 square kilometers (3,166 square miles).

It is a river of very ancient civilizations, which rose at the time of the first settlements in India along the banks of the Indo River, in China around the Yellow River, in Egypt along the banks of the Nile, in Mesopotamia between the Tigris and the Euphrates.

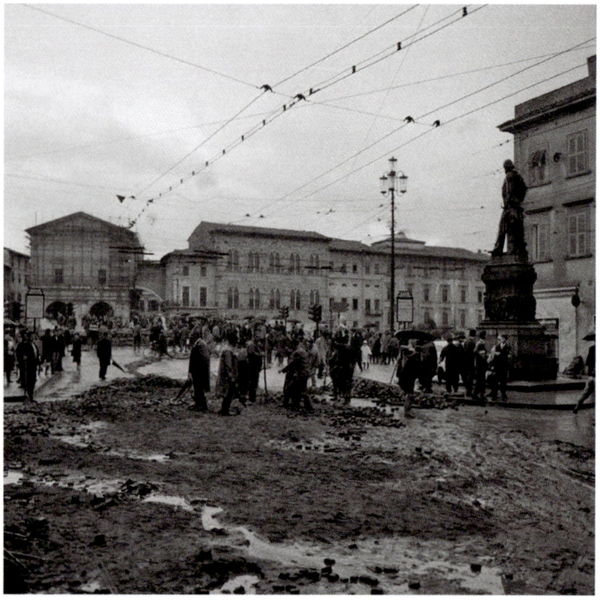

[B] Piazza Garibaldi (Pisa) during the 1966 flood. Citizens and volunteers working to remove mud left by the overflowing Arno River

Although its length is not comparable to those majestic waterways, Poliziano's *Rivo* was already destined to flow in the imagination and in the cultural and artistic veins of the world. When it became tragically famous in the Sixties of the past century for the worldwide media coverage of its flood, it moved and mobilized people everywhere.

It is unfortunately true that the Arno has a rather unruly, impetuous character. It goes from exceptionally dry periods in case of droughts or scarcity of rainfall, to tumultuous floods with catastrophic outcomes. Only one serious flood was considered providential when it occurred, because it happened at a time when Rome was at war with Carthage and contributed, in the spring of 217 B.C., to defeat Hannibal's army. Indeed, the Carthaginian general almost died himself in the flood when, after crossing the Pyrenees and the Alps in winter with thousands of infantry and horsemen, as well as 37 elephants of which only one had survived, he was trapped in the muddy waters of the Florentine marshlands where, as Titus Livius reports, "the Arno in those days was in fuller spate than usual". They fished Hannibal out half dead, and tied him to the surviving elephant, but a severe infection left him almost deaf and blind in one eye. The remaining eye would forever reflect the memory of that horrendous experience.

From the first great flood described in 1177 to the most recent, in 1966, the river has swamped Florence and other communities along its course 56 times, overflowing its banks, and 8 times with "waves similar to those on the ocean, in the raging of the storm", as the medieval historian Giovanni Villani wrote. The terrible years were 1333, 1547, 1557, 1589, 1740, 1758, 1844, 1966. Dante, on December 5, 1288, provides this excellent report of a flood in Canto V of Purgatory:

> When day was spent, the valley he spread o'er, from Pratomagno to the mountain chain with cloud, and made the sky above to lour, so that the charged air changed to water: rain came down and to the rivulets compelled all of it, so that the earth could not contain. And as it merged and into torrents swelled, so swiftly to the royal stream it presst that nothing its impetuous rush withheld.

In 1503, Leonardo studied it at length and drew maps and zones of "routes" writing that "it floods because it is unable to dispose speedily of the water that from the Val d'Arno rushes down to it". Despite some serious misgivings, in that year he accepted the incredible challenge proposed by Niccolò Machiavelli, Chancellor of the Florentine Republic, to design a titanic duplicate of the course of the river, an Arno-bis that would flow around the city to save it from the floods, drain the swamps and deprive its arch-enemy Pisa of water, while gifting Florence with a Mediterranean port of its own. Leonardo drew a plan with detailed maps and an extremely accurate view from above – it is the same route taken by the current A11 Firenze-Mare motorway. The excavation works got under way in Florence at dawn on August 22, 1504, with the labor of 1,000 convicts, guarded by hundreds of soldiers. But the ditch soon flooded and caved in on the poor diggers, putting an end to the project. Florence's conquest of Pisa in 1509 made the duplication of the Arno militarily superfluous, at any rate.

Today we need only read on the walls of countless buildings in the city and, the many open air museums of historic floods, the marks, colors, plaques and stones in perennial memory of the heights reached by the past floods. Sometimes several plaques are lined up one above and the eye jumps quickly to the heights reached on November 4, 1966, by the first widely televised flood that mobilized people all over the world and is still remember as the flood that brought the "Mud Angels", thousands of young volunteers who rushed to Florence to save the city and its people.

The Arno is now, as never in the past, a fluvial ecosystem in equilibrium with the environments it passes through. In the past, it was a powerful source of energy, turning the wheels of the mills, as now it drives the wheels of hydroelectric turbines.

It's perfectly all right to joke about the highs and lows typical of our free-flowing rivers, however, why not? A rather dandified elderly American thought so in 1904, and enjoyed walking along the shore and chatting in his broken Italian with the fishermen, washerwomen and sand diggers. In his book, *The Innocents Abroad* he wrote:

> It is a great historical creek with four feet in the channel and some scows floating around. It would be a very plausible river if they would pump some water into it. They all call it a river, and they honestly think it is a river [...]. They even encourage the delusion by building bridges over it.

So wrote Mark Twain, the famous American writer and humorist, who chanced to visit the city at a time when the river was unusually low. He was nevertheless charmed by it and, If he were to come back now, he'd be satisfied to see a great wide river always full of flowing water "pumped" since the end of the past century from a vast artificial mountain lake called, Bilancino.

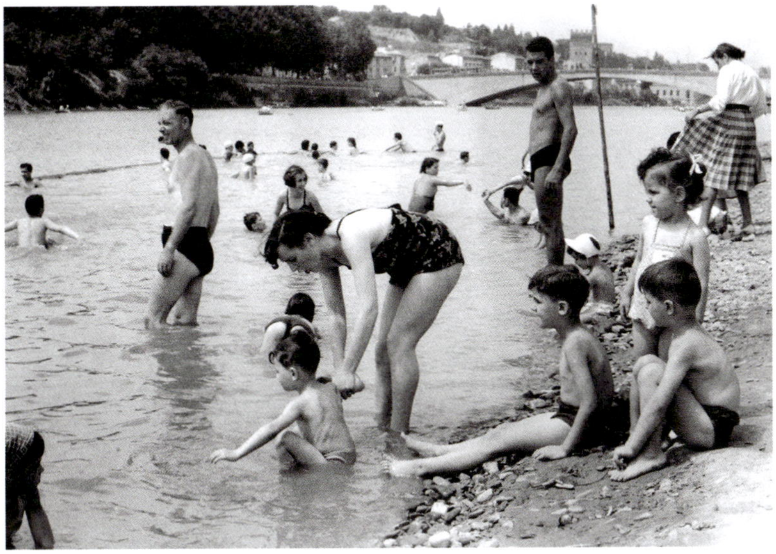

[C] Negative no. 2671, 1953, *Bathing in the Arno*. Historical photograph depicting moments of bathing in the Arno River at a historic Florentine bathing site

An even newer system has added four detention basins above Florence, at Pizziconi, Restone, Prulli and Leccio-Burchio and has plans to increase the depth of the reservoir at Levane, for which financing was allocated in 2017 as part of the government's Technical Structure of the "Italiasicura" Mission. Toward Pisa, he would see the detention tank at Roffia, and the spillway channel that starts from Pontedera, deviating a portion of the Arno in flood for a distance of 28.3 kilometers (17.5 miles) and discharging into the Tyrrhenian Sea below Pisa, protecting the city and its environs. The Arno Basin District Authority, the Tuscan Region with its agency for environmental protection, ARPAT, and the Office of Civil Protection constantly monitor the infrastructures and conditions of the Arno and its tributaries.

When it comes to bridges, indeed, the Arno is second to none – an architectural catalog of crossings. To date, 85 have been built, and the next one will be the tramway bridge at the south end of the city. They are admirable infrastructures, built by Romans on Etruscan remains, and later medieval bridges, first in wood and later in stone. The most iconic is the Ponte Vecchio, the "oldest" of all, which on its upper level connected two buildings, unique in all the world, along the ancient *Corridore*, a masterpiece of art and engineering 1 kilometer (0.6 miles) long, built by Giorgio Vasari in just five months, between March and August, 1565, to link Palazzo Vecchio to Palazzo Pitti. The Medici duke, Cosimo I, asked him to build a safe passage from the ducal residence to the political and administrative center of the city.

Thanks to the colossal and still ongoing labors of Publiacqua, under the leadership of Nicola Perini, the company has succeeded in putting an end to two dramatic decades in which the recurrent inexorable droughts left central Tuscany without drinking water. The water of Lake Bilancino and the other new infrastructures is constantly monitored and subject to quality control at the Anconella aqueduct, one of the most modern in the world. The past crises of the water supply are only a memory now, and the river that flows into the aqueduct is always full of water, with stable loads that have the effect of reducing the risk of flooding. Another decisive action was the construction and expansion of the sewage networks and water treatment plants. Today, the Anconella delivers 82 million cubic meters of drinking water a year into a network of pipelines over 7,000 kilometers (4,350 miles) long in 63 municipalities, to the most outlying houses on the mountains and hills. The pipelines also deliver it chilled, natural or carbonated to 115 drinking fountains – after installing the first of its kind in Italy in 2010 – to plazas and parks. Over 250,000 chemical and biological tests are performed annually to guarantee the maximum quality of the water at all times, everywhere.

In Italy, for the first time, the waters of a major river no longer receive urban and industrial waste. This achievement was possible thanks to the commitment of the municipal administrations, and to the technical and technological capabilities developed by the waterworks along the river, especially Publiacqua, in the central Tuscan portion.

For that reason, the Arno can now be indicated as a European fluvial model of biodiversity, a mixture of natural phenomena with a wide variety of organisms like fish, invertebrates, aquatic plants and algae. They are beautiful to look at, especially in the urban sections. All this makes the Arno a much-beloved river, capable of surprising and delighting us. Florentines can enjoy it and take pleasure in a cooling dive into its protected natural fluvial pools, where the water reflects the iconic sites of its urban crossings, adding Florence to the list of European cities where swimming in the river is allowed, from Paris to Zurich, Amsterdam, Copenhagen and Vienna. In a country like Italy where it is possible to count on the fingers of one hand the urban areas that attempt to give their citizens clean, enjoyable rivers, it is time to rediscover the most extended ecosystem of Tuscany, the vital ecological infrastructure that is its long waterway, and call attention to it as a river that is more than ever clean and safe and can even be enjoyed as a modern *theater of fireworks* or installations of events like those organized in the 14th century by Buonamico di Martino, known as Buffalmacco, a legendary organizer of parties on the river. Isn't it true, after all, that the river is the oldest evidence of our civilization?

Memories and Floods, a Troubled Relationship Between the River and the City

Riccardo Fanti
Full Professor of Applied Geology, Department of Earth Sciences, University of Florence

Relations between cities and rivers are almost always described using "passive" descriptions and verbs: the river "runs through" the city, or the city "is built on the banks" of the river, as if the two organisms were separate and independent neighbors, barely acknowledging each other. Cities and their rivers (or rivers and their cities) are more like marriages, with intense, intimate, lengthy, tumultuous histories, distinguished by the obvious spread of buildings and bridges, but also by events and transformations that the river observes from an eternal and exclusive point of view.

Florence, the Arno and their relations are a paradigm of all this, with a few distinctive features that make their story particularly interesting from the historic and technical standpoint, starting from the geological and geomorphological aspects. Observing the Florentine plain, it will immediately be apparent that the Arno does not flow, as most rivers do, directly through the middle of the city but, particularly in the urban portion, it is "relegated" to the south side, up against the southern hills that close, in a spectacular and unique manner, the urban perimeter of an extraordinary city. These geographical features are the result of a geological history in which the plain that contains Florence was formed in the Plio-Pleistocene era, not by the Arno but by what are now several of its tributaries, coming from the hills to the north, particularly the Mugnone. It was only during the Pleistocene Age that the geological dynamics of the Appennines led to the regional drainage that formed a paleo-Arno, initially on the Florentine plain and later "pushed" south by upward thrusts of the plain caused by tectonic movements during the latter part of the Quaternary(01).

The outcome is that of a geographical and urban asymmetry, which is reflected in the toponymy: in Florence, regardless of where one happens to be, "this side of the Arno" and "that side of the Arno" indicate the right and left banks, testifying to the substantial preeminence of the former, where, in fact, the history of the city began. After its foundation, another thousand years would pass before the city of Florence would effectively reach the left bank, marking the start of its effective and turbulent relationship with the Arno.

The Roman city was, in fact, founded on the plain, on a slightly elevated area north of the Arno, where the river was – and still is – rather narrow, plausibly making it easy to cross at fords and bridges. The early Florentines probably found it more logical to consider the Mugnone the city's waterway, using it in various ways as a defensive element and hydraulic reference. In time, the Arno became the city's fluvial highway, however, and at the same time a critical element for the construction of its road system, as it was necessary to provide a fixed crossing with a bridge toward the southern part of the city. Archeological and historical research indicates that already in the 1st century A.D., there was a bridge at the point where the Ponte Vecchio now stands(02), and it has occupied that spot in its current form at the center of the urban scene since the middle of the 14th century, when it was rebuilt after the flood of 1333.

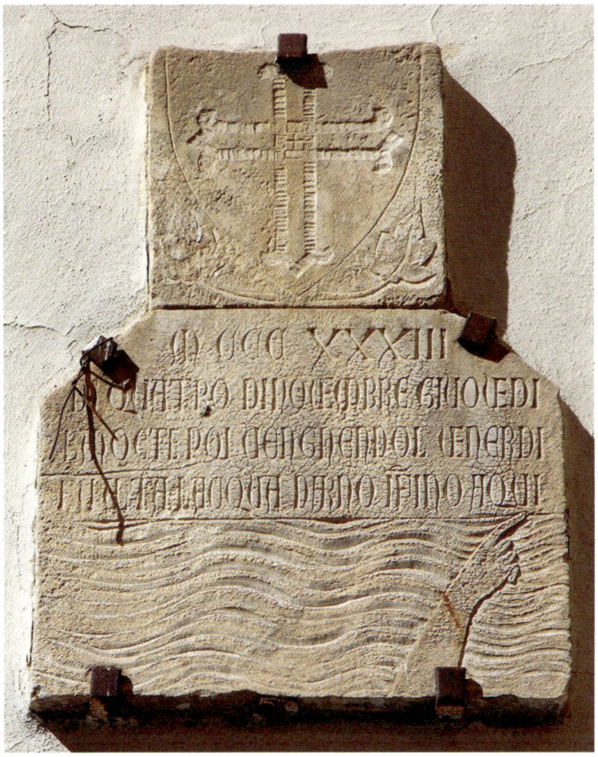

[A] Stone plaque from 1333 located in Via Giancarlo Setti, Florence. The plaque marks the water level reached by the November 4, 1333 flood at Canto dei Soldani, in the Santa Croce district: the inscription above the hand indicates the water's height and reads "MCCCXXXIII: On the night of Thursday, November 4, followed by Friday, the Arno River rose to this height"

Already in the previous century, however, relations between the city and its river had become stable and mature, as evidenced by the construction of at least three more bridges (Ponte Nuovo, later renamed Ponte alla Carraia, built in 1218; Ponte Rubaconte, later called Ponte alle Grazie, built in 1237; and Ponte Santa Trinita, 1252). The history of the bridges of Florence continues through the centuries, with repeated episodes of destruction and reconstruction, up to the tragic consequences of the Nazi fury in 1944. But the main villain of the story was the Arno itself, with its floods and disastrous

(01) Massimo Coli, Pietro Rubellini, *Geological anamnesis of the Florence area, Italy*, in *Z. Dt. Ges. Geowiss. (German J. Geosci.)*, 164 (4), pp. 581–589.

(02) Pasquino Pallecchi, Marco Benvenuti, G. Carlotta Cianferoni, *The water in the development of Florence (central Italy) between the Roman and the Renaissance ages: the resource and the hazard*, in *Il Quaternario, Italian Journal of Quaternary Sciences*, 23 (2Bis), 2010, pp. 323–334.

surges that damaged the bridges and caused their collapse, so that they had to be rebuilt or repaired over and over.

Floods were what marked the relationship between Florence and the Arno, with a myriad of direct and indirect effects on the history of the city, in a complicated dance between dynamic, geomorphological, hydraulic, urban and architectural elements(03,04).

Traditionally, the flood of 1177 is considered to have been the first great flood of Florence, but there is no doubt that even in the preceding centuries the river had flooded during its seasonal exceptional peaks over large areas along its course, spreading over a vast and mobile area which illustrates the peculiar morphology typically associated with rivers and their characteristic movement and deposits of solid material.

The current aspect of the river, proceeding in a relatively straight line bordered by weirs, embankments, walls, levees and bridges, represents the late stage of a complex history, as observed above, in which the floods marked the peak times of crisis and were particularly frequent in less favorable climatic periods(04,05).

In the 13th century there were at least five Arno floods, some responsible for the destruction of the newly built bridges, as mentioned above. The flood of 1333, however, is considered the first of the city's catastrophic floods, with the destruction of Ponte Vecchio and terrible inundations of which there are still physical traces, which can be found poking about among ancient documents but also keeping an eye out for the plaques on the streets showing the levels reached by the floods through the centuries(05).

In the late 13th century, the city was developing rapidly and tumultuously, and had decided to merge forever with its river, regulating its course and allowing it to run alongside the urban circle designed by Arnolfo di Cambio, which incorporated over 400 hectares (1.5 sq. mi.), intended for urban development that would not be completed, however, until at the end of the 19th century.

There have been several dozen historic floods of Florence since the 14th century, with particularly difficult periods in which the Arno chose to visit its city repeatedly. There were at least eight floods in the 14th century (in addition to the one in 1333) and six in the 14th century. The worst century was the 16th, however, marked by severe climatic conditions that generated a sequence of floods: there are about ten on record, including some with disastrous consequences, especially in 1547, 1557 and 1589(04).

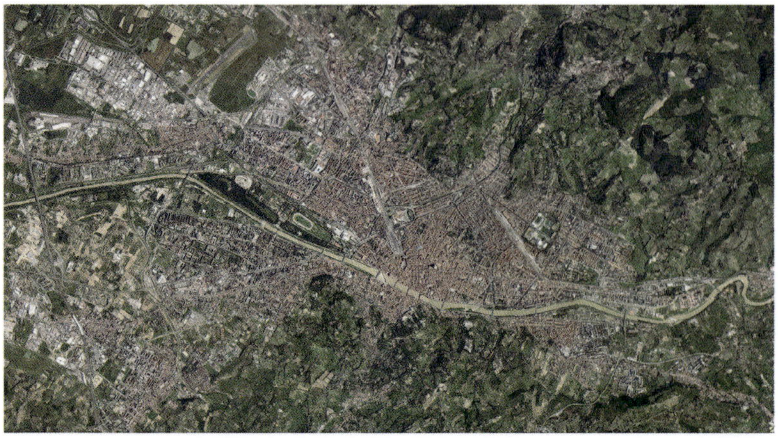

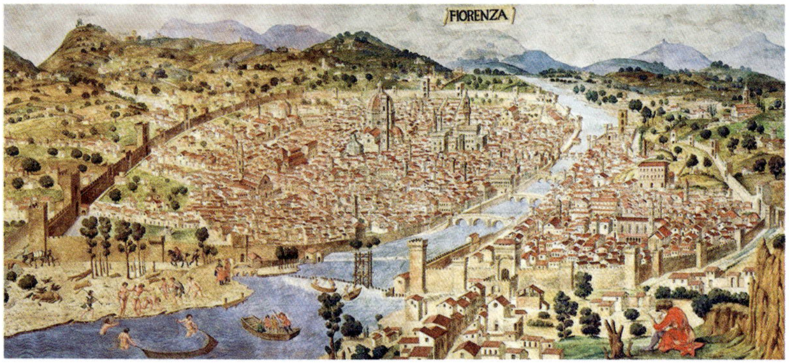

[B] Florence and the Arno seen from the satellite
[C] *Veduta della Catena*, 1887, attributed to Francesco and Raffaello Petrini, a painted reproduction of the woodcut (1471–82) by Francesco Rosselli, Museo di Palazzo Vecchio, Florence. Florence and the Arno have long coexisted symbiotically, though upstream and downstream the river maintains its natural character

Even later, relations remained unsettled: there were 14 events in the 17th century and nine in the 18th, when the floods of 1740 and 1758 were particularly bad. The hydraulic history and urban development of the city were at times profoundly transformed, since after every event, especially during the centuries of greatest splendor and wealth of the city, studies and countermeasures were undertaken, among which a number of prestigious, bold projects including the celebrated studies and drawings of Leonardo da Vinci.

The most recent history of relations between the city and the river is, we think, the most intense and interesting, also for the extraordinary urban redevelopment and for the records that are in many cases still living memories with tangible and intangible effects on the history of Florence and the Arno.

In the 19th century, there was only one flood, but it was particularly bad: it occurred on Novem-

(03) Ferdinando Morozzi, *Dello stato antico e moderno dell'Arno e delle cause e de' rimedi delle sue inondazioni. Ragionamento istorico matematico*, Stocchi, Florence, 1762.
(04) Enrica Caporali, Massimo Rinaldi, Nicola Casagli, *The Arno River floods*, in *Giornale di Geologia Applicata 1*, 2005, pp. 177–192.
(05) Gerald Galloway, Giovanni Seminara, Günter Blöschl, Marcelo Horacio Garcia, Luca Solari, *Saving a world treasure: Protecting Florence from flooding*, Firenze University Press, Florence, 2017.

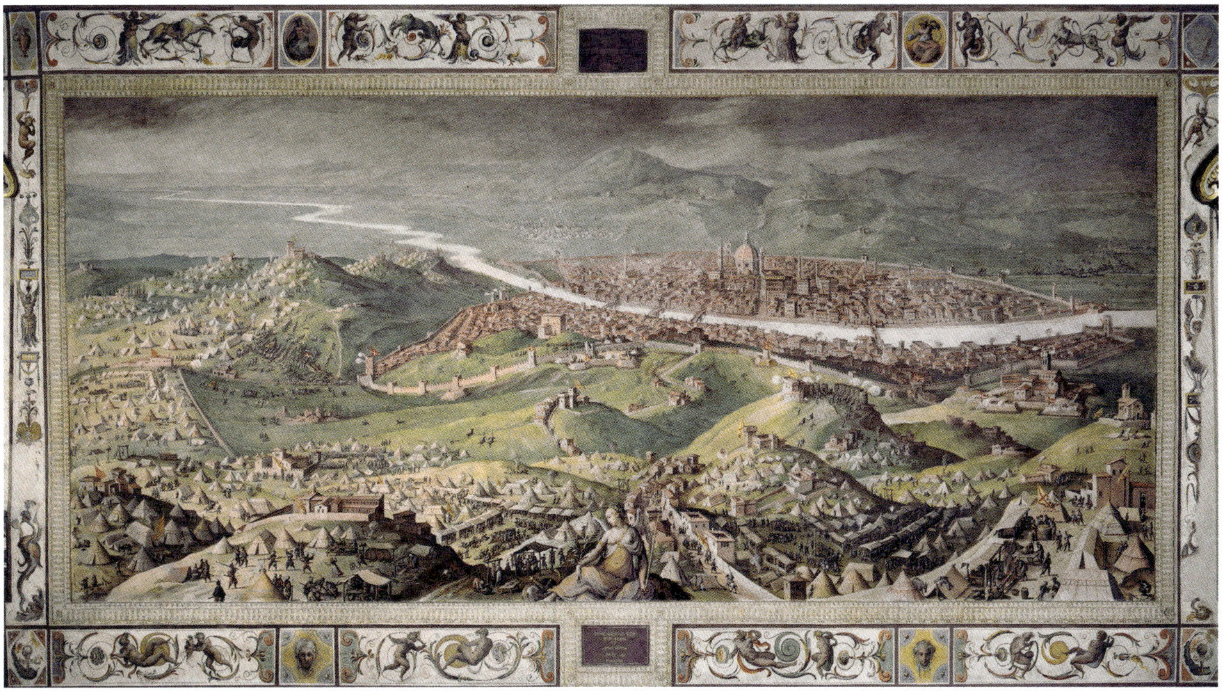

[D] Giorgio Vasari (and workshop), *Siege of the City of Florence in 1530*, ca. 1560–62, fresco, Salone di Clemente VII, Museo di Palazzo Vecchio, Florence. Documentation confirms the participation of Vasari's workshop and collaborators, including Giovanni Stradano, in the overall decoration of the frescoed halls

ber 3, 1844, and impressed itself indelibly on the memory of the city. Almost a century from the previous major flood in 1758, the Arno reminded Florence that nature is not always an easily managed factor in their relationship, after leaving the role of reminding people of the continuous hydraulic risk to its lesser tributaries for many decades.

Indeed, the Florentine territory outside the 14th century walls was marked by numerous large and small waterways (Mugnone, Terzolle, Affrico, Fosso di San Gervasio, Fosso di Ricorboli, Fosso di Gamberaia, Fosso di San Rocco) which frequently escaped their beds, but the city was able to ignore them by closing its gates and remaining in the company of the Arno alone within its borders. In 1844, all these hydrographic elements suddenly came to the fore, however, when Giuseppe Poggi was assigned the "Project of Works for the Enlargement of Florence".

Reading the book of the same title, written by Poggi(06), we observe that from the outset, there were three "very serious" problems that the City Council wanted to resolve with this Project, which had nothing to do with urban embellishment or the need to guarantee its military security by creating appropriately broad avenues for the cavalry, but the city's "hydraulic defense, also considering that the walls were to be eliminated". We should note here that the other two issues concerned maintenance of the city's tolls and the construction of two railway stations.

The city has completely resolved the problem of tolls, at this point, merely by reason of exogenous factors, but the hydraulic problems remain, although the work planned and carried out by Poggi contained extraordinarily farsighted and revolutionary elements for the city. For example, in the early projects. the ring of boulevards were supposed to be elevated to ensure that, even in the absence of the walls, the city would maintain a physical barrier or protection.

The overall project of Poggi and the works on the Arno and its tributaries brought the city into the 20th century profoundly redesigned, although still exposed to the hydraulic risk. The Arno would have to wait another century before it could assign to the memory – personal and familial to many Florentines still alive today – the records of the most terrible flood of all, that of the November 4, 1966.

Since then, Florence and the Arno have continued in their impetuous, volatile relationship, with repeated warnings of crises (in 1992, 2014 and 2025) that never actually led to flooding, but that never fail to generate a deeply rooted awareness and attention. The proud residents of Florence watch the Arno intensely at times like these, while trying not to seem to. Her older inhabitants linger nonchalantly along the riverside walls, gauging the levels of the water or following with an apparently languid gaze the rapid transit of the water under one of its bridges. With that watchfulness that we like to imagine has been the same through the centuries, the indelible genetic imprint of the river on its city is further reinforced.

(06) Giuseppe Poggi, *Sui lavori per l'ingrandimento di Firenze,* G. Barbèra, Florence, 1882.

1

DECODING SIGNALS

For human beings, living in this world often means inserting a system of analysis between ourselves and what is around us. Observing, classifying and decoding are actions we use in an effort to make diversity comprehensible. We see this clearly in the relationship between Florence and its river, which is structured through the interface of measurements.

The city, viewed as an extension of the social body, has learned to live with the Arno by turning it into a signal, translating matter into data. Beyond its molecular structure, the river appears in this view like a flow of information through the landscape, giving a direction to the course of our imagination.

This work re-examines the data collected, comparing the measurements taken in the heart of the city with those received from the river's upper basin.

It is not simply a matter of comparing data, but of drawing a map of that matches distant zones, between the mountain and its valley, between the center and its suburbs. In the digital environment, these relations are translated into animated visual flows, where the data acquire shape and movement.

A chromatic study based on Plutchik's Wheel of Emotions guides the affective interpretation of the landscape: every variation of intensity triggers a corresponding variation of emotion, where distance becomes echo and information comes back as perceptible matter.

1.1

Data Crossover: Hydrometry-Pluviometry

The first correlation to be reinterpreted by the artist concerns the relation between rainfall upstream and the variation in the water level observed farther downstream.

The rainfall measurements were made at various points through the area considered the "upstream basin" of the Arno River, which covers the entire Mugello district across the Casentino up to the outskirts of Arezzo. The data collected here were matched with the hydrometric levels recorded by the Florentine measuring station Uffizi 3, located along the Arno between Via dei Georgofili and the Uffizi Gallery, a key fluvial observation point in the heart of the city.

The measurement, made on a daily basis, highlights three specific points in time – selected in the years 2004, 2012 and 2025 – which have been isolated to illustrate anomalous situations of particular intensity with respect to the climatic context in the reference year. Each event is compared with the relative annual average, generating a visual tension between the state of normalcy and the critical condition. The work transforms these data points into dynamic flows that vary in the intensity of their color: the pluviometric variable passes from the yellow of a calm situation to the orange of watchfulness, while the shade of the river goes from the green of acceptable conditions to the blue of more threatening ones.

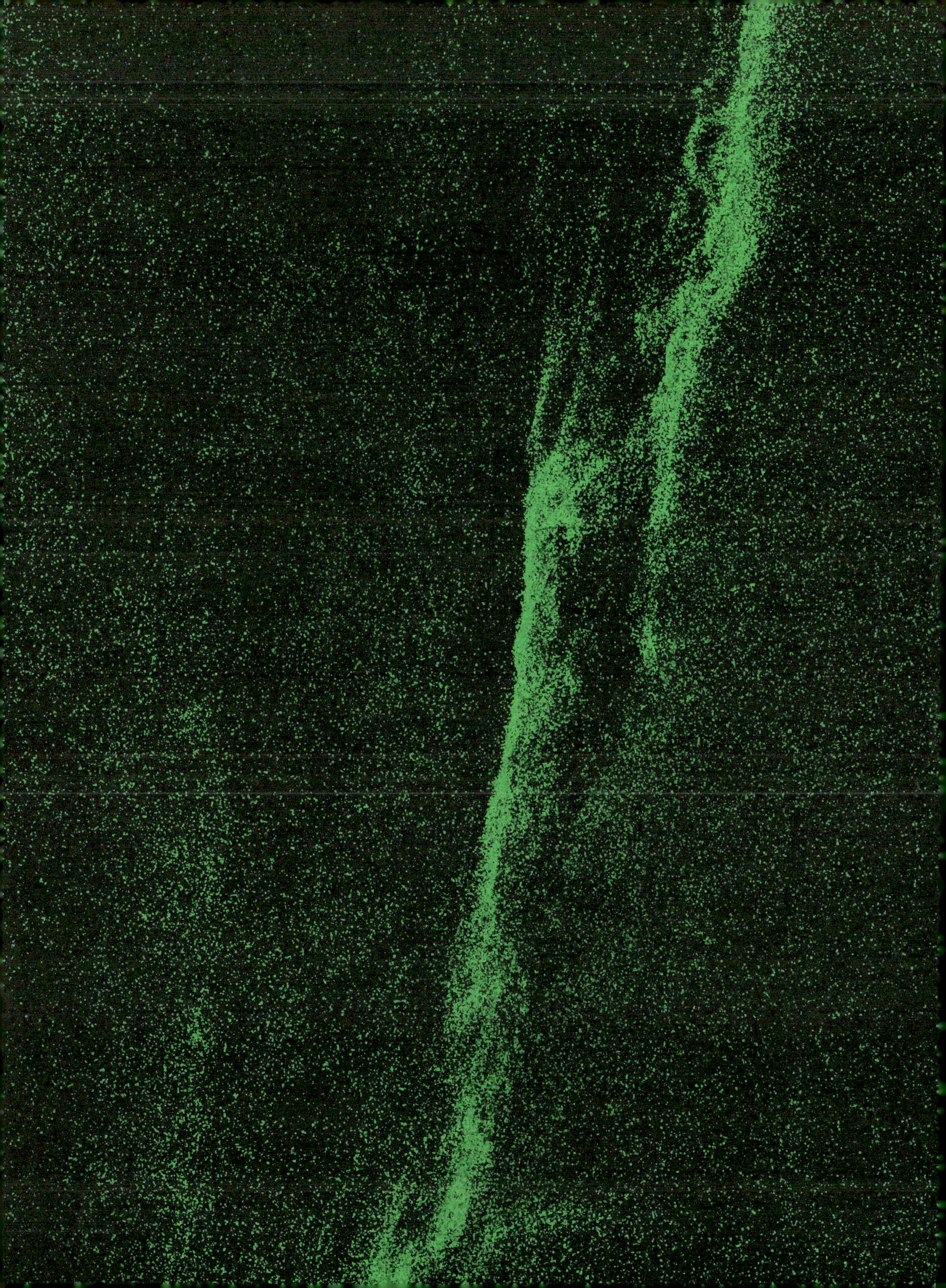

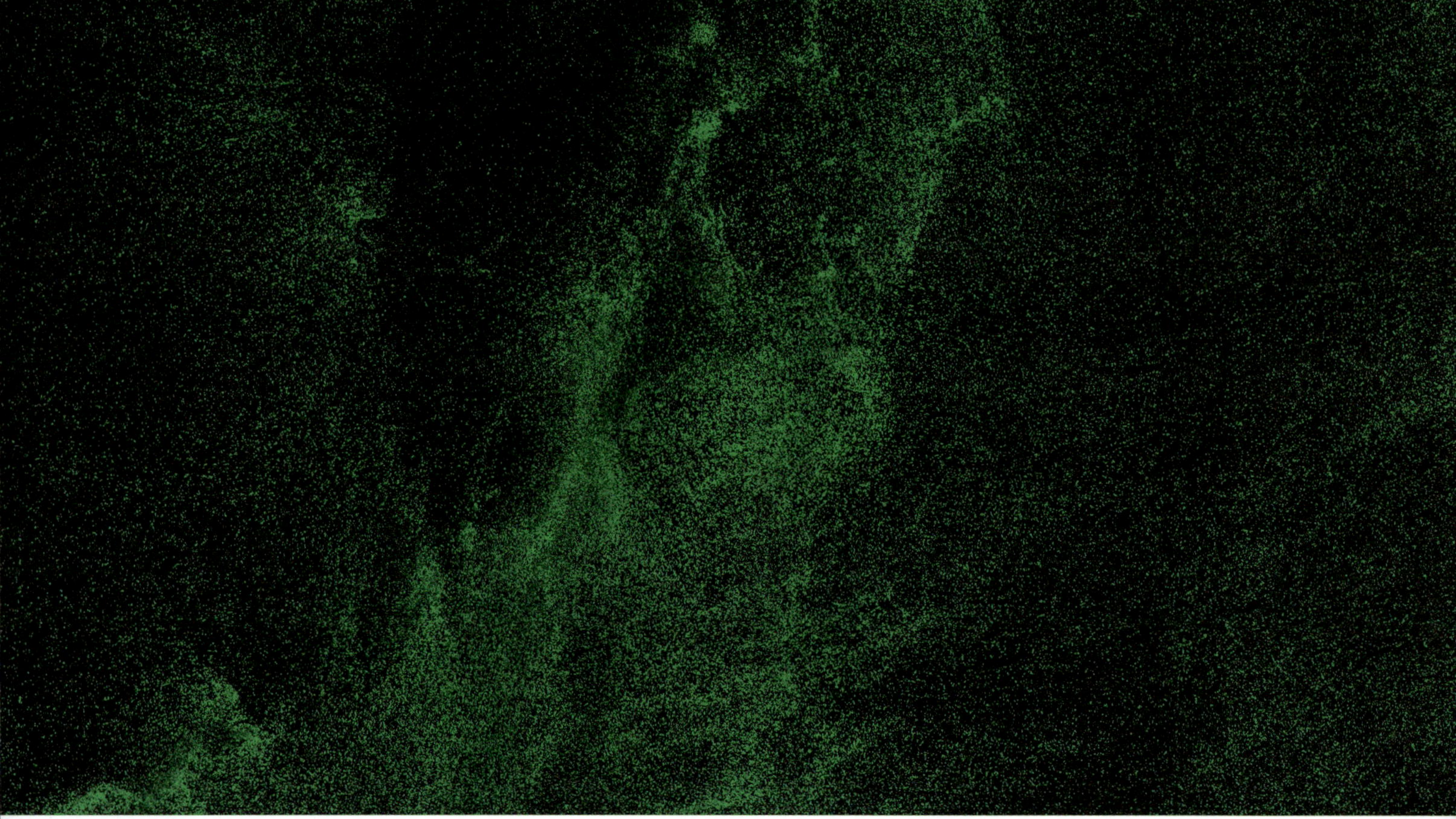

Light green, the color of balance and stability, represents the hydrometric baseline data recorded at the Florence Uffizi 3 station – specifically, the annual averages for 2004, 2012, and 2025. The particles flow slowly and harmoniously, following a smooth, stable path that reflects the river's equilibrium: 0.6997 m in 2004, 0.5974 m in 2012, and 1.1555 m in 2025.

This is the Arno's natural breath – a state of hydrological calm that conveys optimism and security. During this phase, the river absorbs rainfall without stress, maintaining a calm, regulated rhythm.

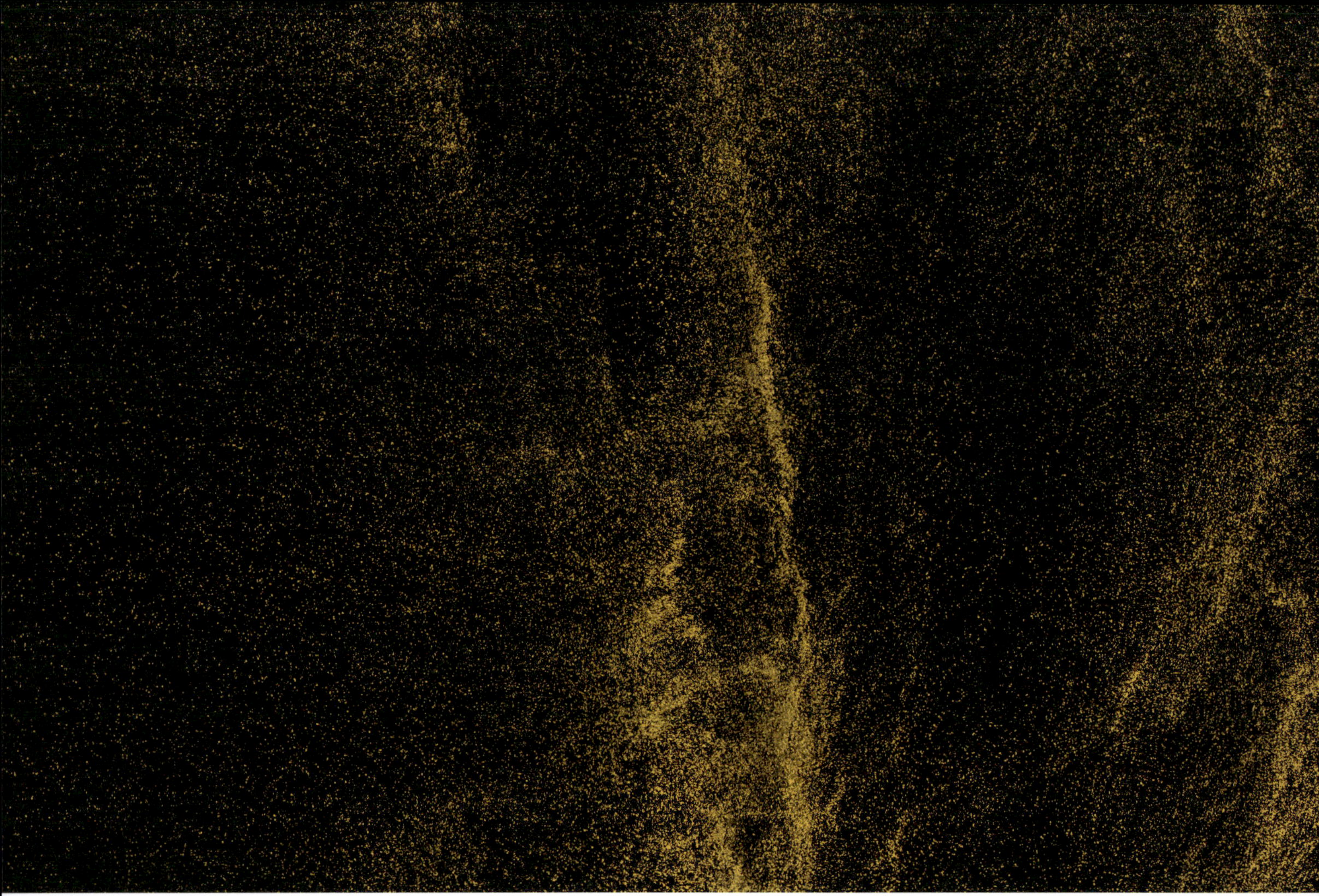

Yellow, the color of serenity, reflects hydrological conditions with moderate rainfall in the upstream basins of Florence. Daily average rainfall values – 3.25 mm in 2004, 2.73 mm in 2012, 4.90 mm in 2025 – indicate a hydrological condition that appears stable, yet remains vulnerable, with particles flowing in a steady, ordered motion.

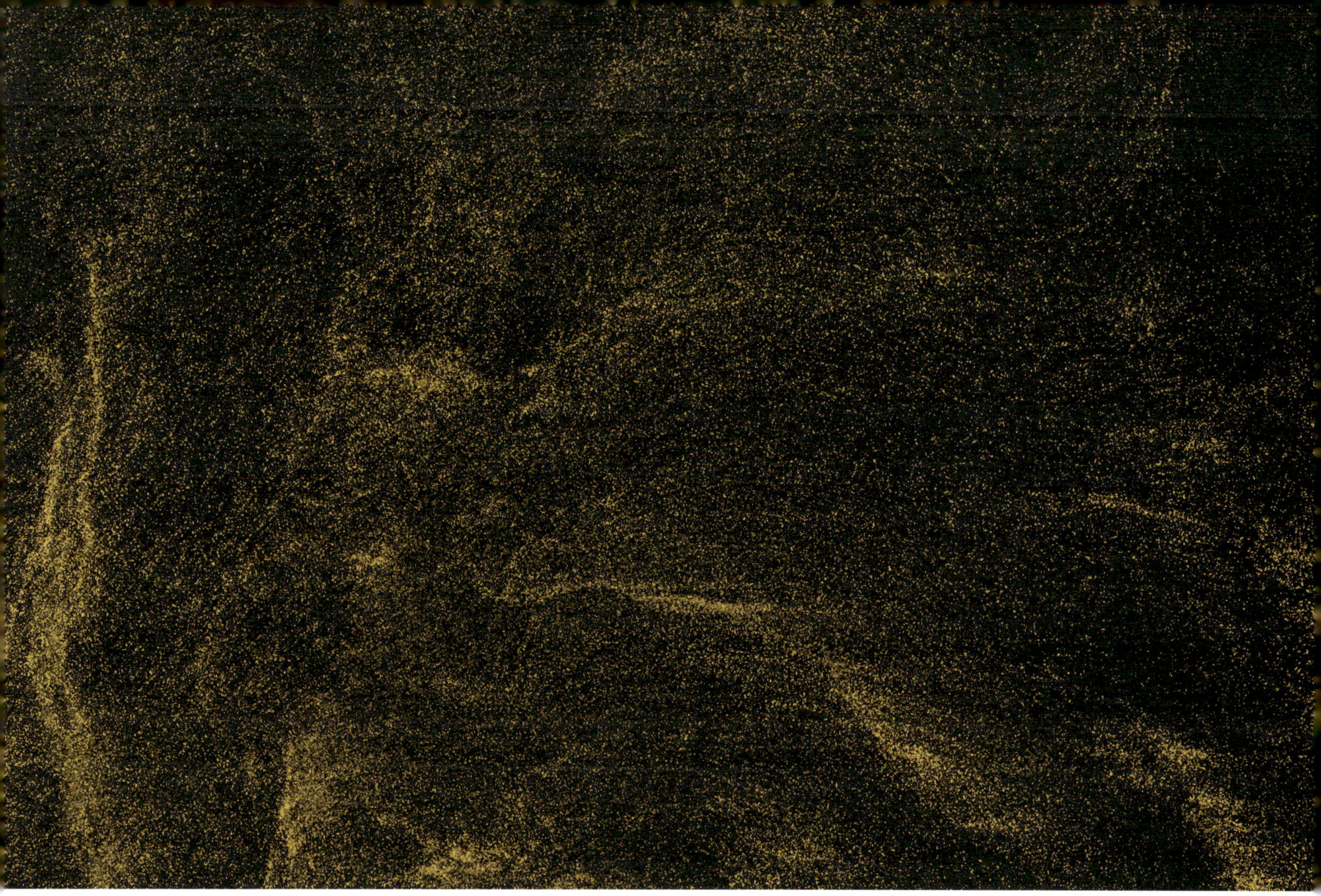

This is rain that nourishes without overwhelming, accompanying the river without pushing it to its limits. Subsequently, blue emerges – the color of distress – with dense and accelerated particles in response to exceptional rainfall. Hydrometric peaks – 2.65 m in 2004, 2.63 m in 2012, 3.28 m in 2025 – mark a critical phase of sudden and dramatic changes in the river's level.

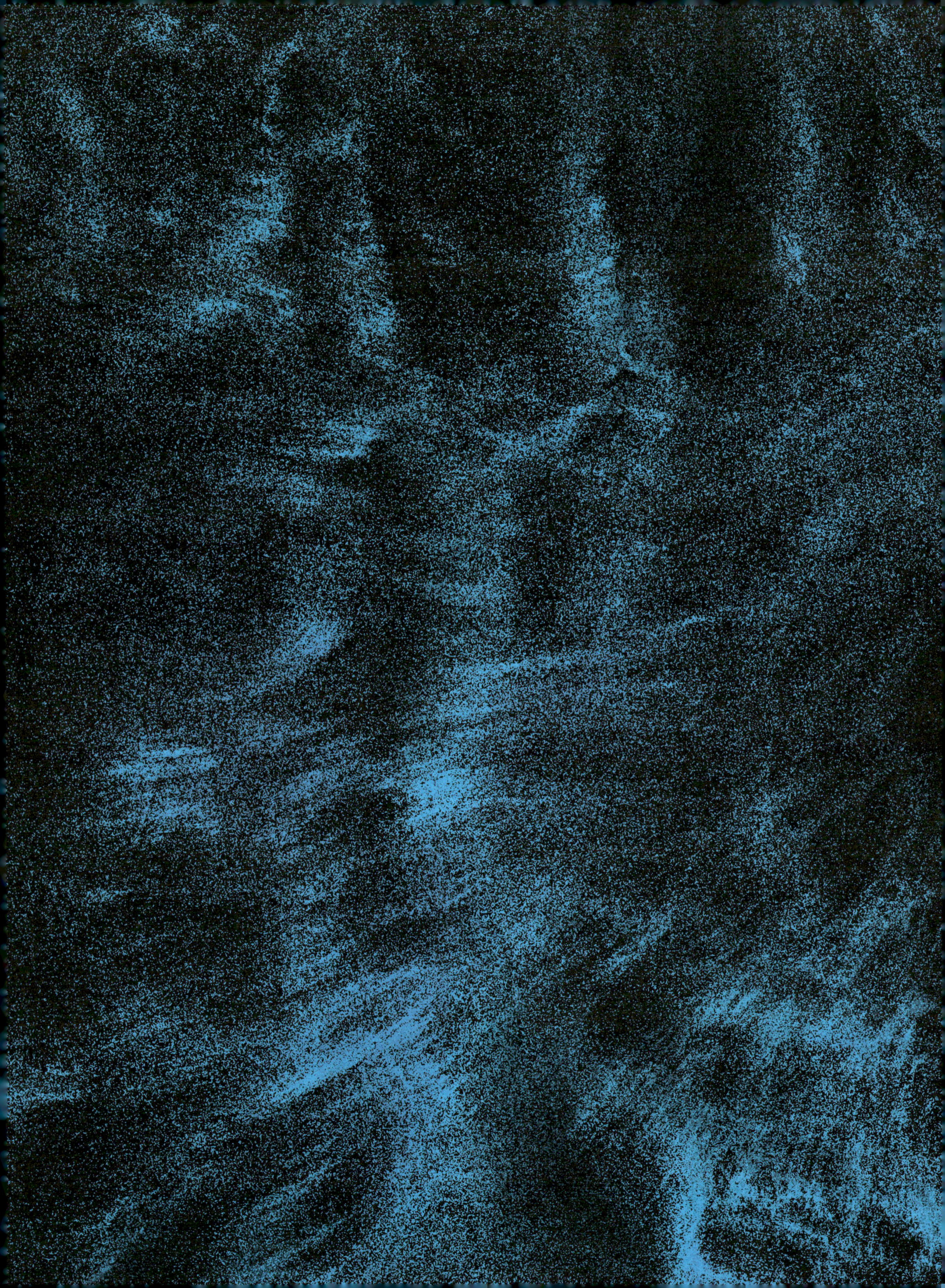

1.2

Data Crossover: Hydrometry-Thermometry

The correlation explored in the second act illustrates the same comparative method applied between the temperature variations recorded in the area of the Arno basin and the changes in the water level observed in the city center.

The analysis, made on data recorded between 2012 and 2024, points to a complementary behavior with respect to that examined in the first act: as temperatures rise in the upstream areas, the level of the Arno in Florence tends to decrease noticeably. The river, in other words, tends to shrink when subject to prolonged thermal stress. This indicates a state of tension in the river, revealing the fragility of the fluvial system in the presence of extreme climate conditions.

Three unusual heat events, recorded respectively in the years 2012, 2017 and 2024, were compared with the annual averages to highlight the difference. Here again, the data are illustrated as perceptible emotional states: the temperature is translated into a color scale that passes from orange to the red of rage; the level of the river moves from the yellow of joy to the purple of loathing. The interaction between physical variables and affects generates a real visual grammar of climate instability, capable of revealing the emotional impact of otherwise invisible environmental phenomena.

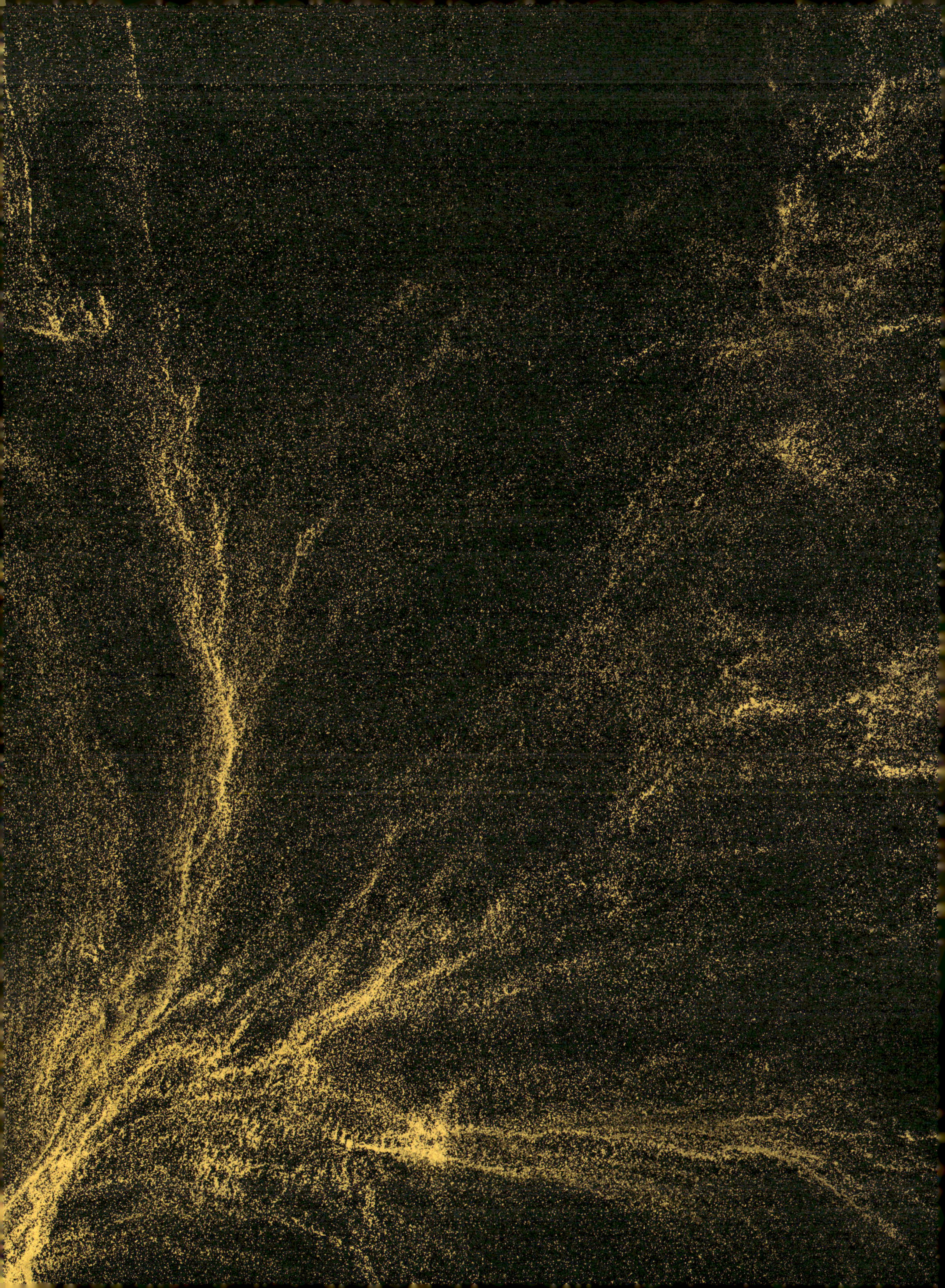

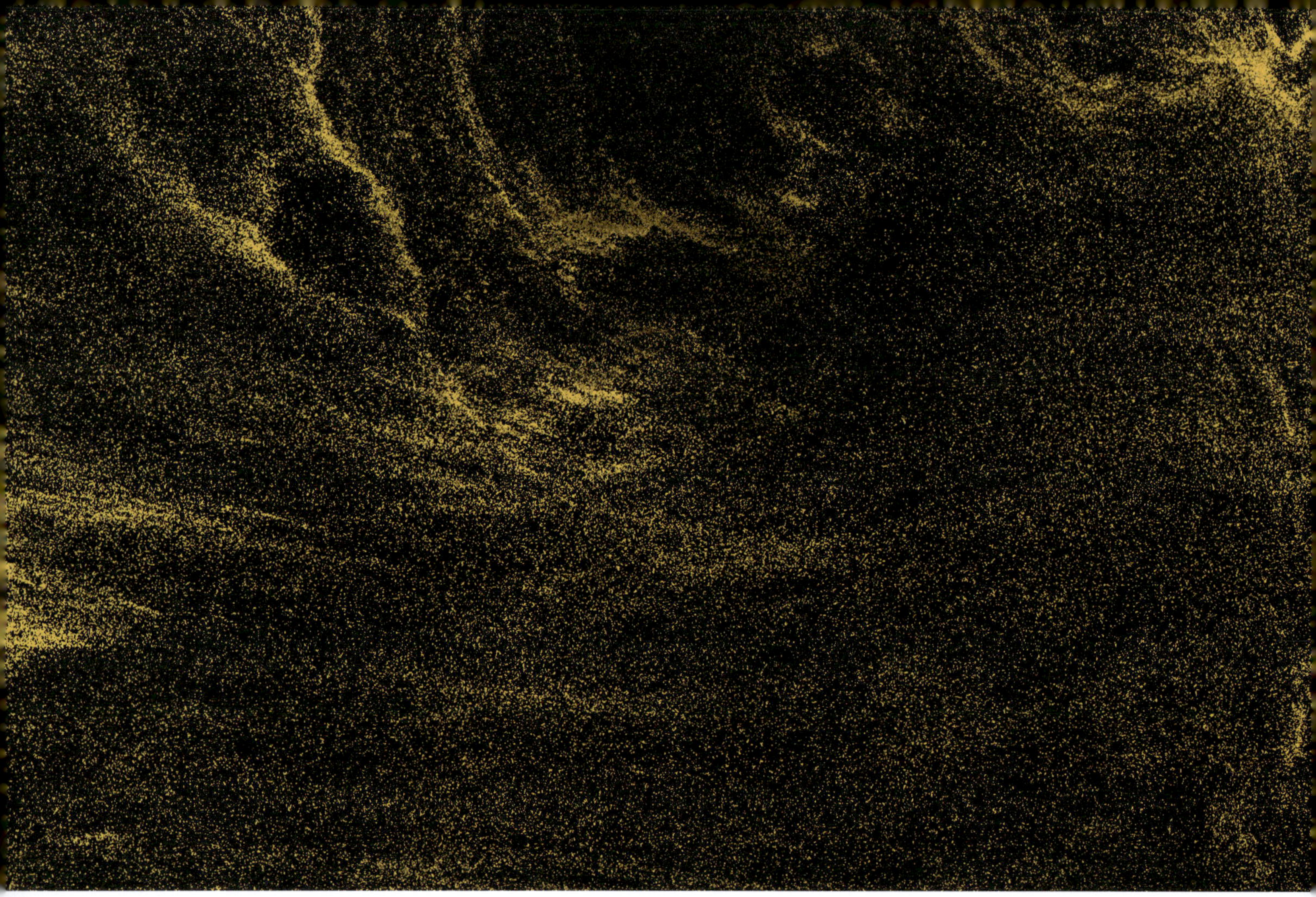

In examining the relationship between upstream temperature and downstream river level, yellow again denotes the river's calm – this time referencing the baseline level downstream. The particles move broadly and steadily, suggesting the apparent calm of the river under normal upstream thermal conditions.

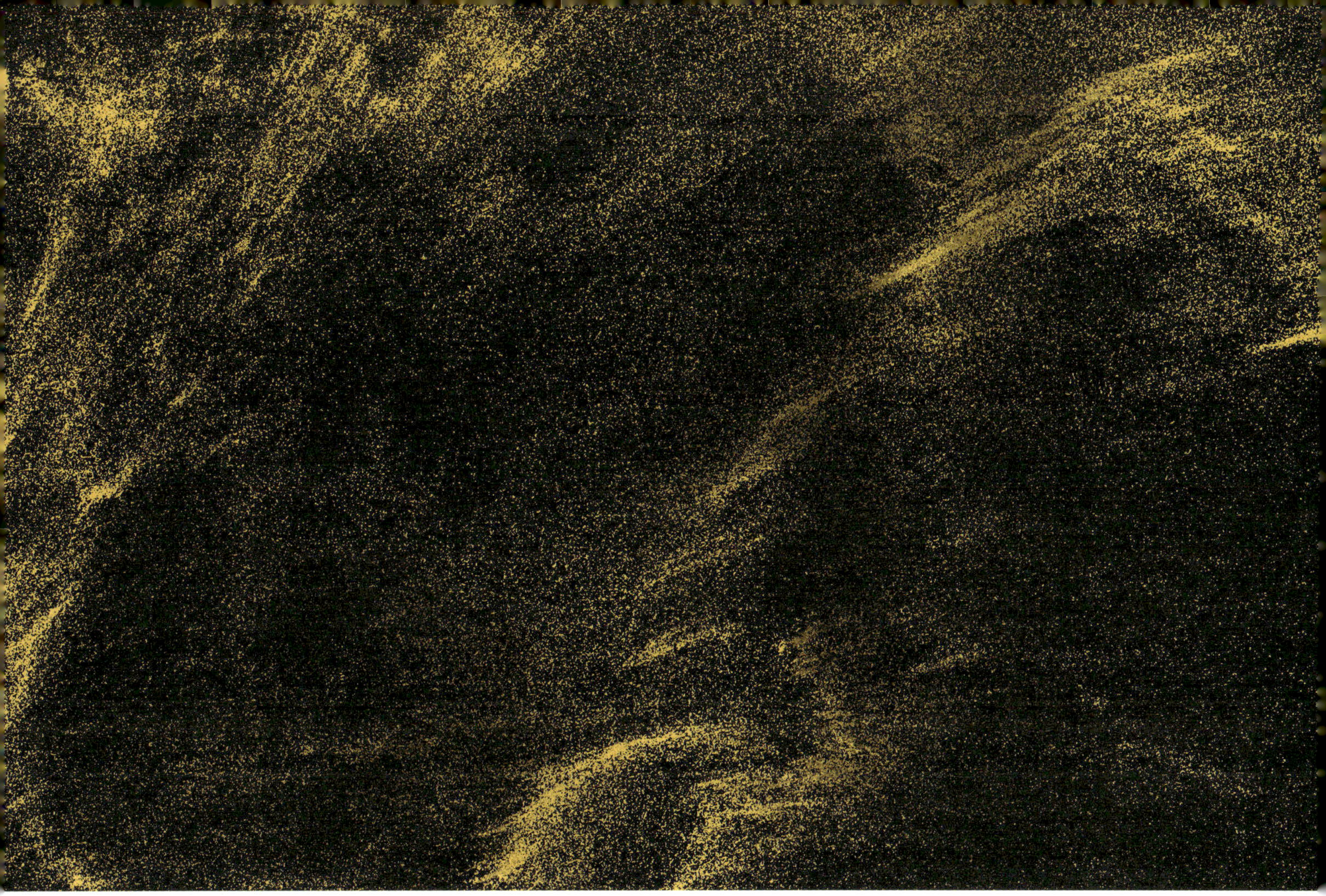

Annual hydrometric averages – 0.597 m in 2012, 0.764 m in 2017, 0.876 m in 2024 – describe a regular flow not yet impacted by drought. This is the baseline: an equilibrium that begins to falter only when heat intensifies and the river begins to recede.

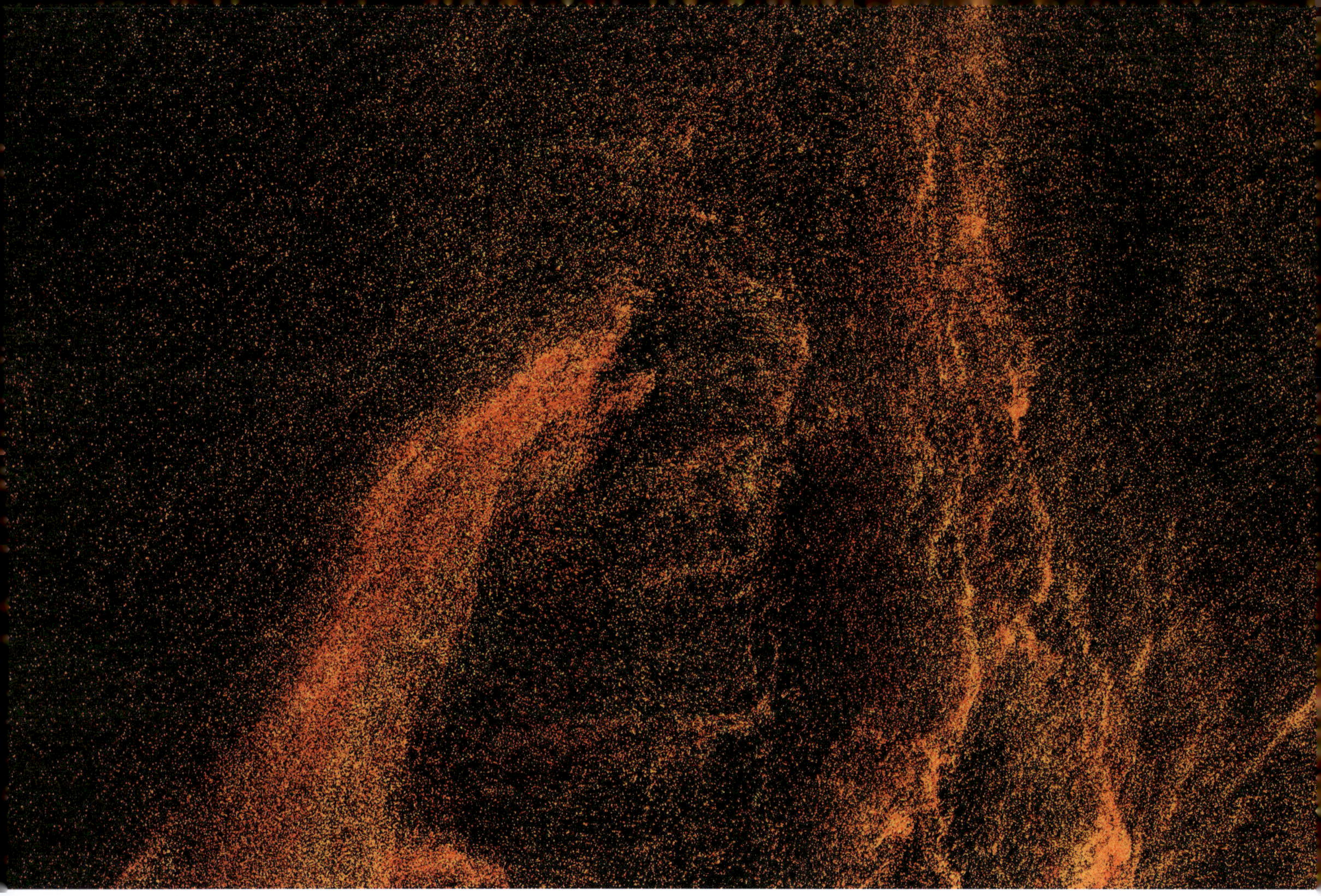

As temperatures rise, the particles shift chromatically from yellow to soft orange – a symbol of watchfulness and anticipation – then deepen into intense red, the color of irritation and anger. The baseline range of 16–19 °C is surpassed by extreme peaks: 34.28 °C in 2012, 37.92 °C in 2017, 36.62 °C in 2024. This heat accelerates the flow and induces vibration – signs of agitation within the river system and of an approaching crisis.

Before this critical threshold is reached, purple appears – the color of aversion – representing the river's retreat under thermal stress. Water levels drop sharply: 0.02 m in 2012, 0.55 m in 2017, 0.64 m in 2024, signaling a contraction phase that precedes the most acute stage of thermal collapse.

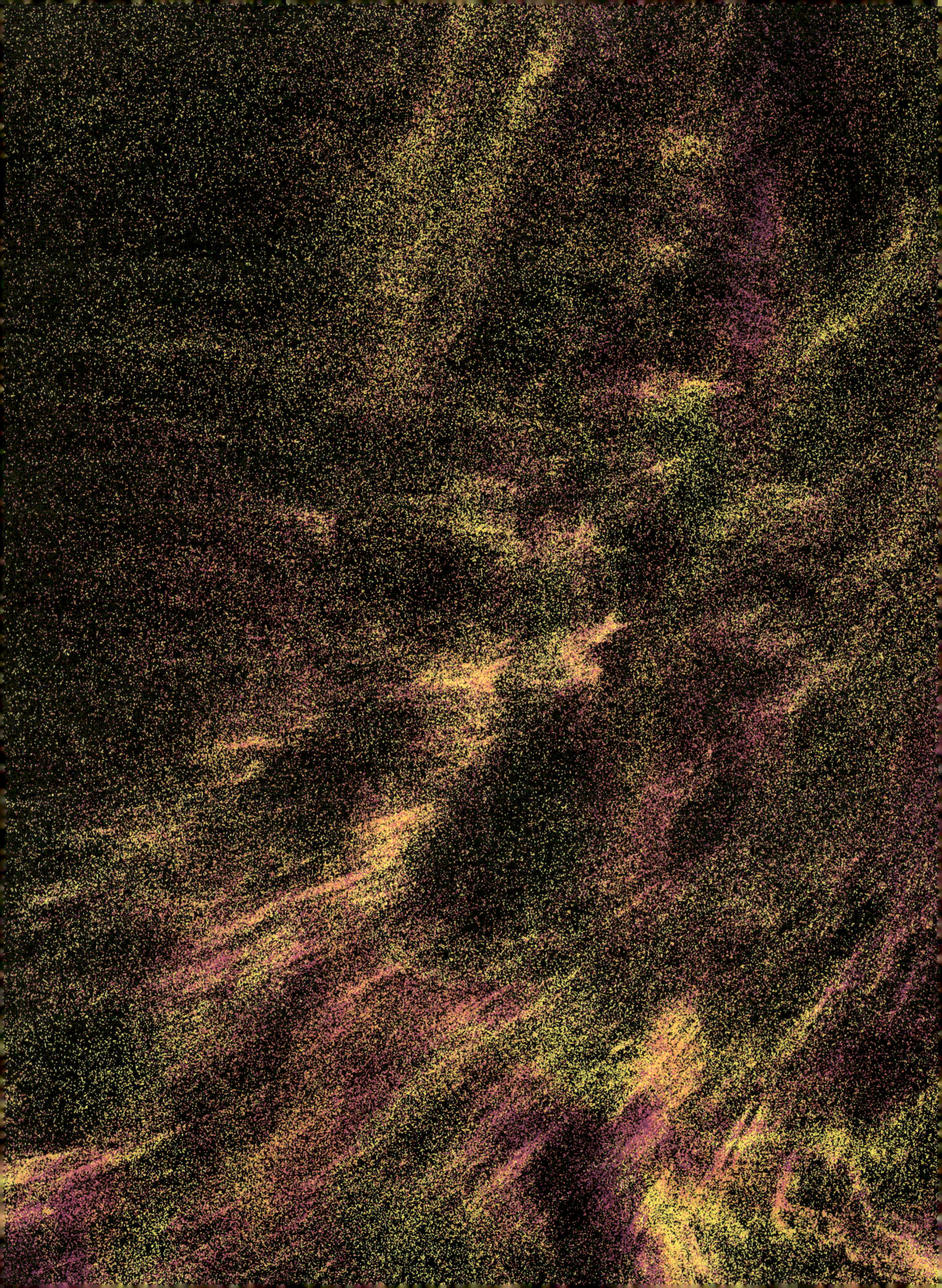

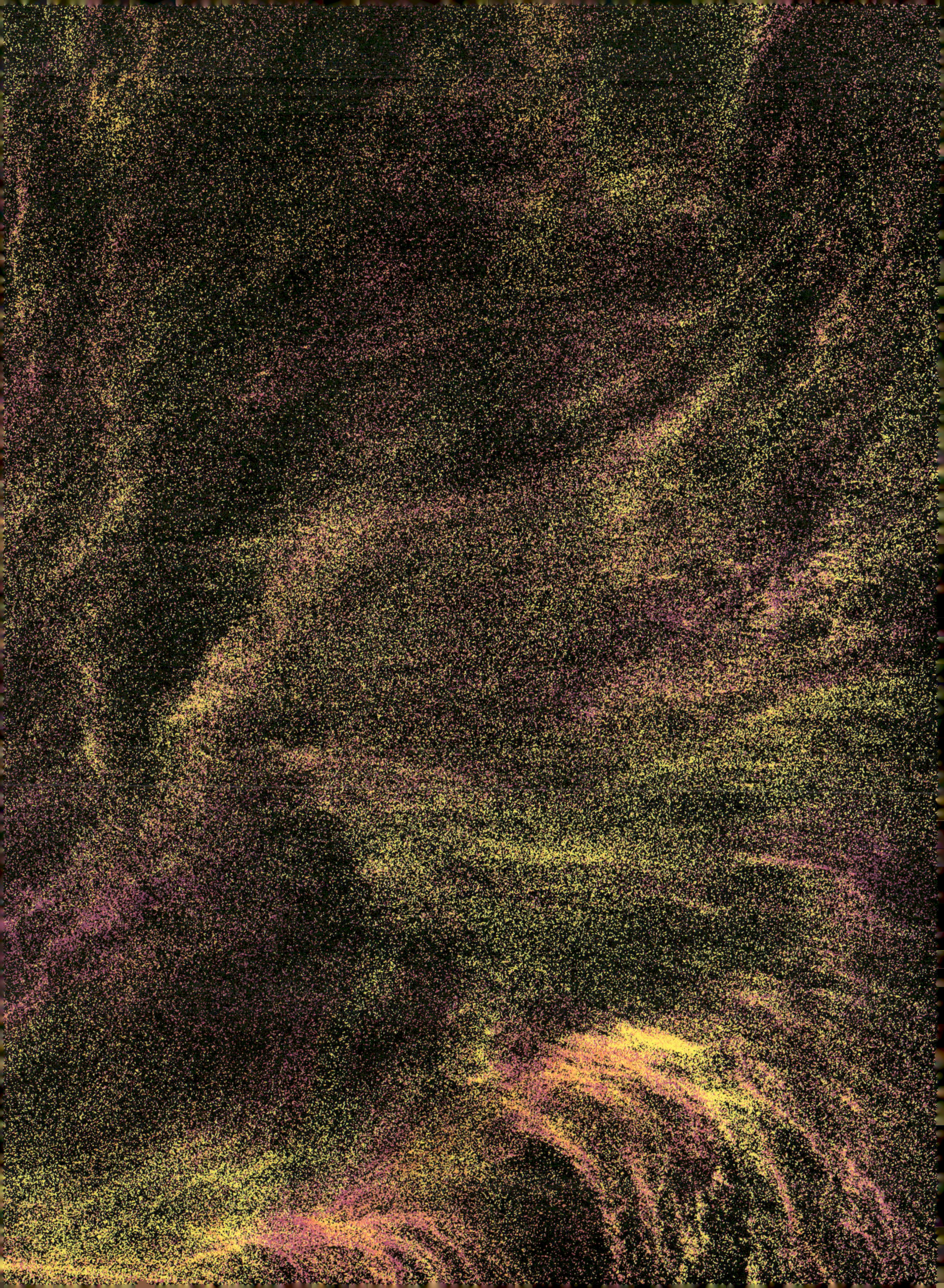

1.3

Seasonal Patterns: Annual Cycles

In this act, the correlation concerns the seasonal changes of the river, viewed as a physiological system subject to expansion, contraction, accumulation and release. The crossover analysis of historical data relative to the water levels and average monthly rainfall provides a model of the recurrent temporal structure: in winter, the water rises gradually, anticipating the high levels typical of the spring; in summer, we see a marked reduction, while in autumn a new cycle of rising levels starts.

To render this cyclicity visually, the year is divided into twelve sections. Every month is represented by a cluster of particles in a state of continuous flux, where colors and movements change constantly, evoking the regular breathing of the river. This representation conveys the impression of a profound regularity, which does not necessarily coincide with stability: it is, rather, the effect of a horizon expanding in time, absorbing anomalies in the larger flow of repetition. Unlike the previous acts, concentrated on critical events and on tension, here we discover a long-term poetic.

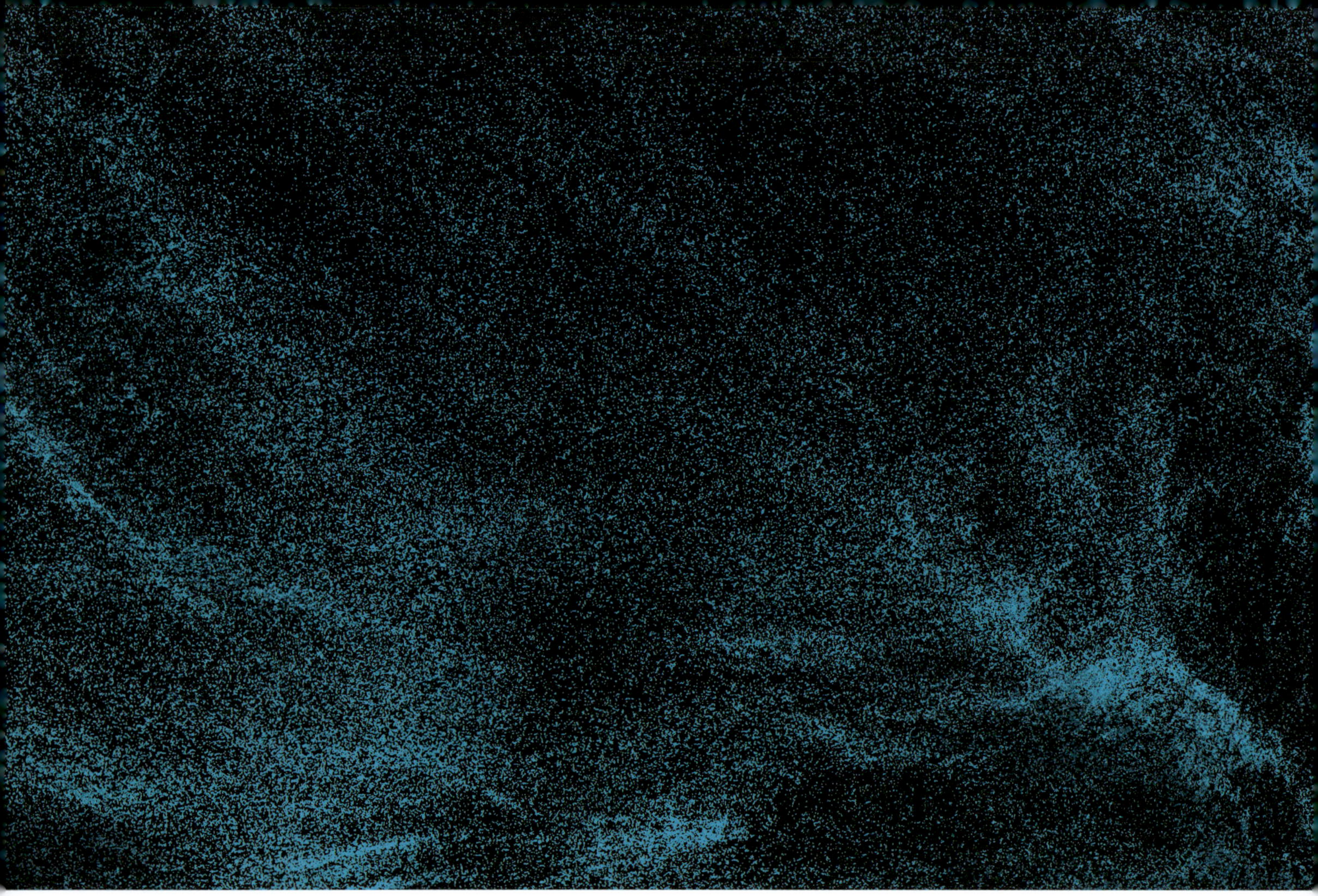

In the annual cyclical sequence, blue – a symbol of sadness – marks the transition from a phase of calm to one of gradual contraction. From April through June, the particles begin to lose their sinuosity; rainfall decreases and hydrometric levels fall: from over 1 meter in February–March to 0.74 m by June.

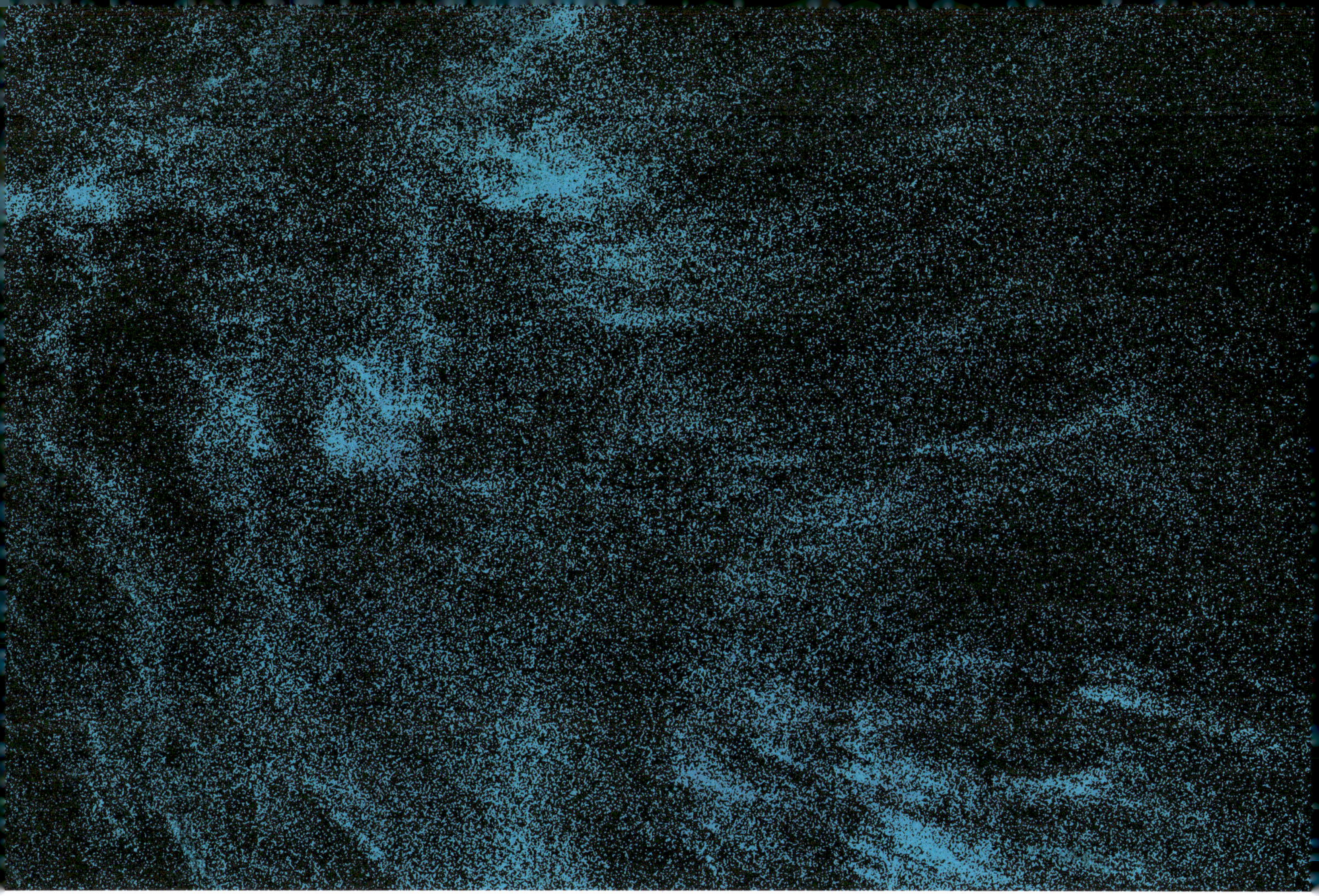

The river starts to lose momentum, revealing a hydric melancholy, as though the floodwaters had left behind only their absence.

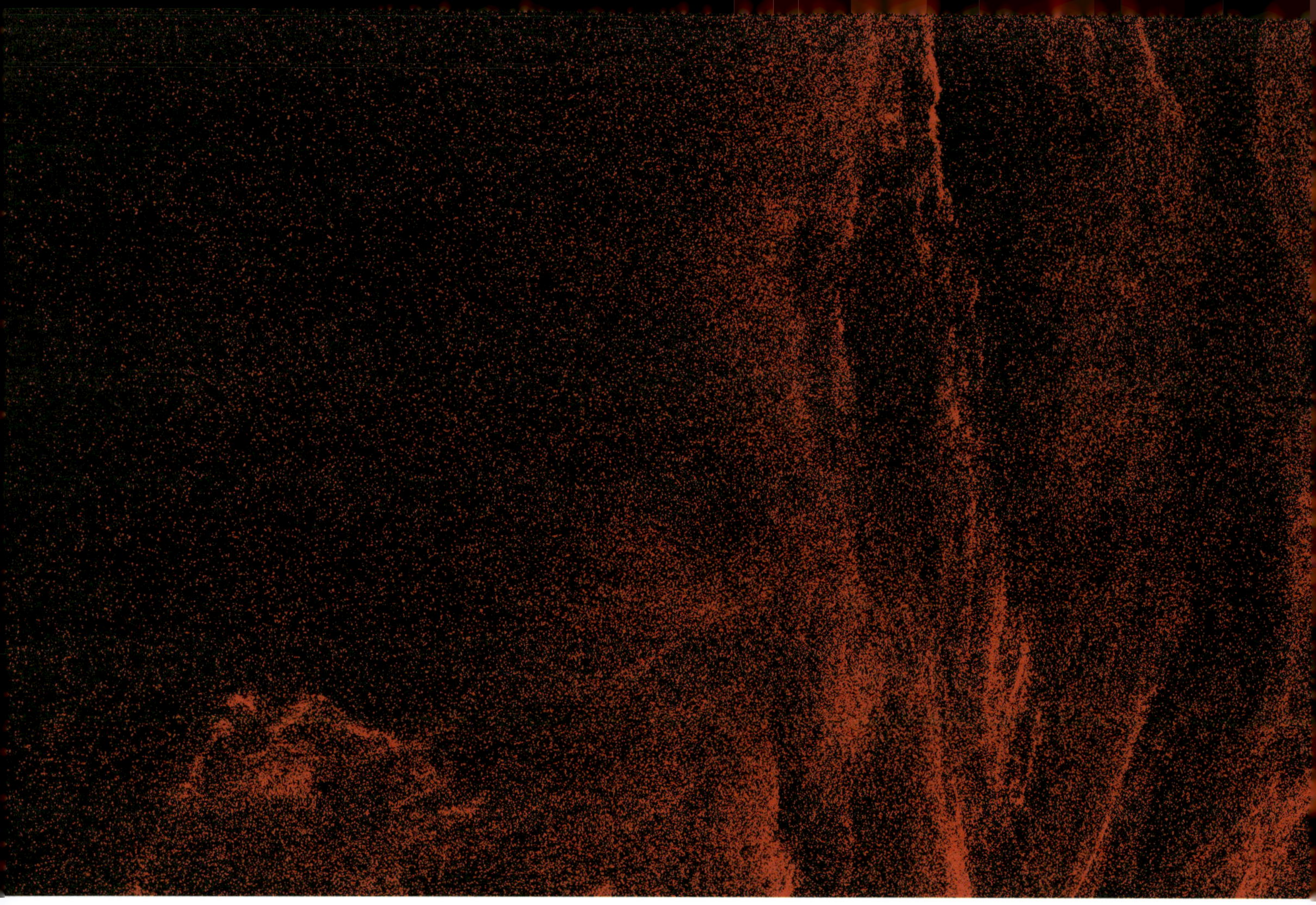

In July and August, red – the color of anger – dominates, marking the peak of hydrological stress. Particles become fragmented and erratic, embodying a river shaken by drought. Average rainfall drops to 0.95 mm in July, and the water level plummets to 0.64 m in August – the height of seasonal tension, as if the Arno were rebelling against its own scarcity.

A transition then begins: shades of red and purple accompany the shift into autumn. Between September and November, signs of strain persist but begin to ease, with rainfall increasing and levels rising above 0.8 m. With December and January, tones shift from orange to yellow, introducing a sense of relief: precipitation begins to stabilize between 2 and 3 mm, and the river level rises above 1 meter in February, signaling a gradual return to equilibrium.

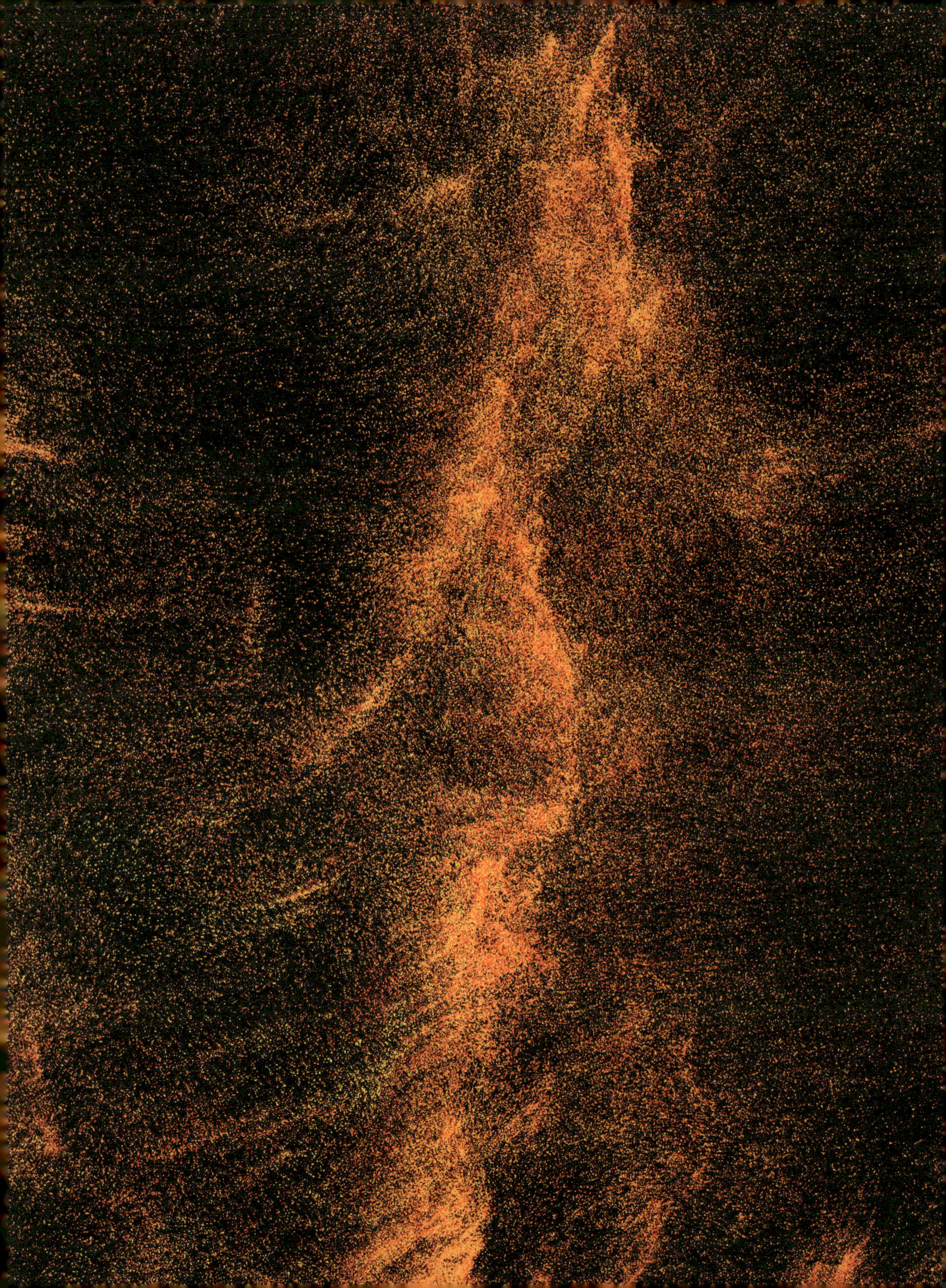

1.4

1966: Hydraulic Record of a Historical Flood

The fourth act deals with an event that deeply affected the relationship between Florence and its river: the flood of November 4, 1966. In a matter of hours, the Arno swept through the city with exceptional violence, submerging entire neighborhoods, devastating the cultural heritage and forever scarring the collective imagination.

The elaboration refers to fragmentary analogue sources: hydrographic records, historical tables, hand-drawn curves preserved among the documents of the time. In particular, one graph reconstructs the progress of the rising level between November 3 and 5, showing a synchronized action of the waters past several measuring points. Between 4 p.m. and midnight on November 3, the river reached simultaneous peaks along various points of its course: it was a deep and dramatic collective indrawn breath, a sob that was the final straw.

That convergence has been turned into a single digital wave that crosses the exhibition space like a living thing, increasing in size and speed. The colors become deep, movements frenzied and shapes lose their stability. The instant stirs a memory that rises to the surface and becomes real, evoking an event that still shapes the way we think about the river.

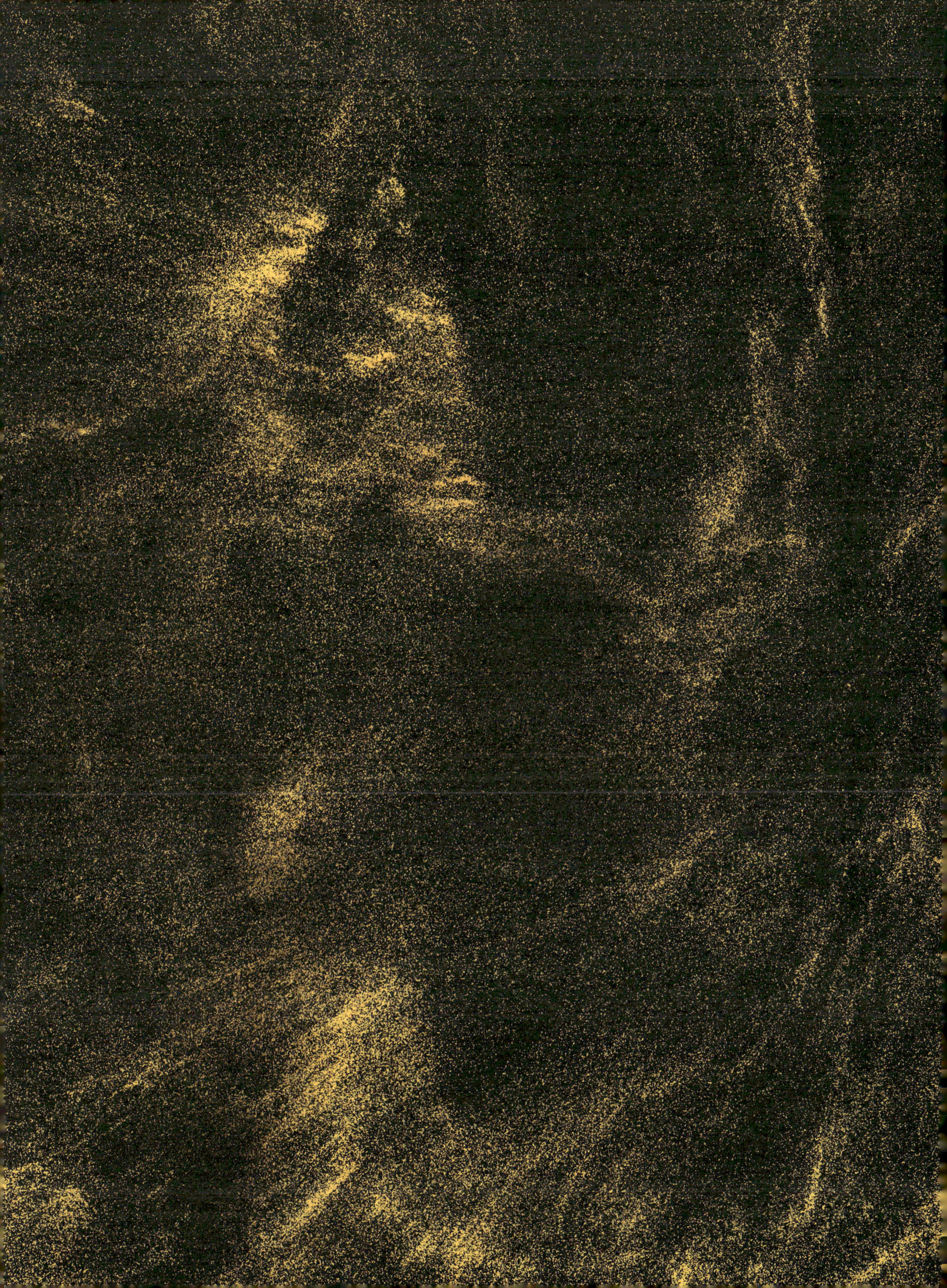

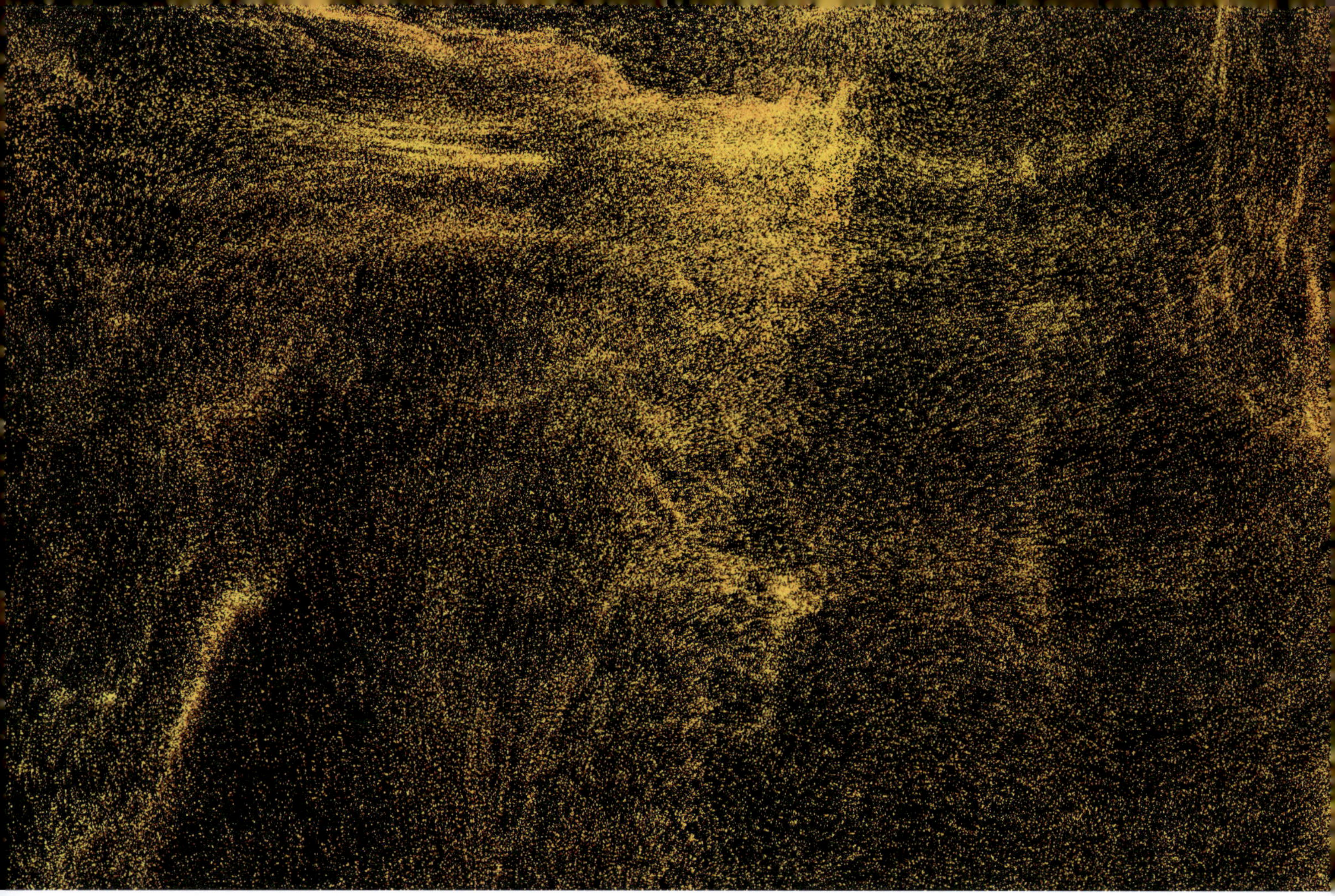

Yellow, a symbol of tranquility and stability, reflects moments of apparent calm during the 1966 flood. In the early hours of November 3, between 4:00 and 12:00, discharge levels remain below 200 m^3/s at all measuring stations – from Nave di Rosano to San Giovanni alla Vena – suggesting a precarious hydrological balance.

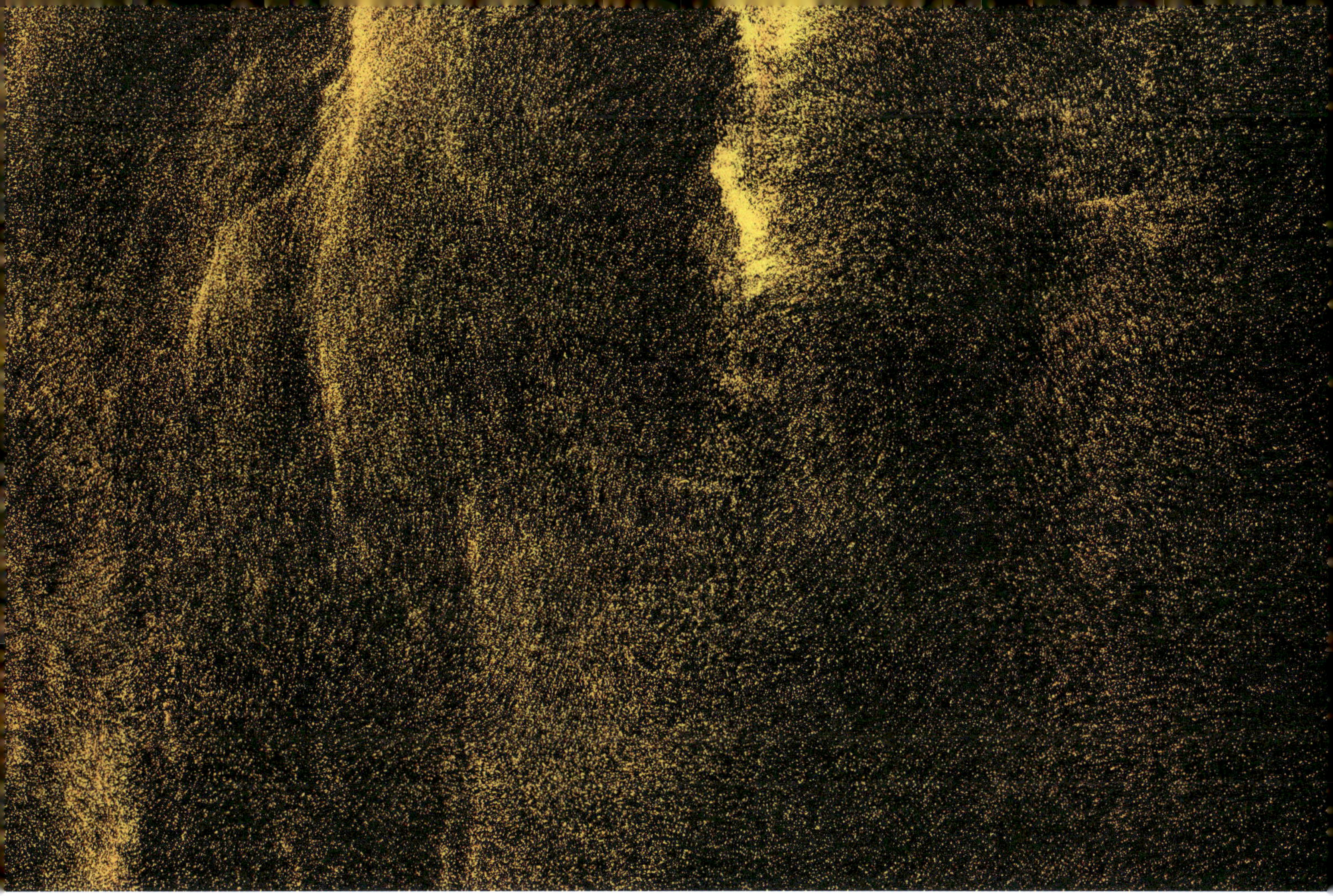

Particles flow smoothly and evenly, indicating a river still containing its potential energy before the surge. Following the peak, yellow re-emerges from 12:00 on November 5, when flow rates fall below 500 m^3/s. The particles return to a steady motion, signaling the slow re-establishment of stability after the extreme event.

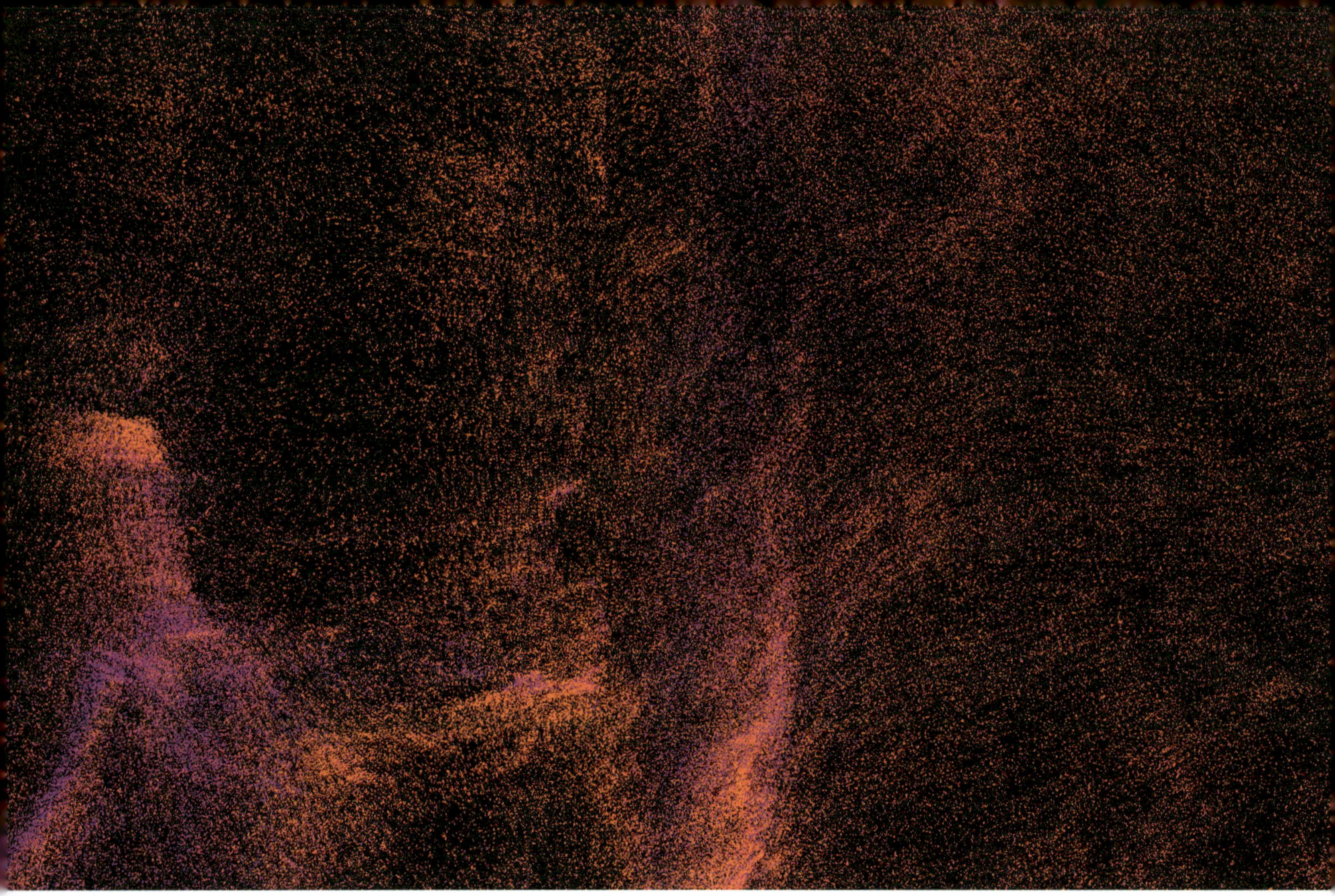

With orange – symbol of alert and vigilance – the river enters a phase of rapidly increasing discharge. From the afternoon of November 3, at 8:00 p.m., with 700 m^3/s recorded at Nave di Rosano, the flow accelerates beyond 3,000 m^3/s by midnight.

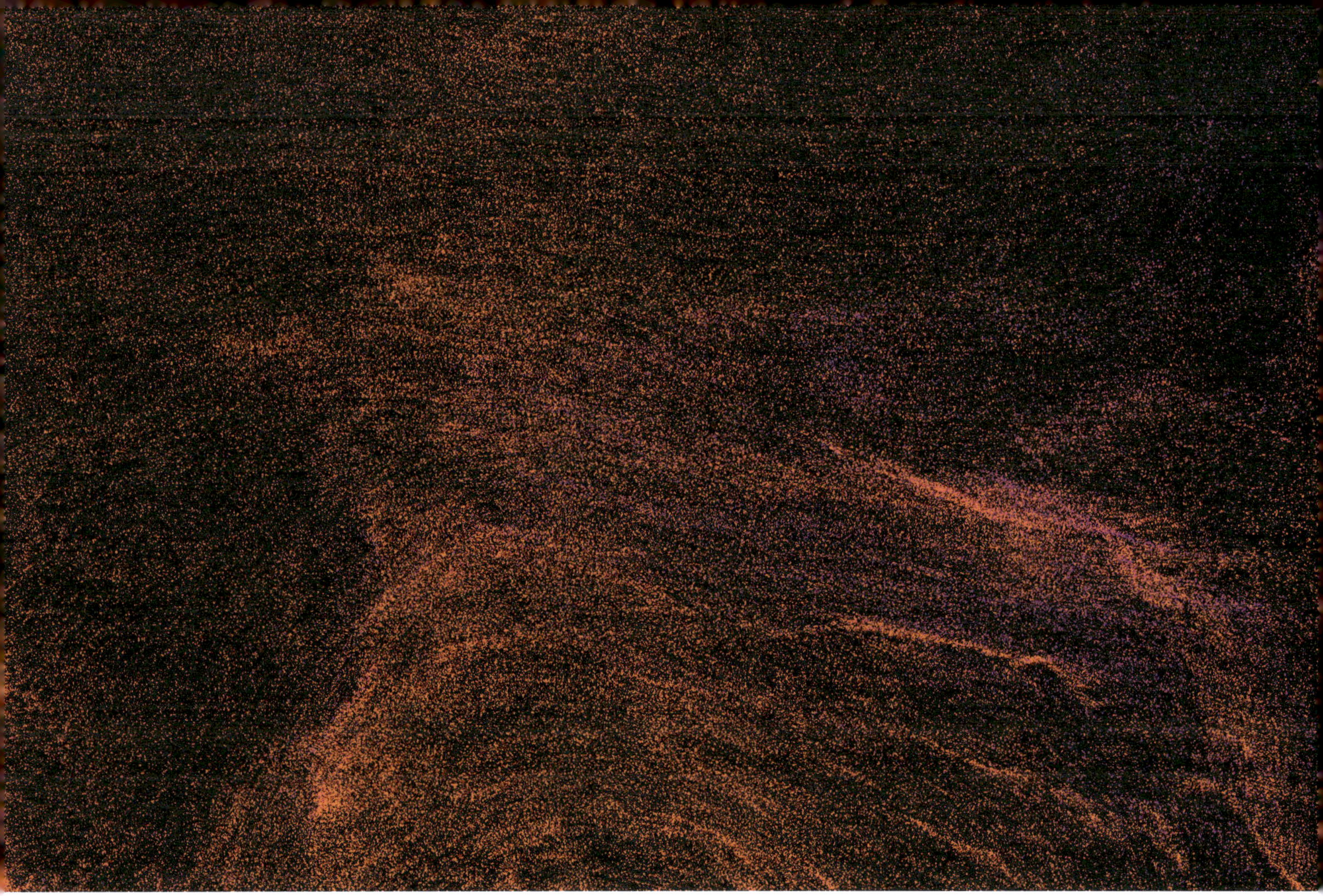

The particles condense and begin to vibrate, anticipating the flood, before exploding into chaotic vortices. The colors shift between red and purple, capturing the moment of maximum violence as the Arno breaks its banks and overwhelms the city.

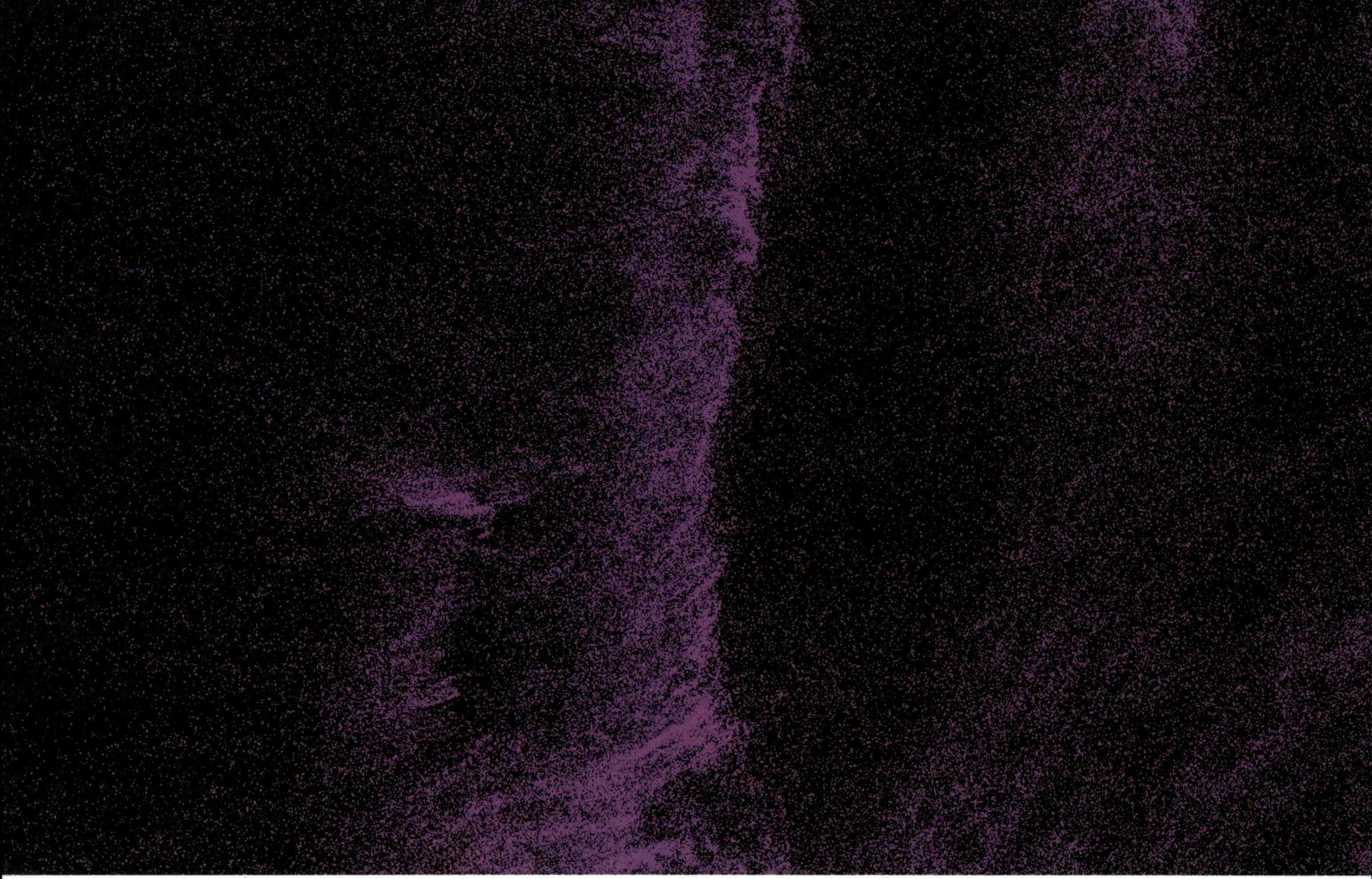

Over the next 24 hours, purple – color of aversion – dominates. On November 4, the discharge peaks at 3,900 m^3/s at 2:00 a.m. and again at 4:00 p.m., with San Giovanni alla Vena also registering a maximum of 2,300 m^3/s.

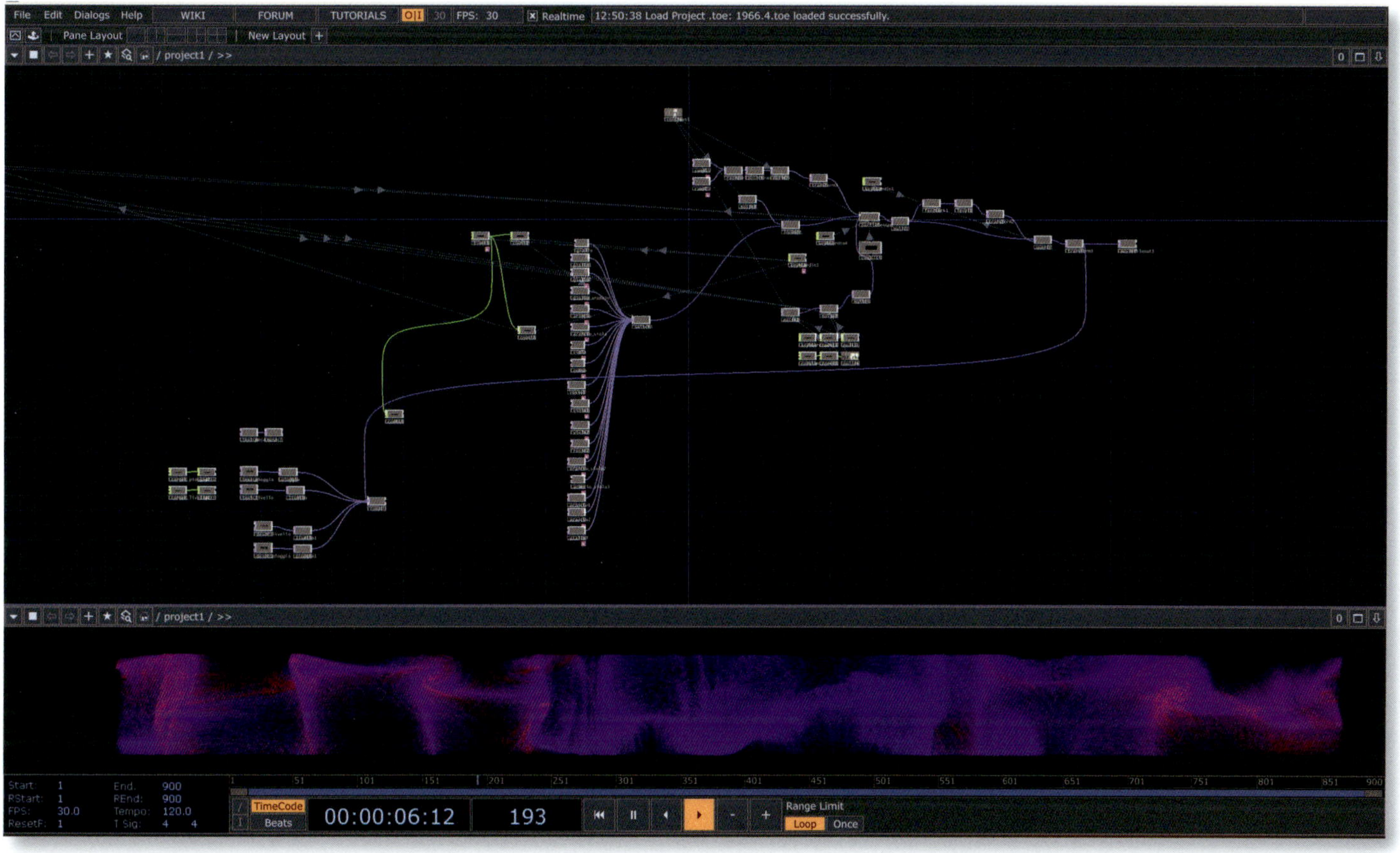

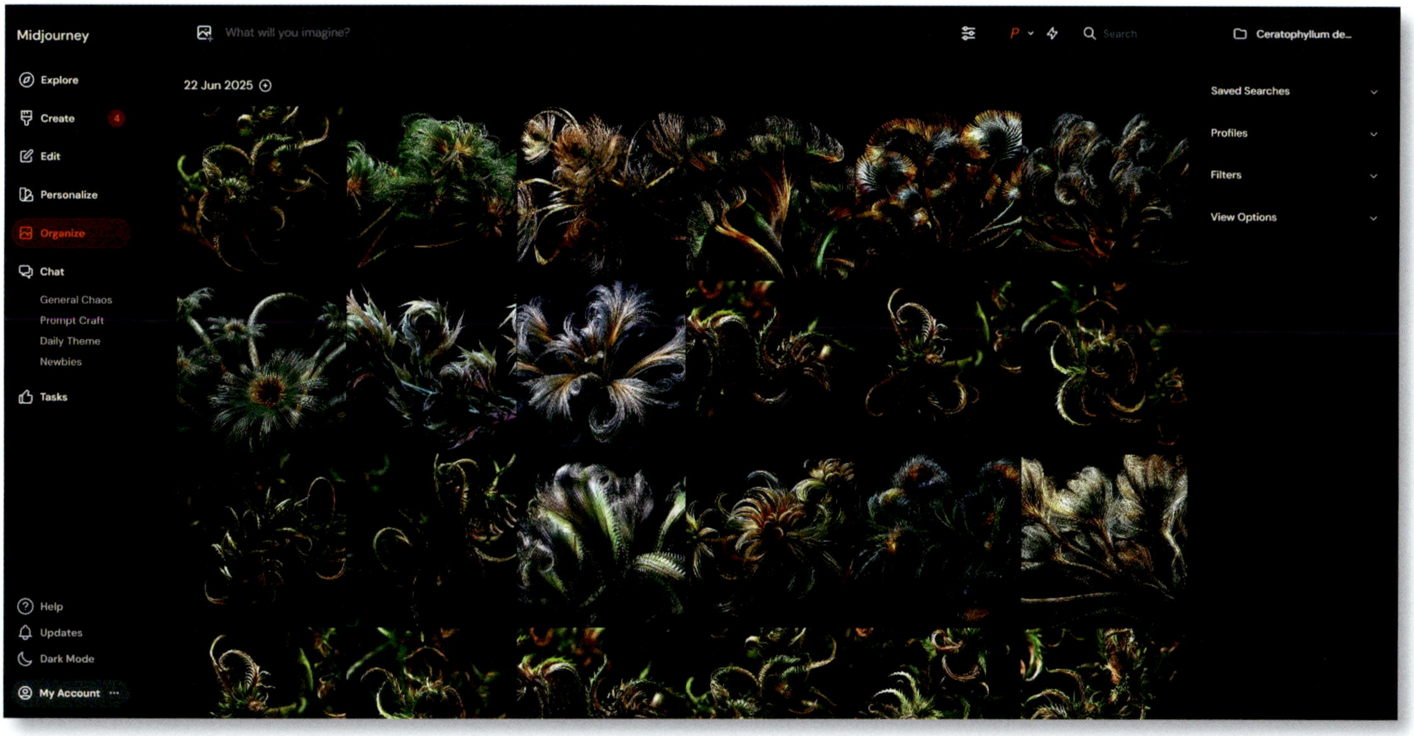

[C] Workflow in TouchDesigner for the dynamic reconstruction of the 1966 flood, with particle flow visualization dedicated to section 1.4 '1966: water chronicle of a historic flood'
[D] Visual processing on the MidJourney platform for the dynamic exploration of the shapes of *Ceratophyllum demersum*, integrated into section 2.5 'Life: River Ecosystems'

2

ENCODING VISIONS

An enthralling visual flow, generated using models of artificial intelligence, gives shape to a fascinating speculation that explores the relationship between nature and culture through the imaginary view of the Arno River. Along its course, an impossible Florence emerges where past and future merge, overseen by a non-human intelligence: that of the river, to which a voice is finally given.

This second chapter is divided into five scenes, each with its own subjective, emotional, heart-rending narrative. It is the river itself remembering, observing and reporting. Its voice is not made of words, but of images, rhythms and flows. Through visions that combine historical truth, scientific accuracy and visual invention, the river reveals fragments of its existence and of the forces that govern its movement and affect the lives of all those who live along its banks.

The project presents the Arno as a living, pulsating organism, capable of evoking images, asking questions, absorbing our full attention. Its intent is not to give back a faithful, documentary reproduction of nature, but to give shape and intensity to what has often remained invisible: a living, undefined nature that takes form here in an archetypal and visionary manner.

The artwork invites us to step aside from our own centrality and listen to another kind of narrative: one told by a body of water that has seen it all and that – in its unending flow – can never stop remembering.

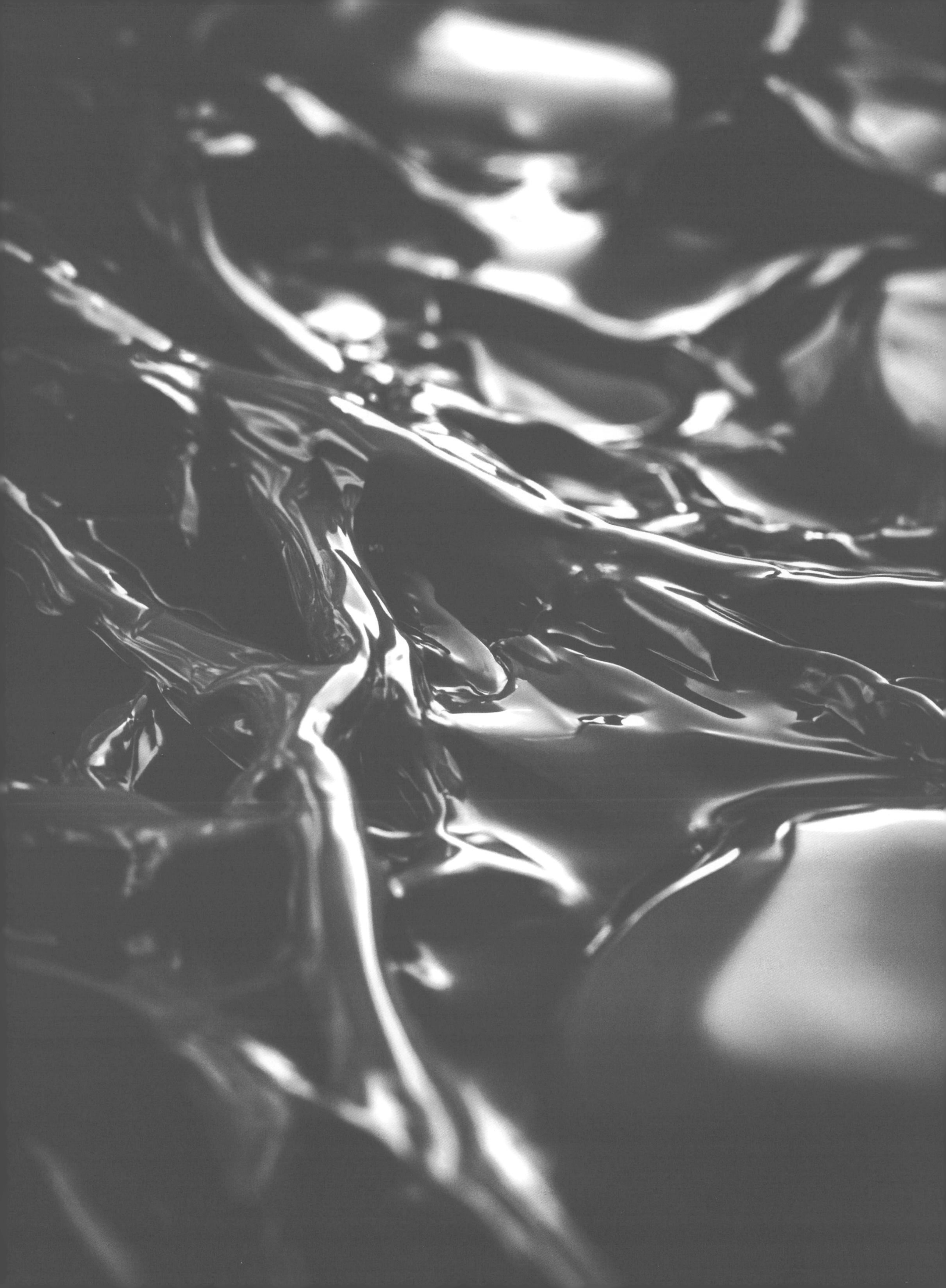

2.1

Space: From the Source to the City

A dynamic, uninterrupted flow follows the course of the Arno River, from its crystal-clear source amid the Casentino peaks to the beating heart of Florence. The story opens on a scene of uncontaminated, primordial nature, travels through the neat rows of agricultural fields dotted with clusters of buildings, to finally reach the urban environment, where the interaction between the land and human settlement becomes more complex and stratified.

The visual impression is of rapid, dizzying motion, capturing the energy and vitality of the waterway, with fluid, enveloping sequences that carry the view along the flow. The space is not mere background, but living, reactive matter: the river does not merely glide seaward, but absorbs and remembers the shapes of the landscape. In its visual progress, it alternates broad panoramic views with intimate glimpses, building a geography that combines precise analytical detail with poetic imagination.

As the landscape changes – in the density of the elements, the colors and structure of the surroundings – it tells a story that explores the fragile balance between natural and artificial. The water's constant flow acts as like a narrative voice, quietly underscoring and providing connection between the multiple dimensions of the landscape, telling of the continuous changes that the river itself experiences and travels through.

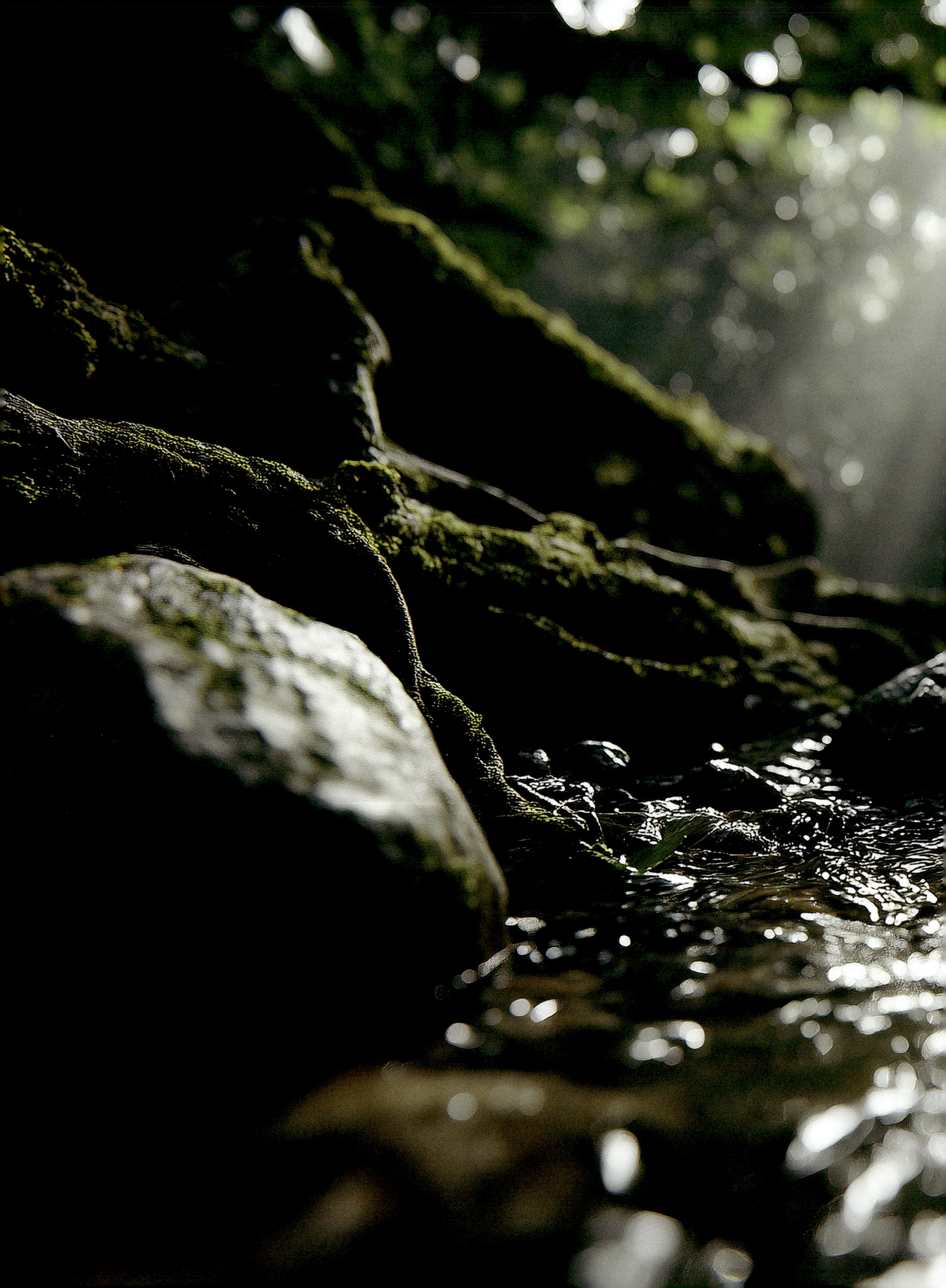

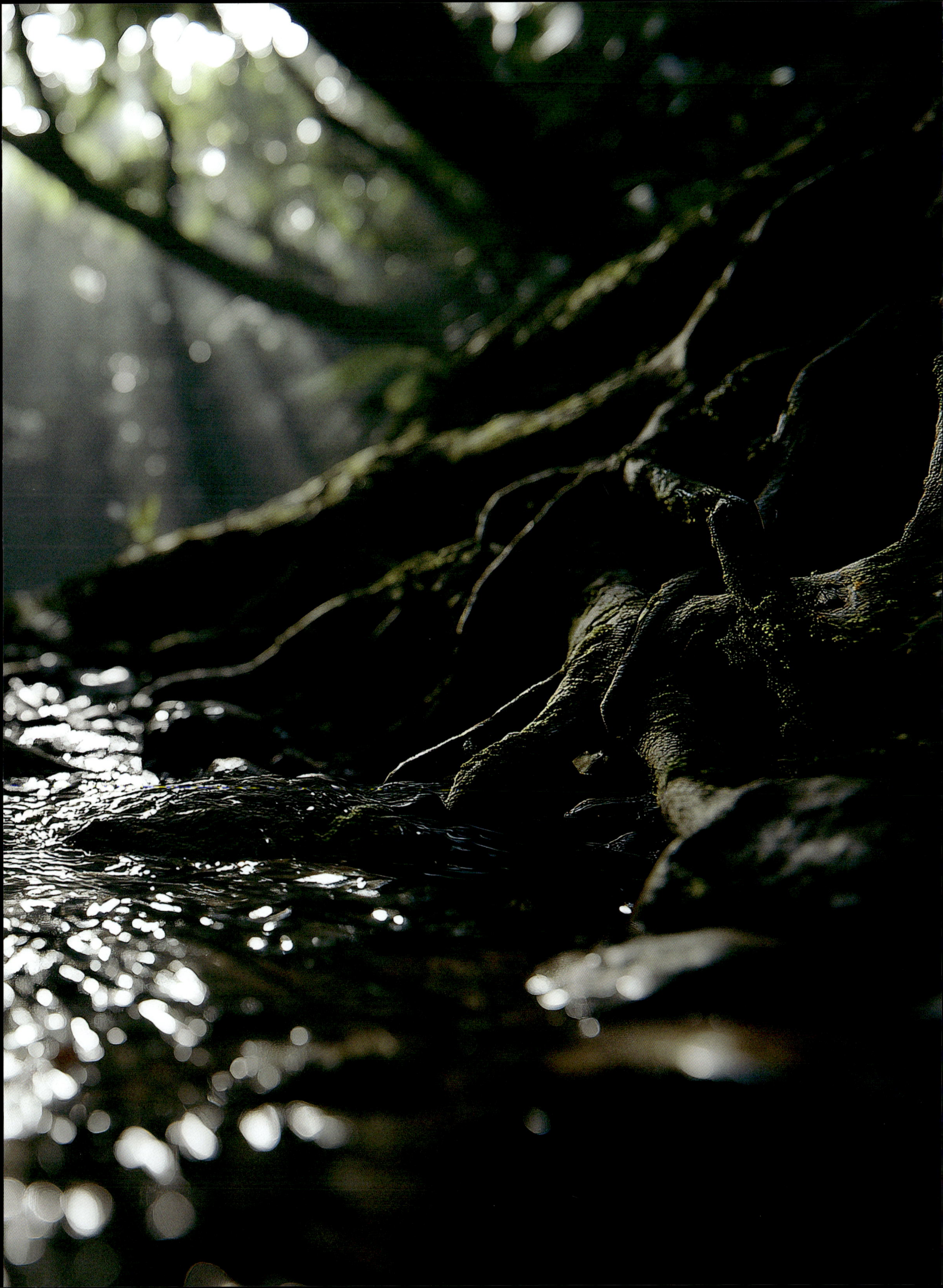

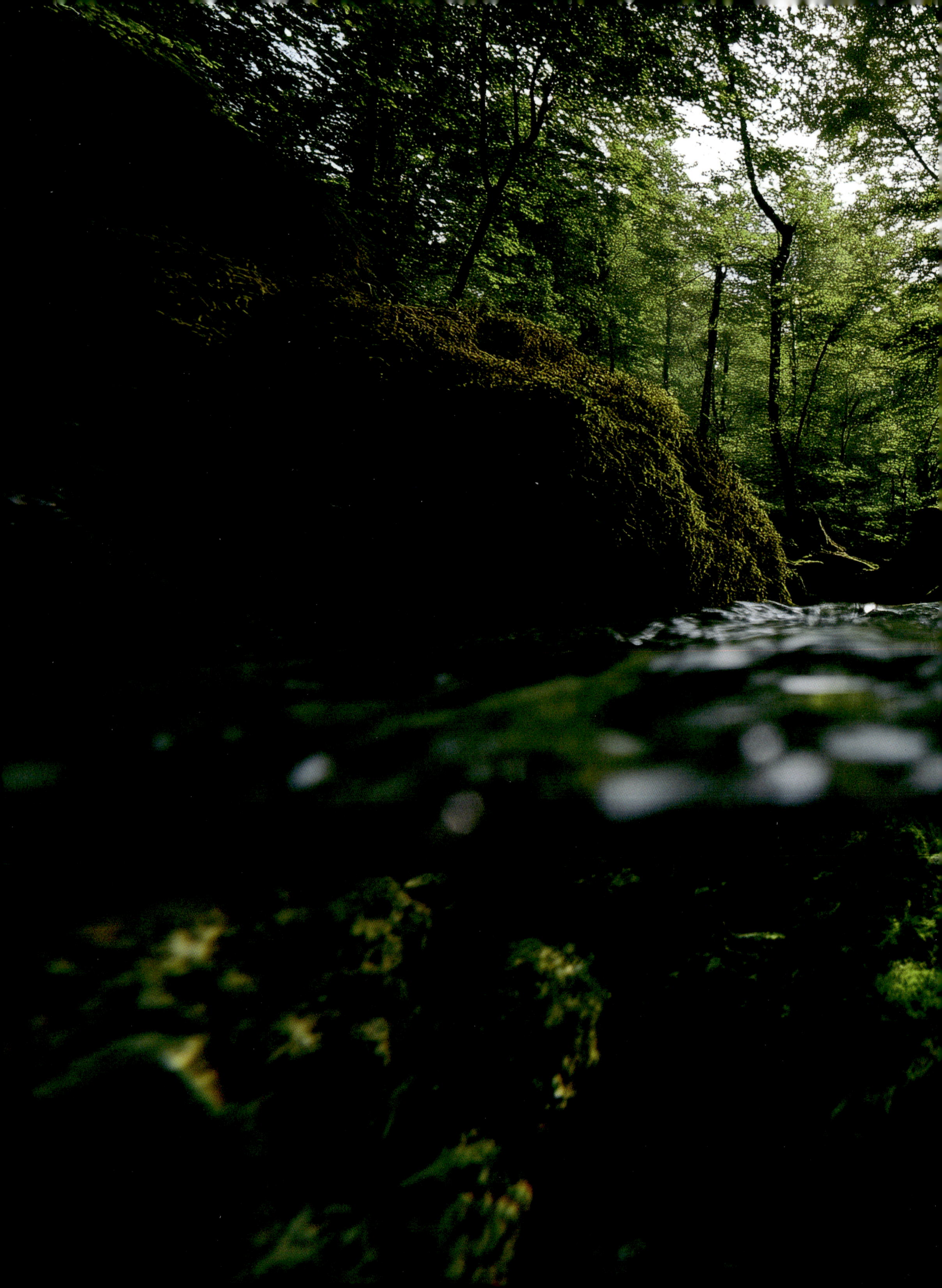

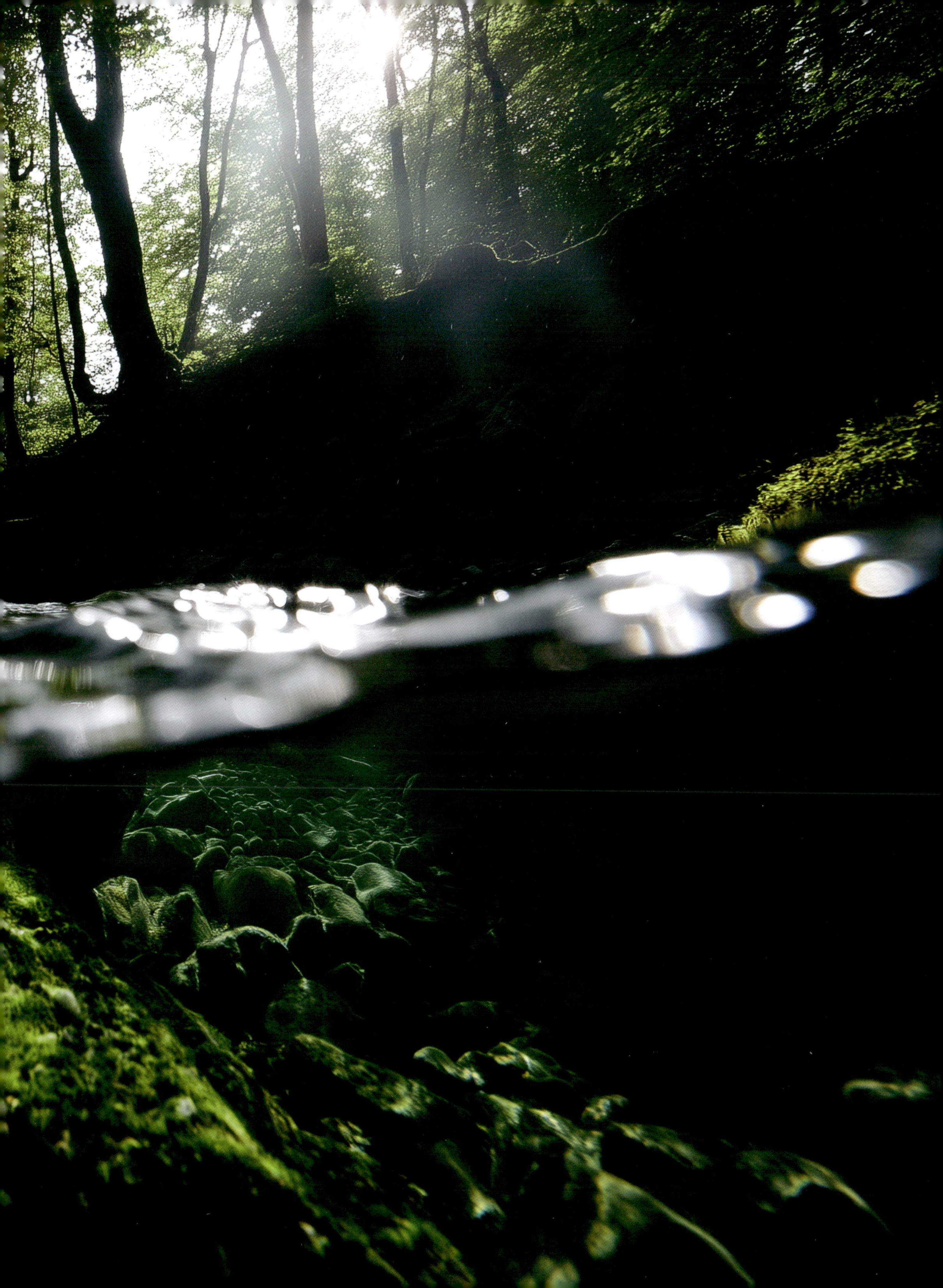

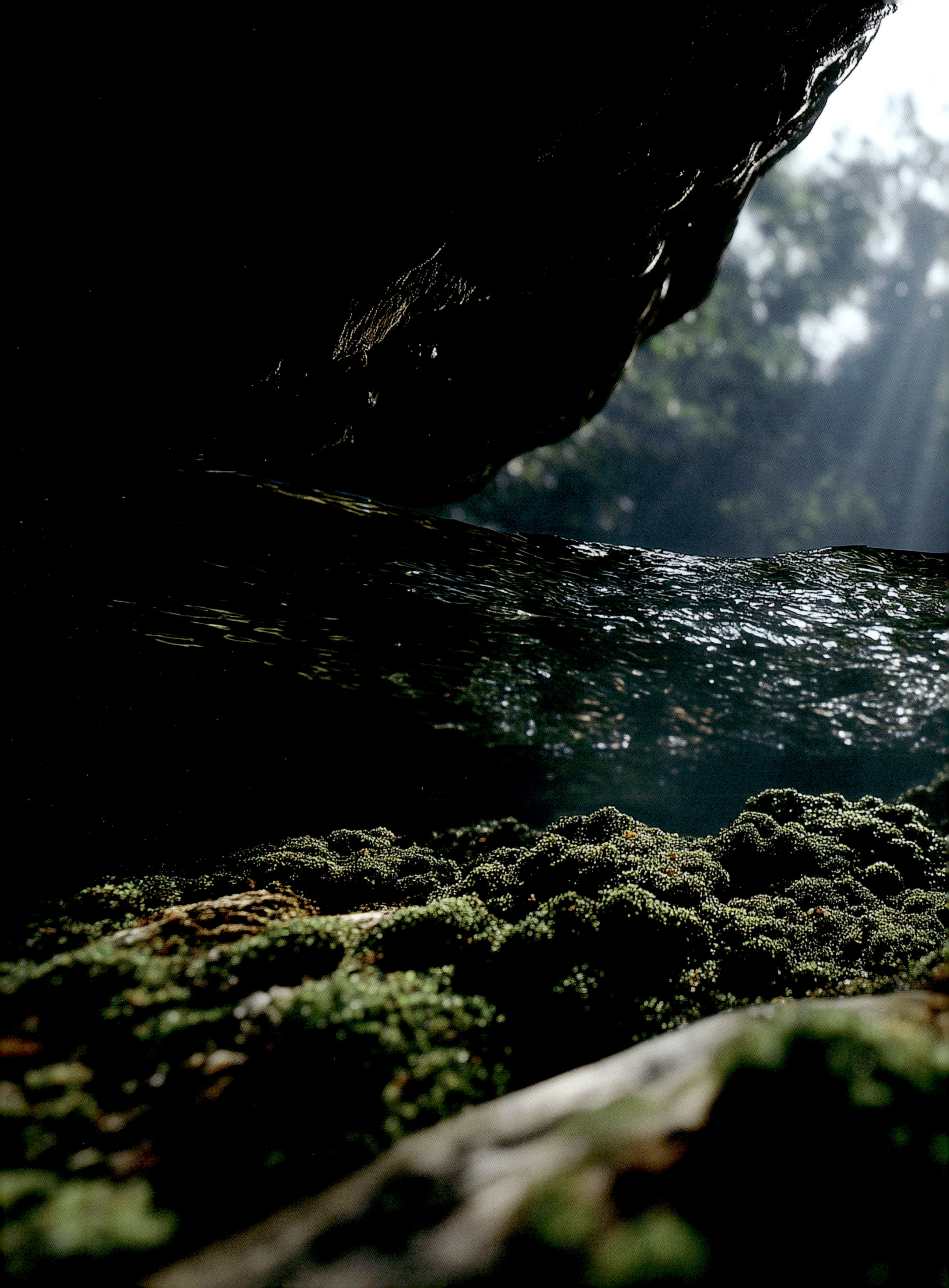

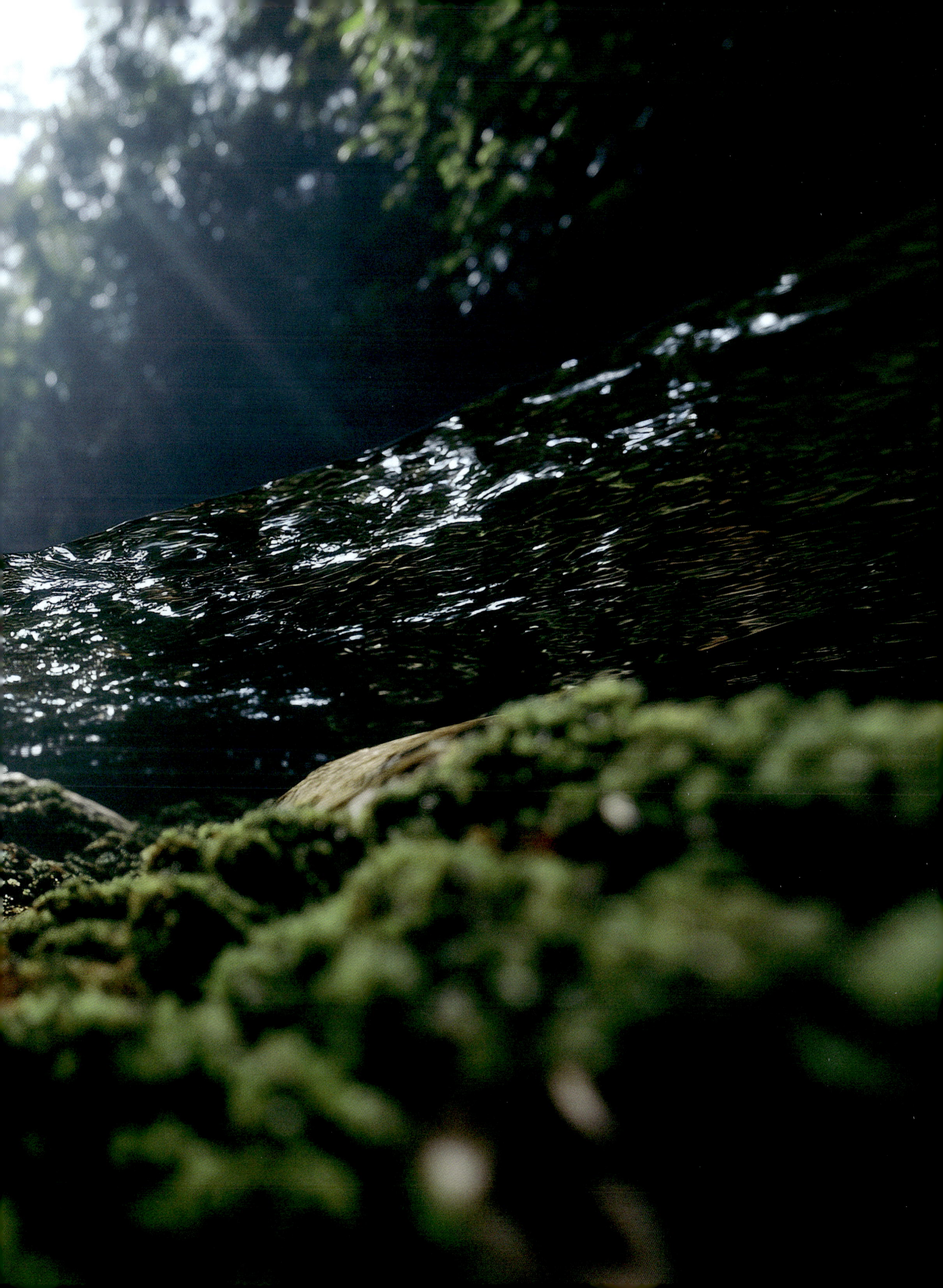

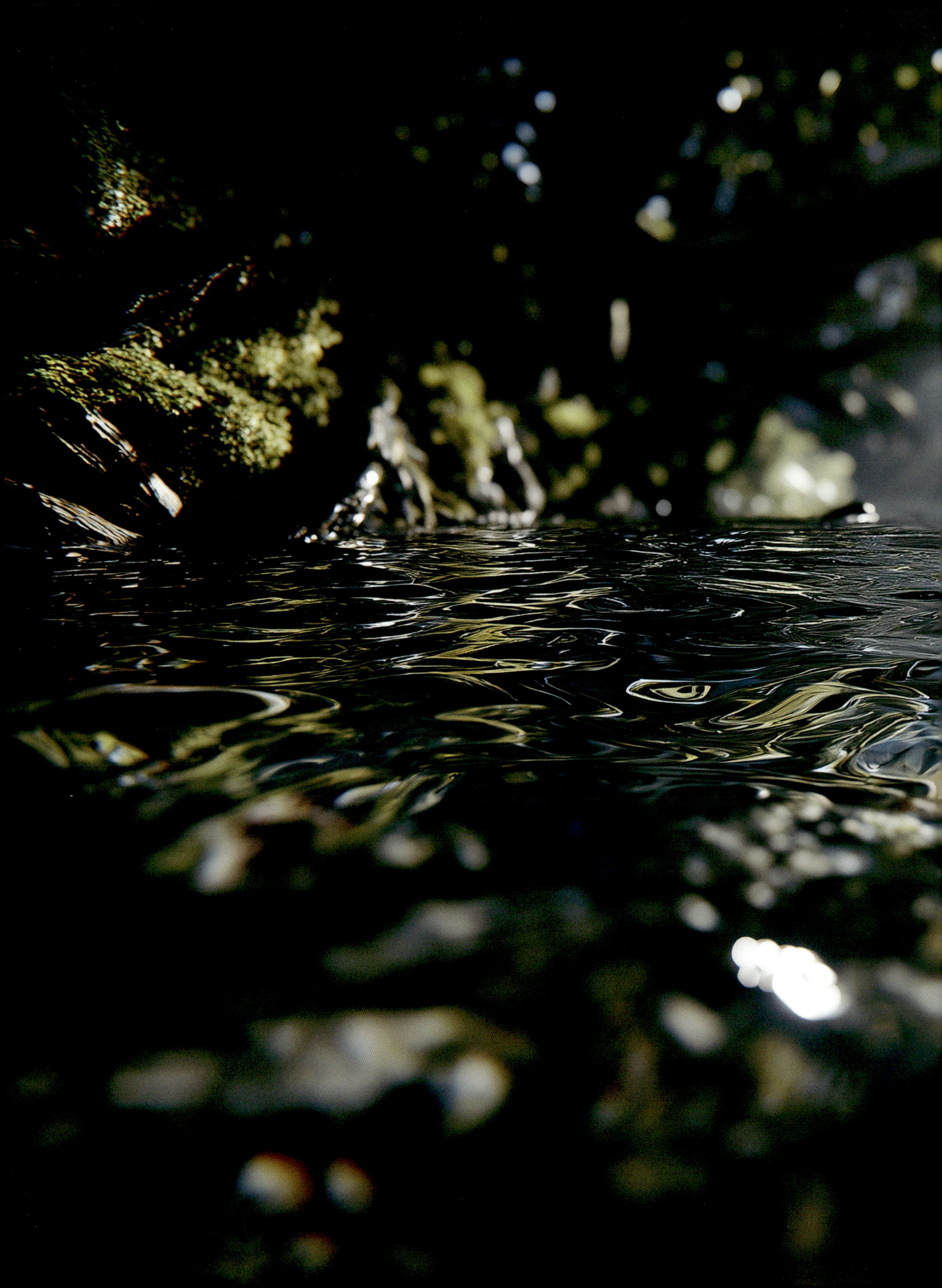

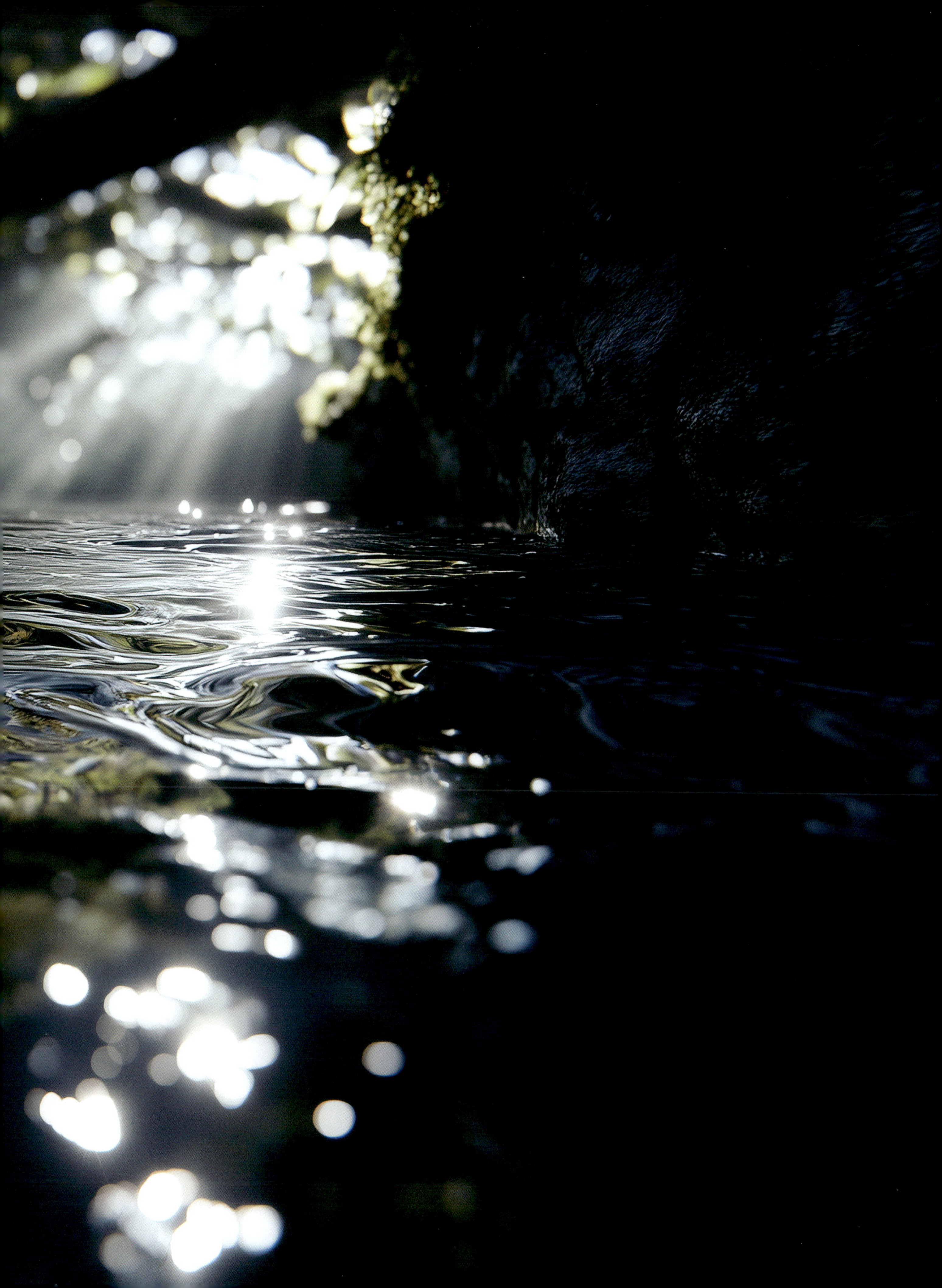

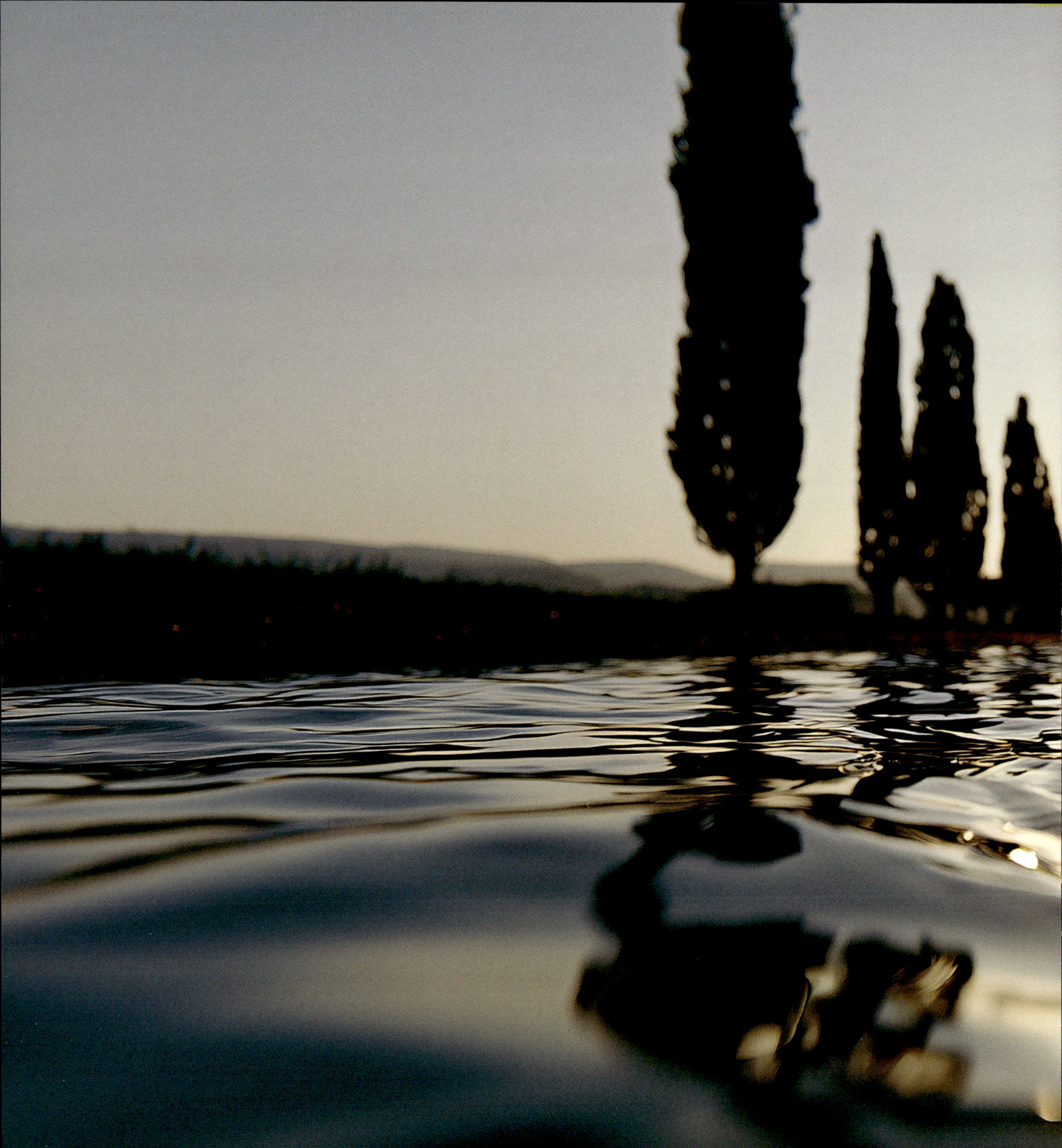

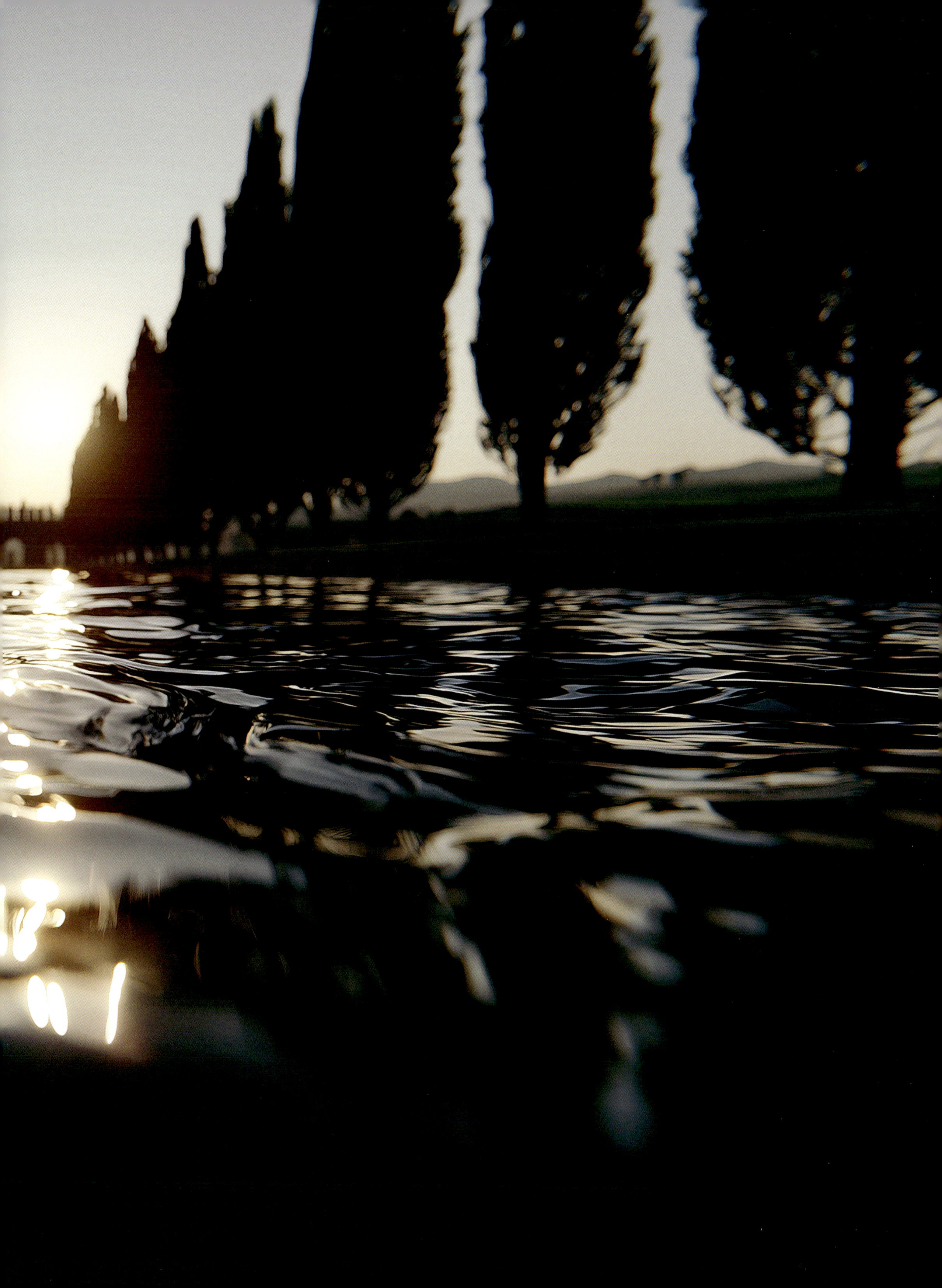

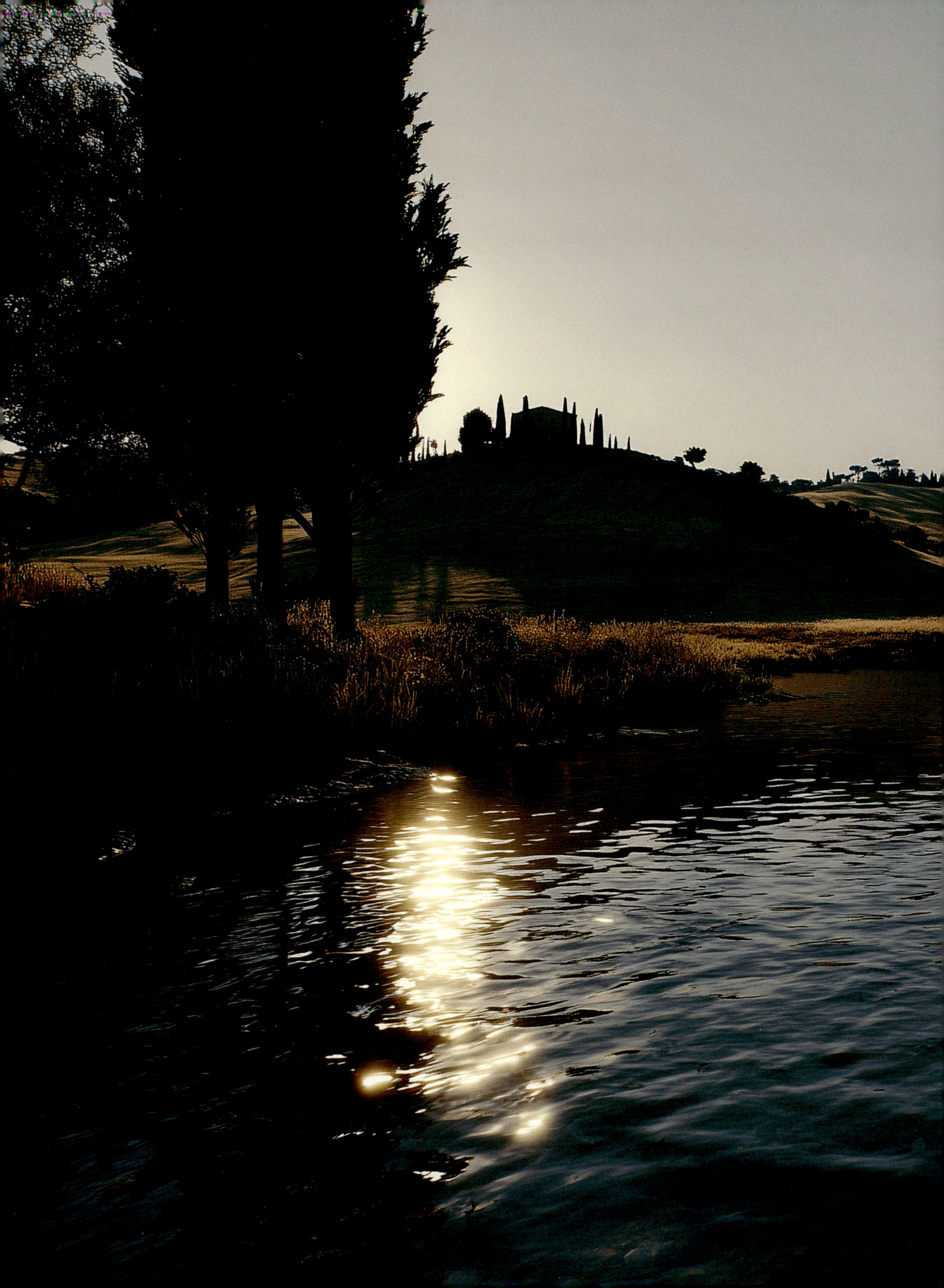

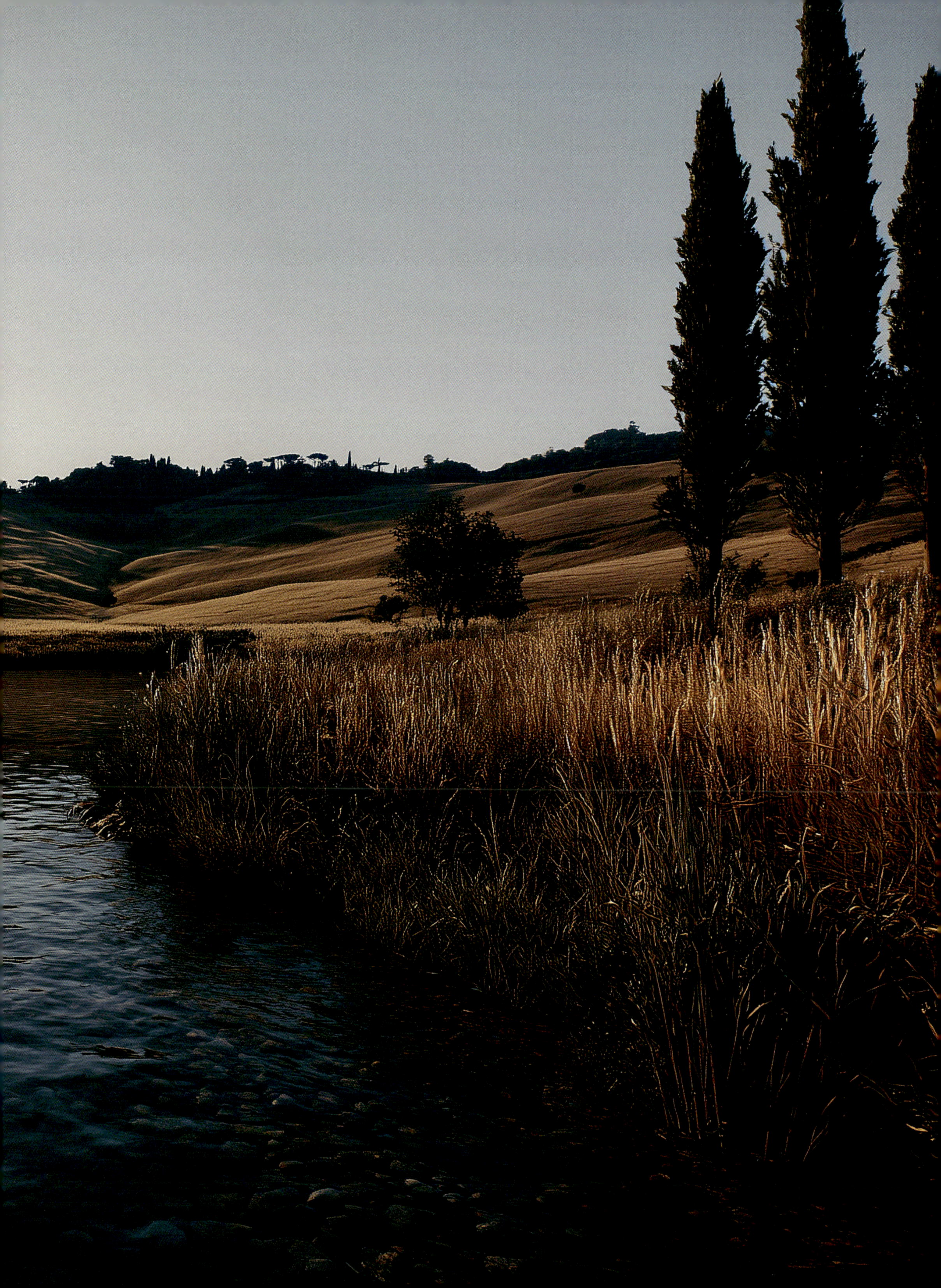

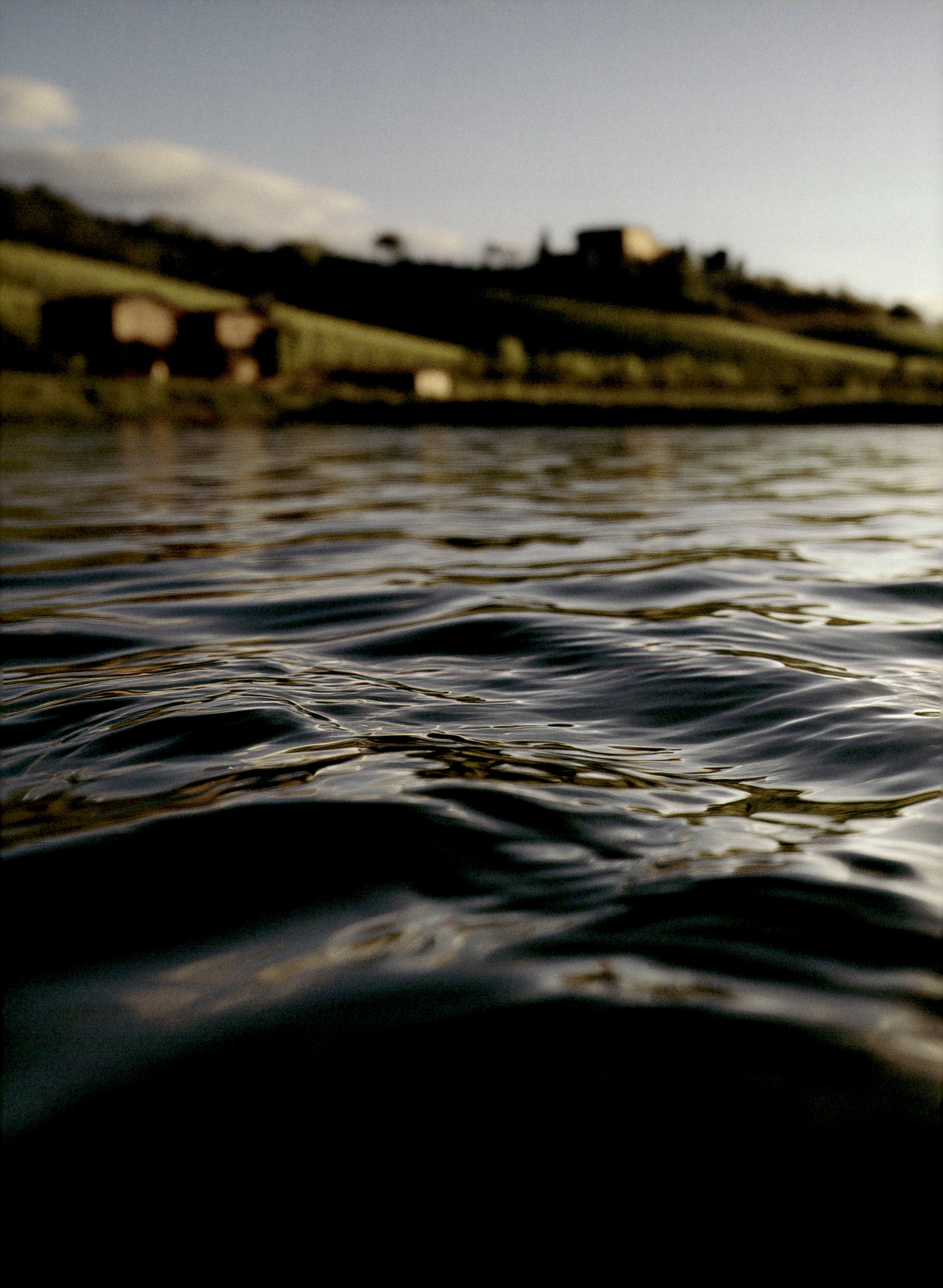

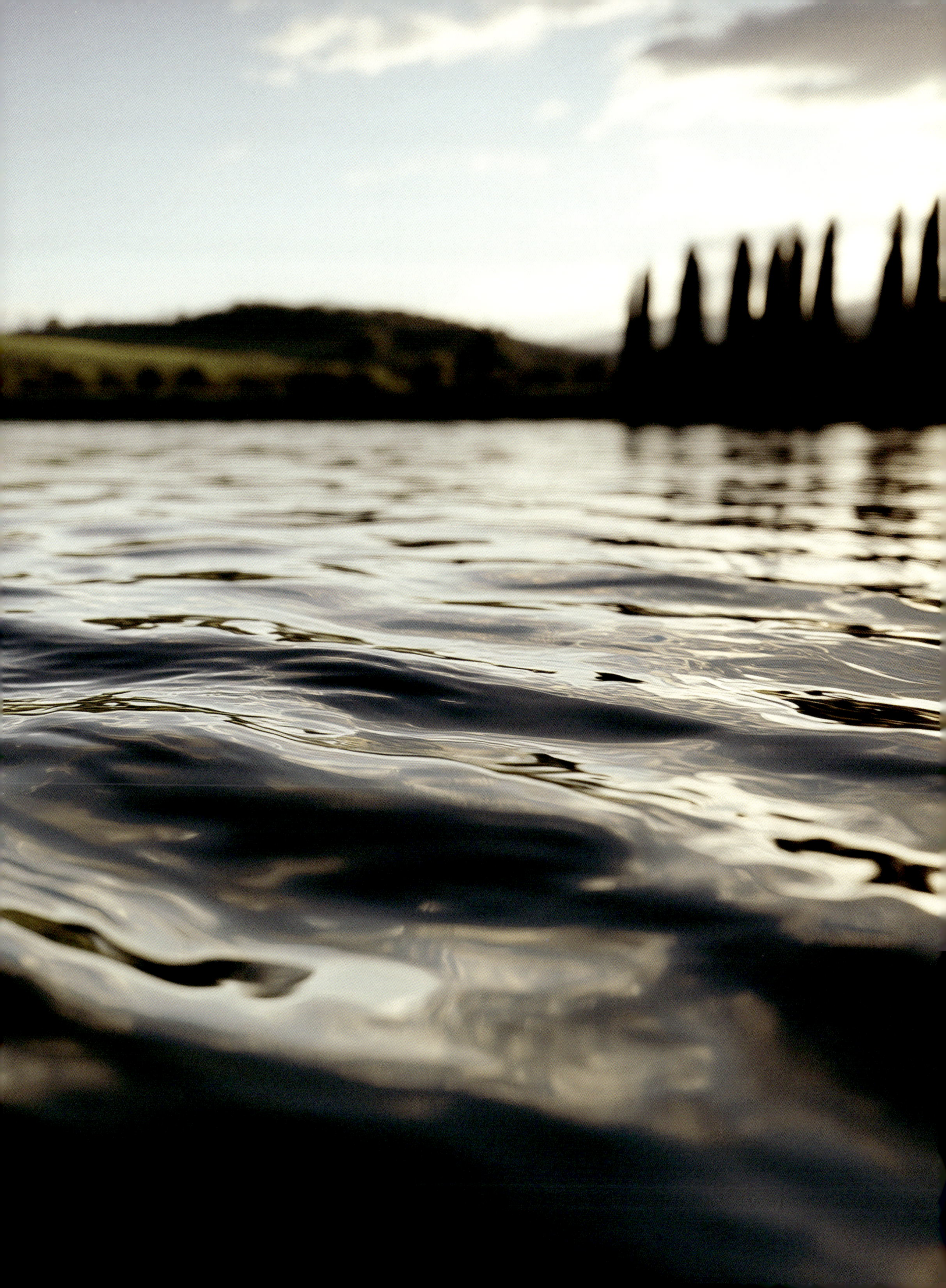

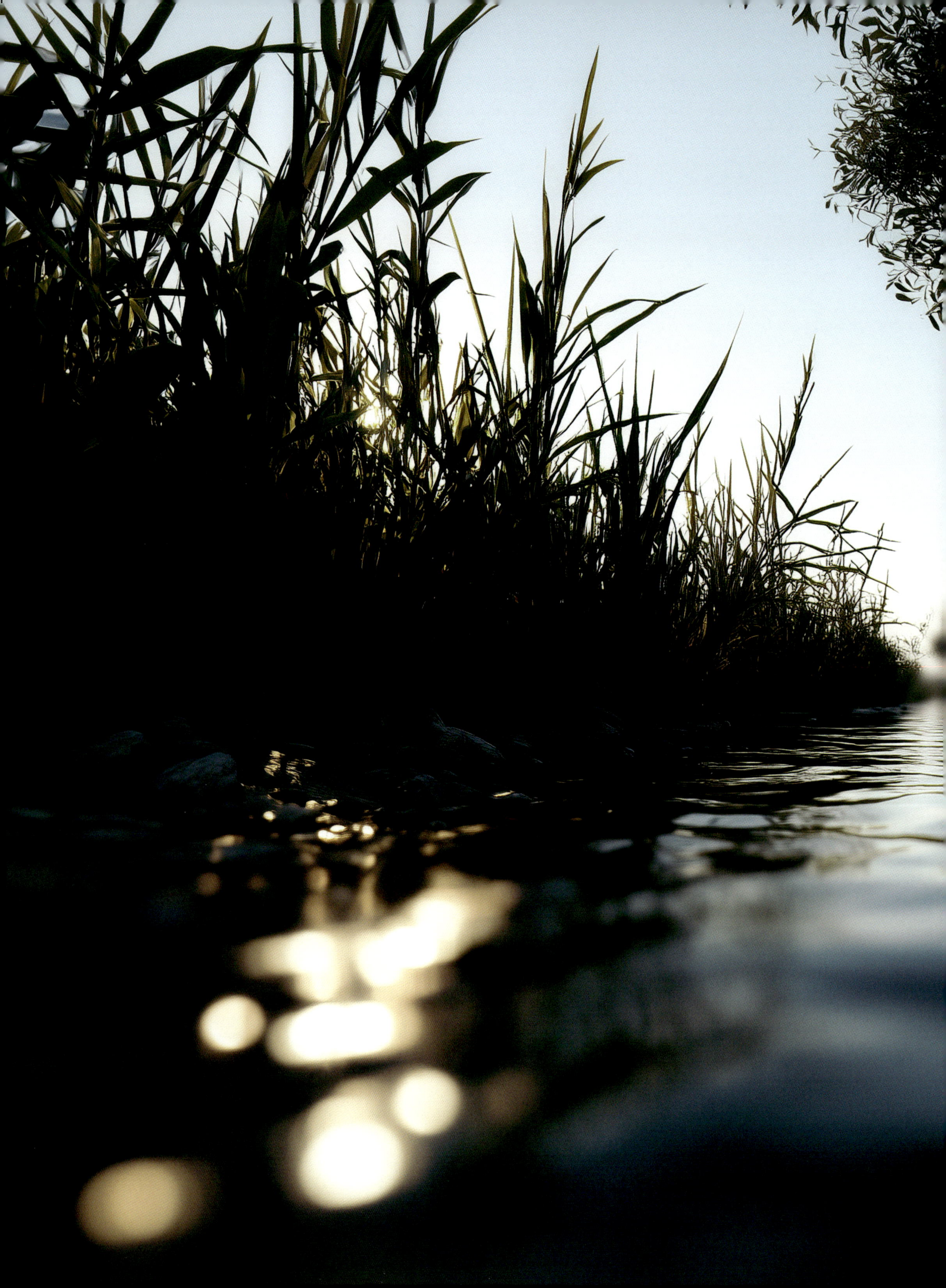

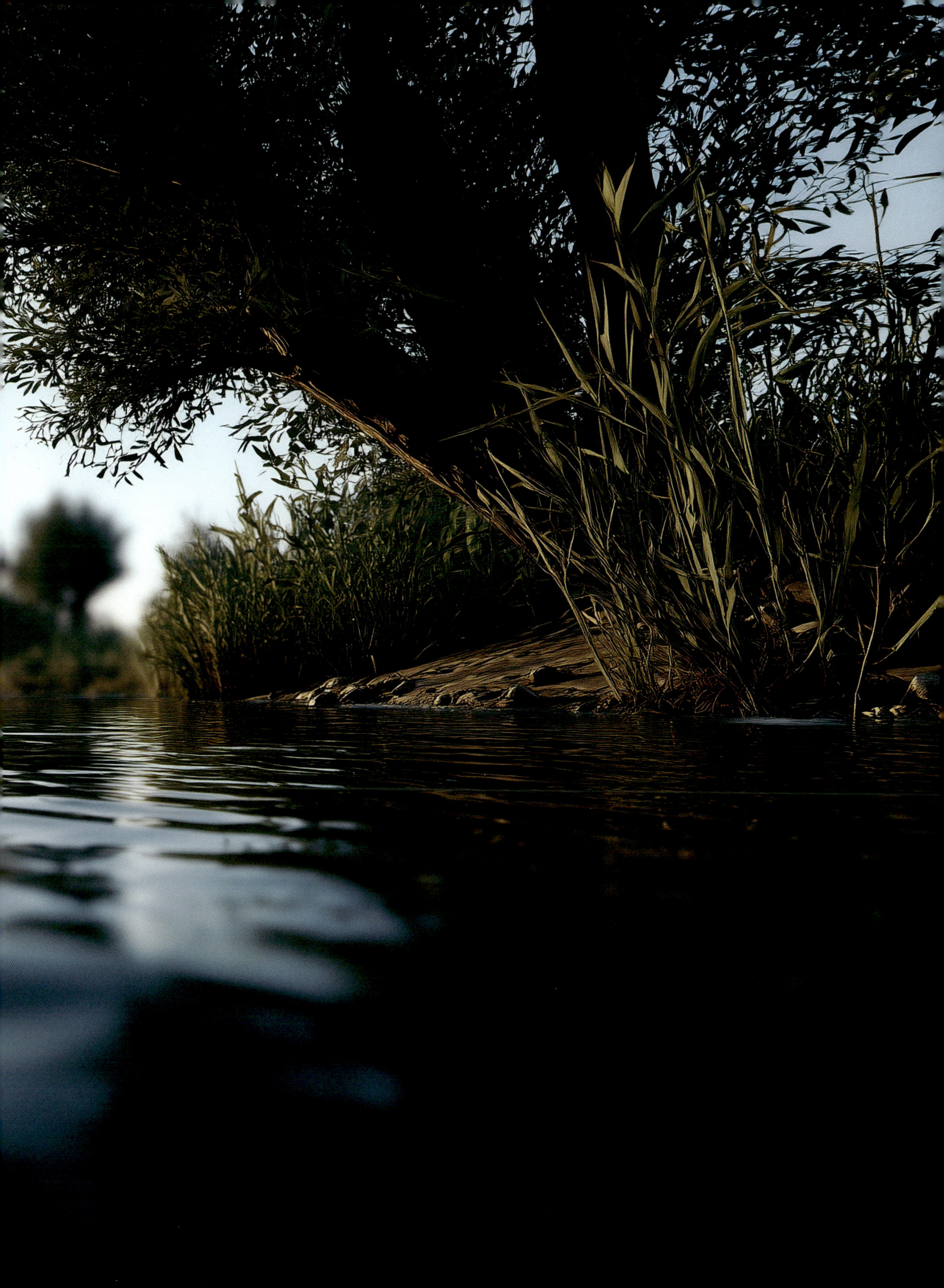

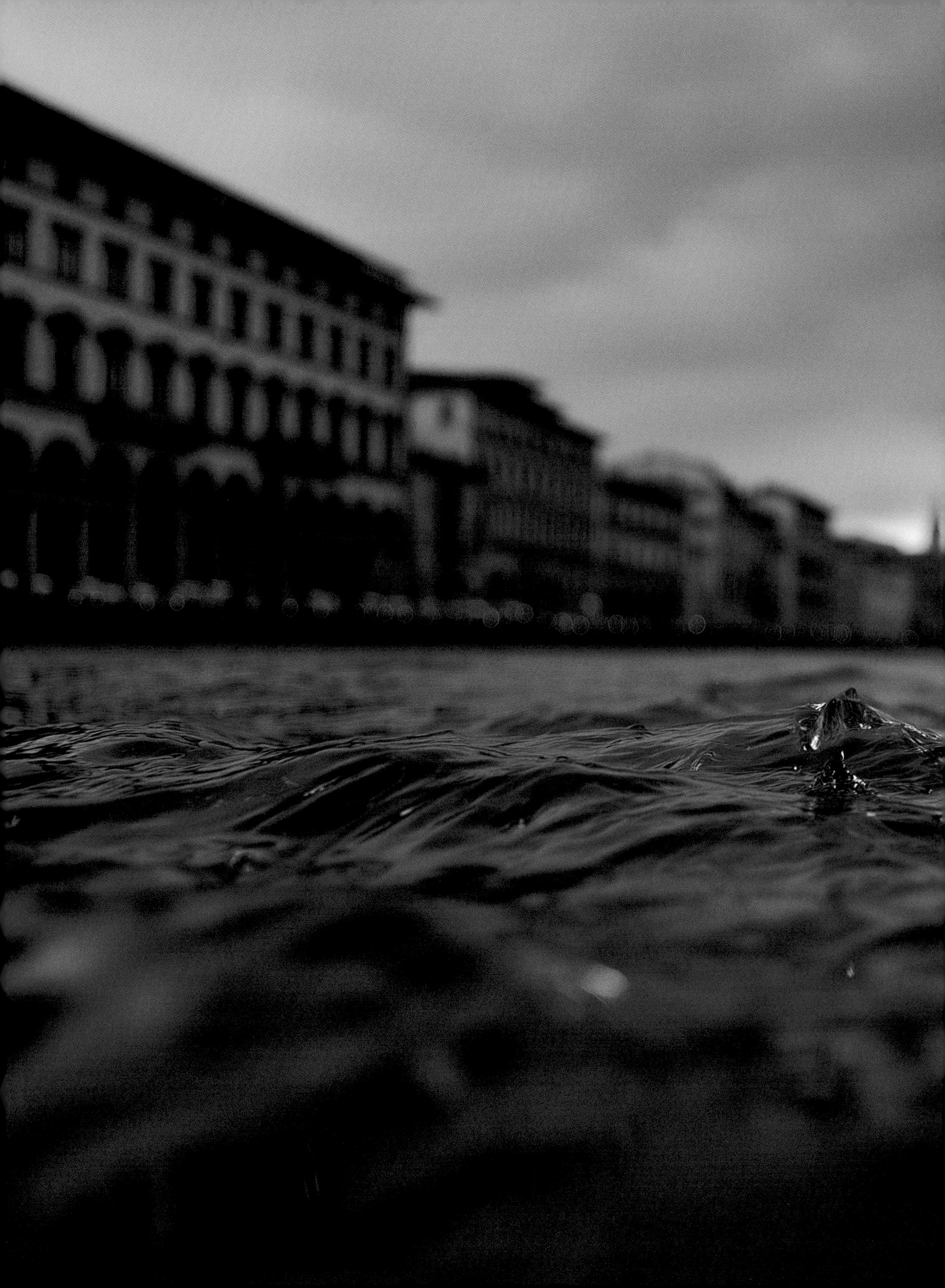

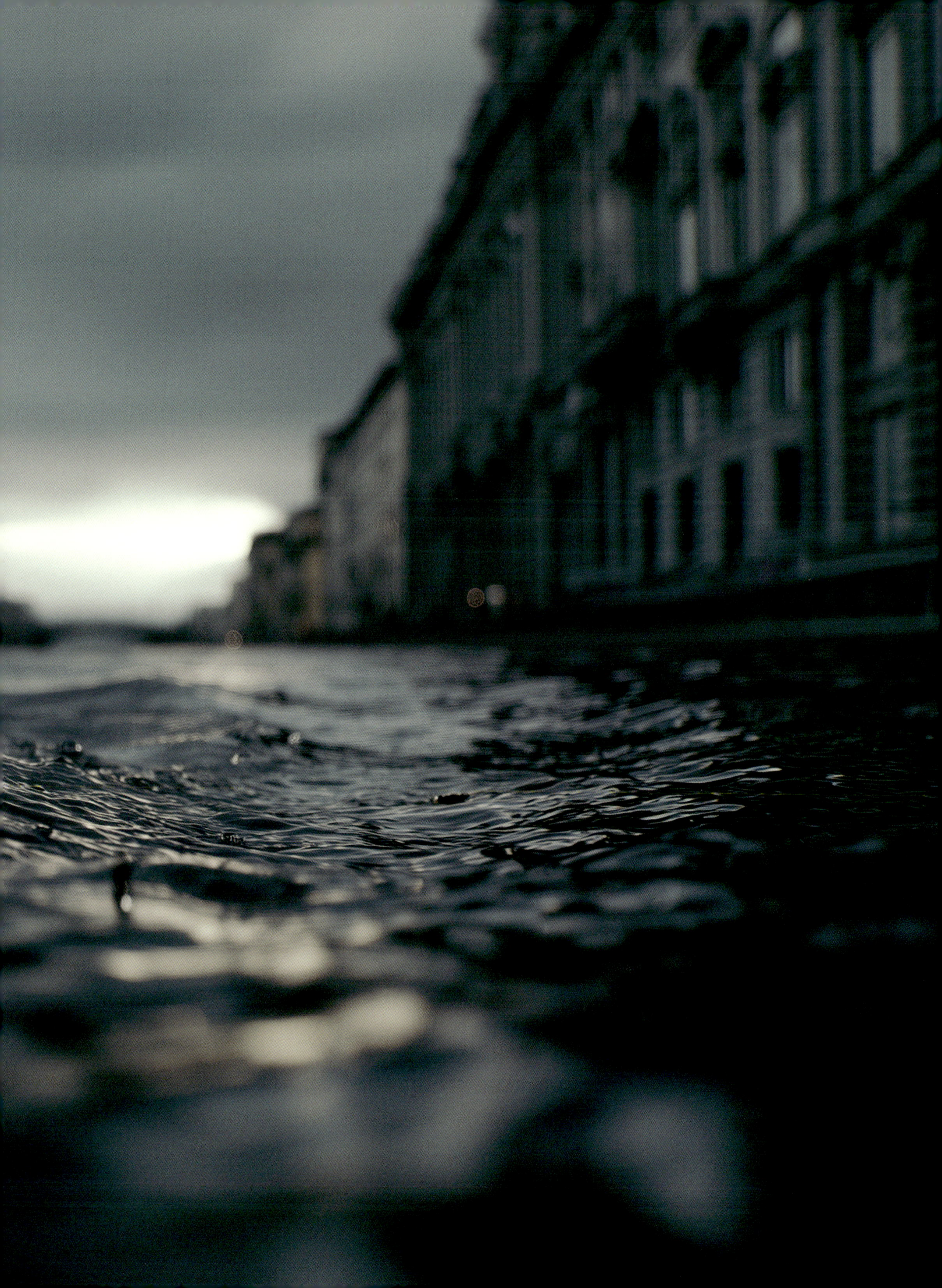

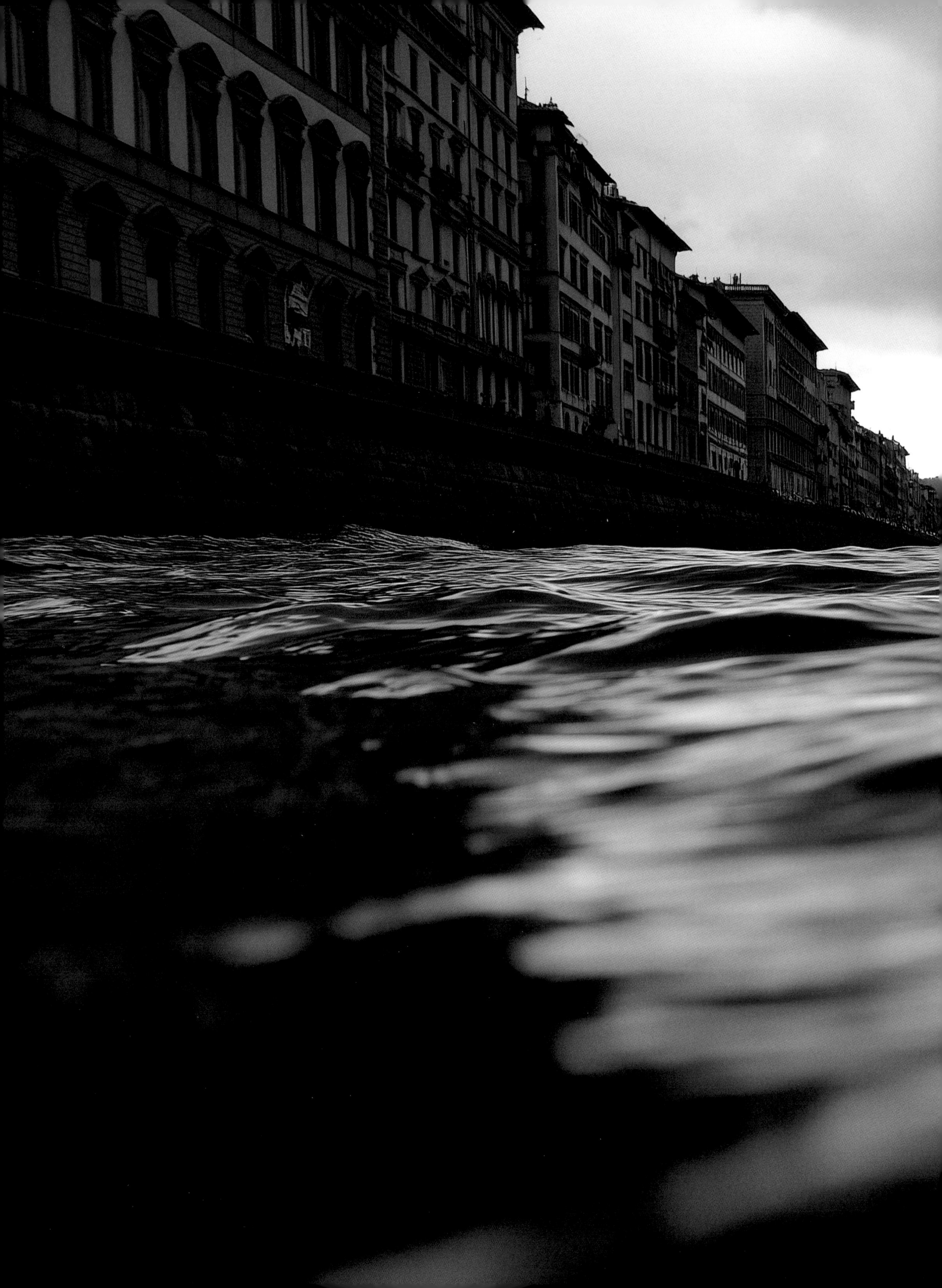

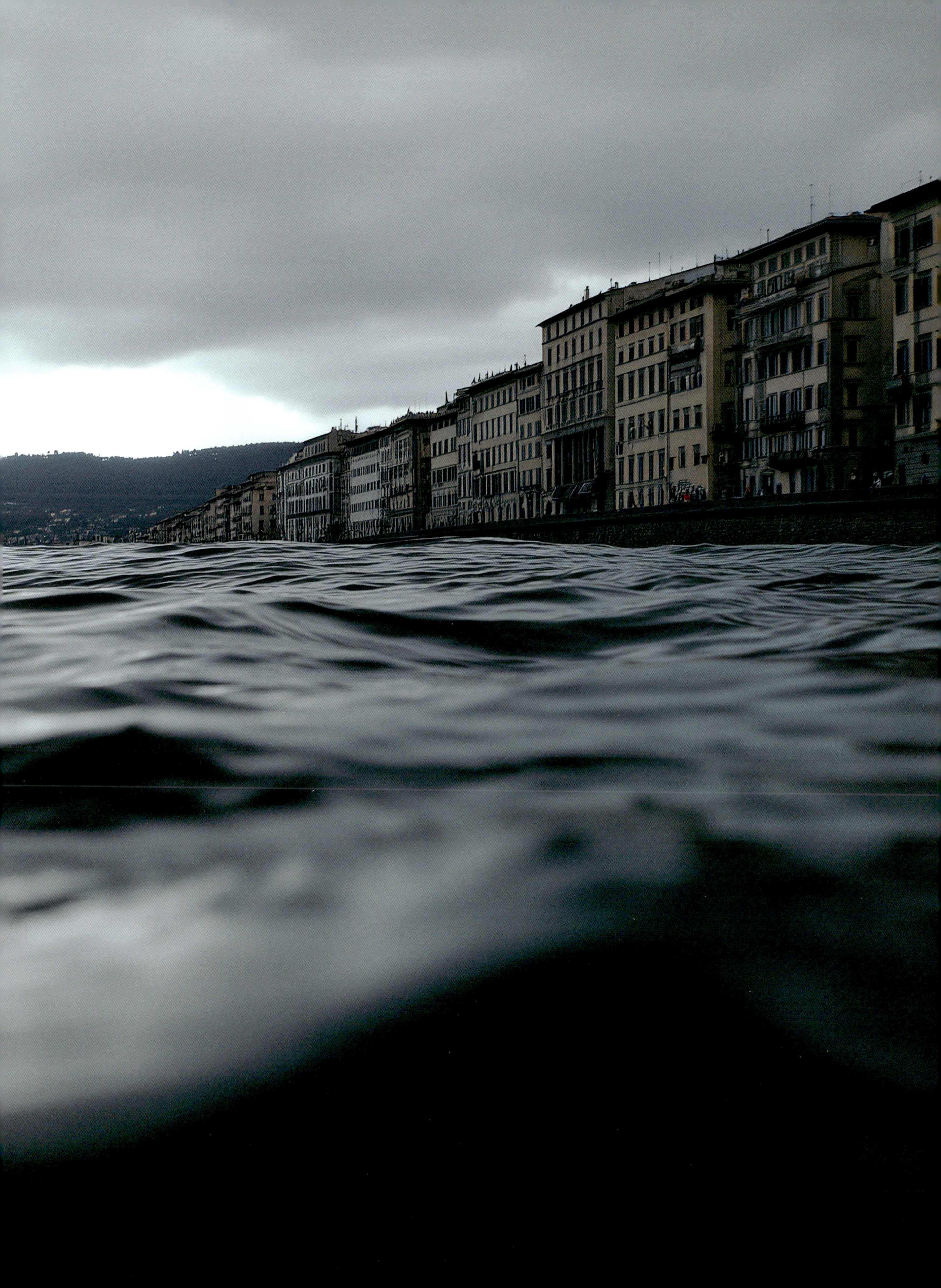

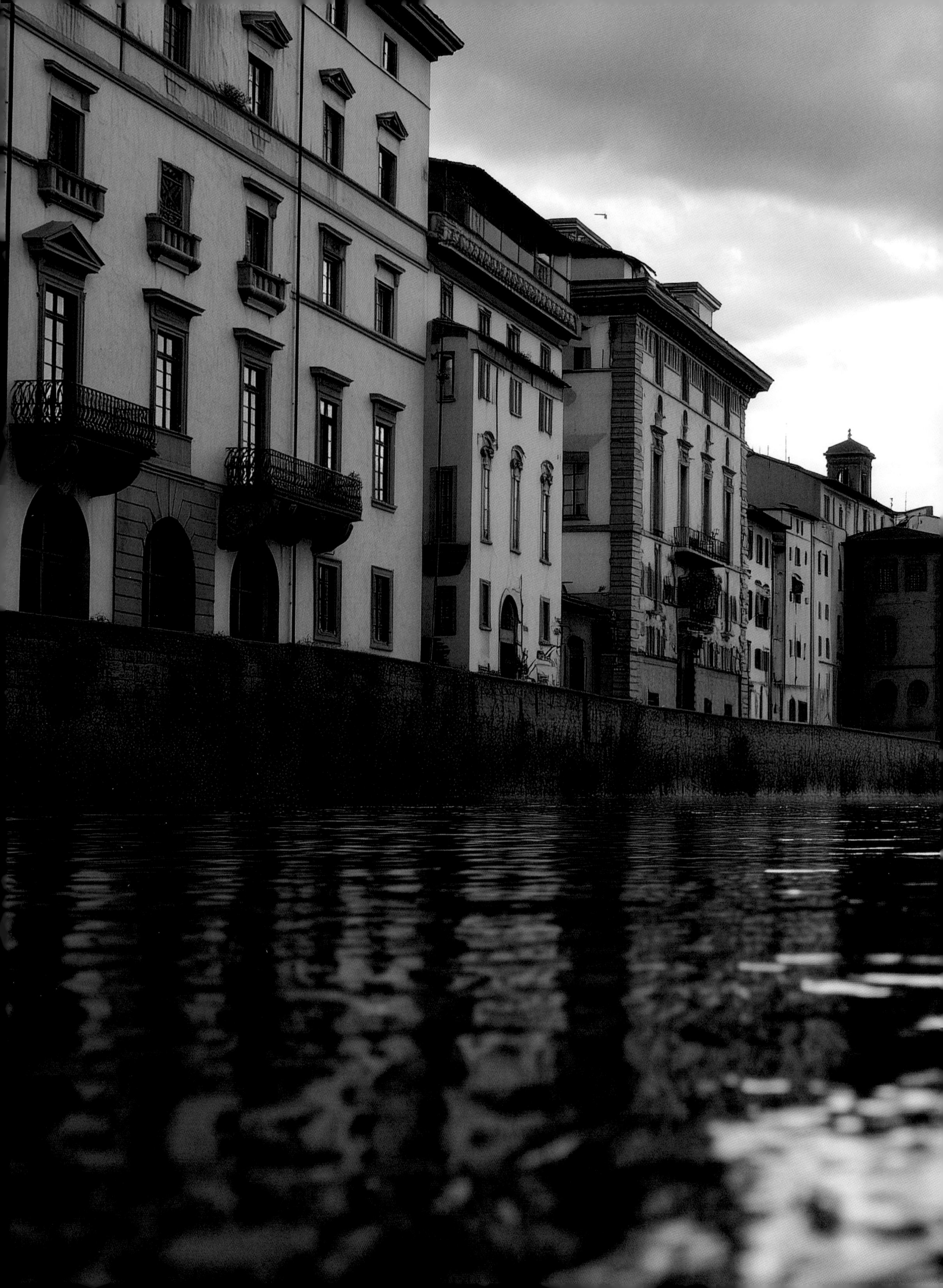

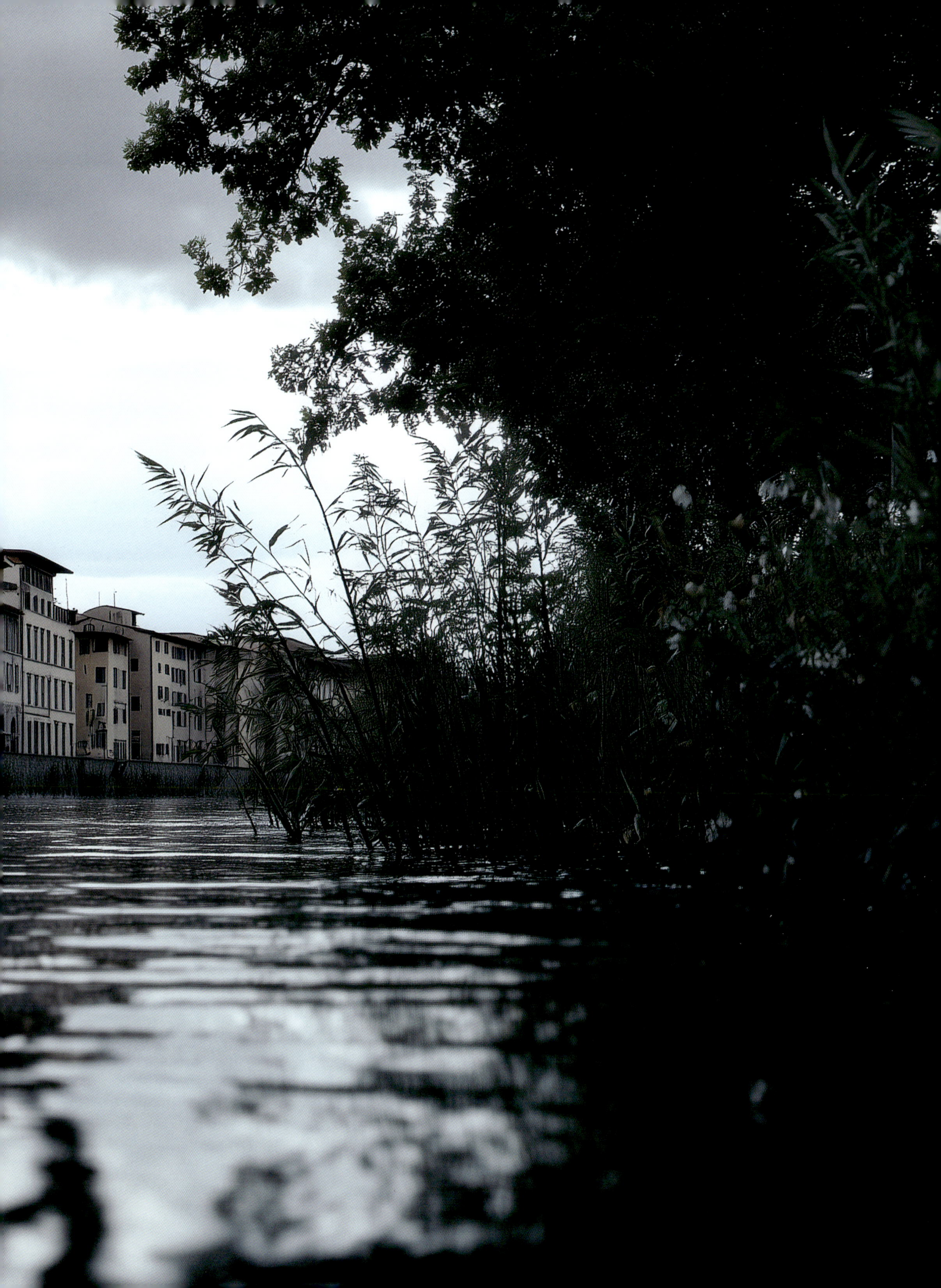

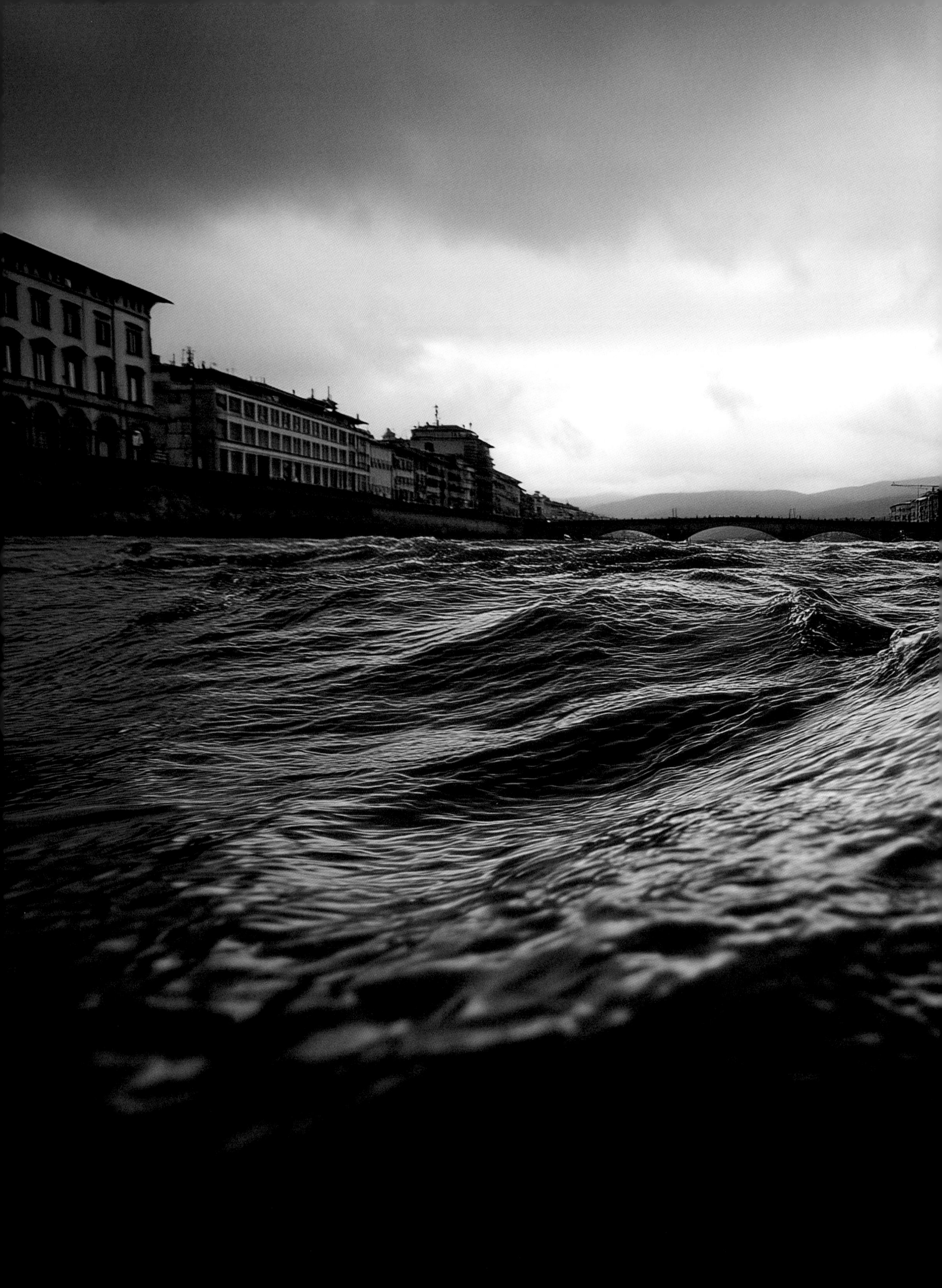

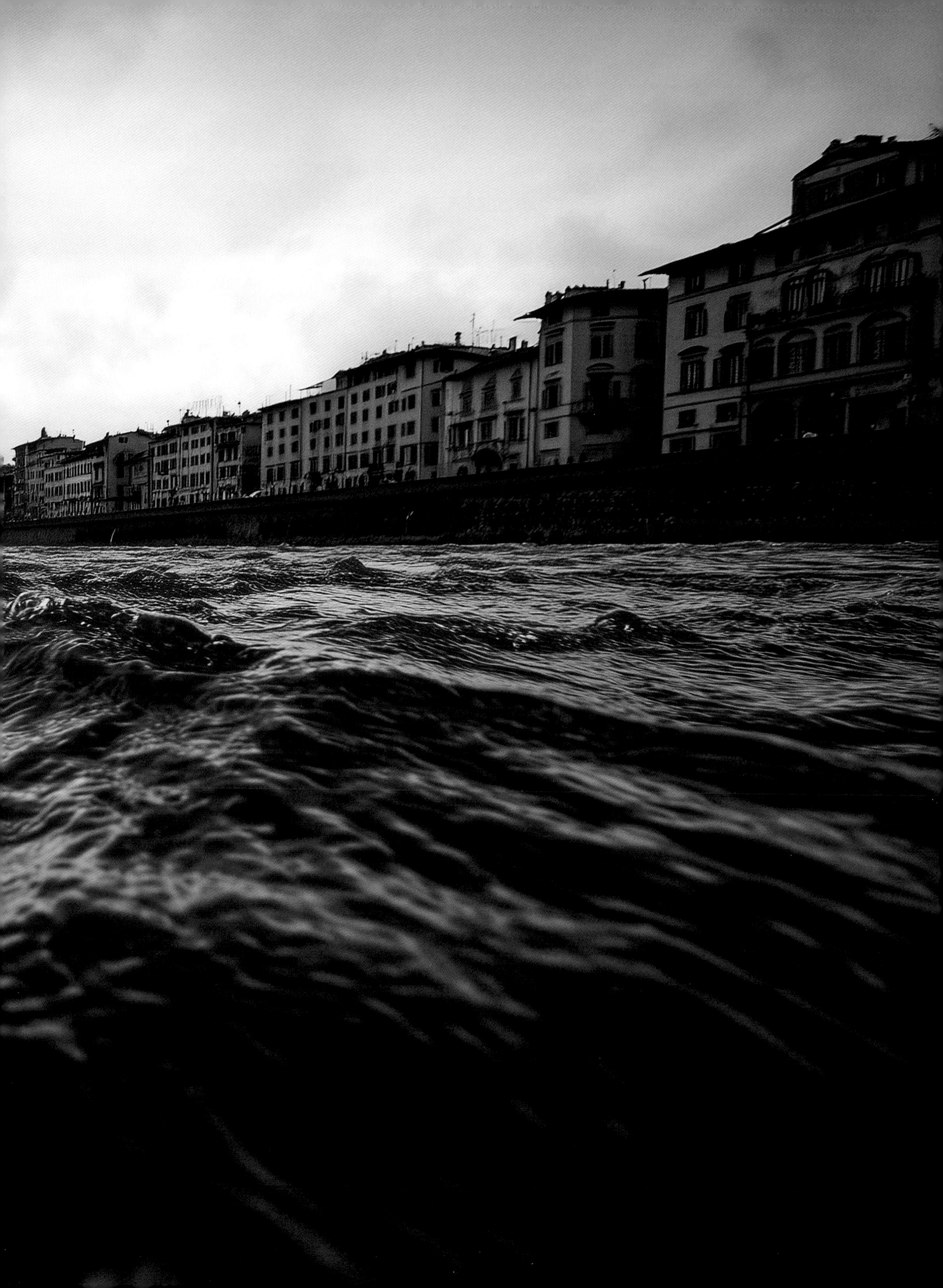

PROMPT_01 [low-angle view from Arno river source, crystal clear mountain stream flowing between mossy rocks and roots, lush ancient forest in background, early morning mist, sunlight beams through foliage, realistic water texture, cinematic light and shadow, vivid natural colors, depth of field --chaos 15 --ar 16:9 --raw --stylize 50]

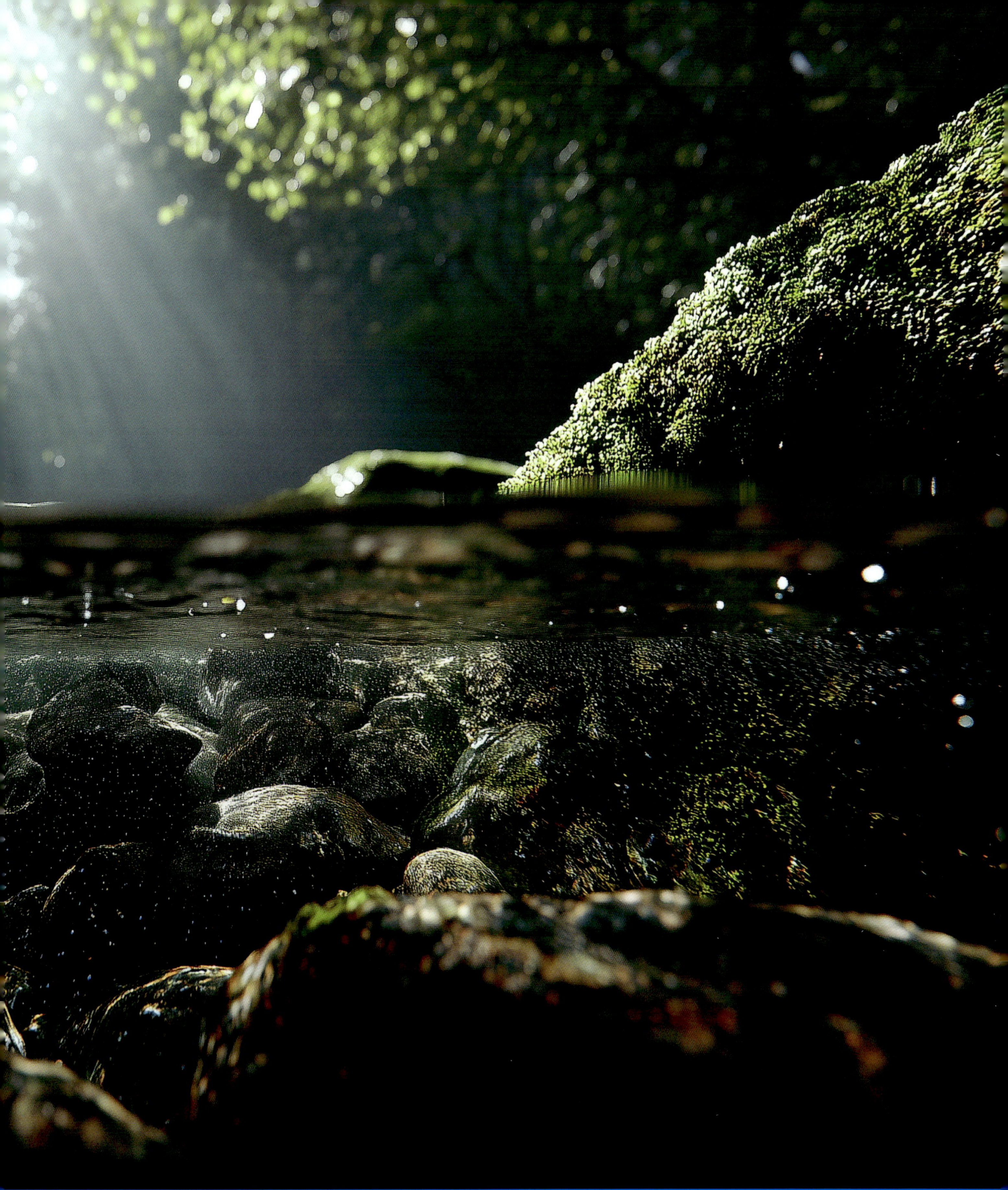

IMG_01

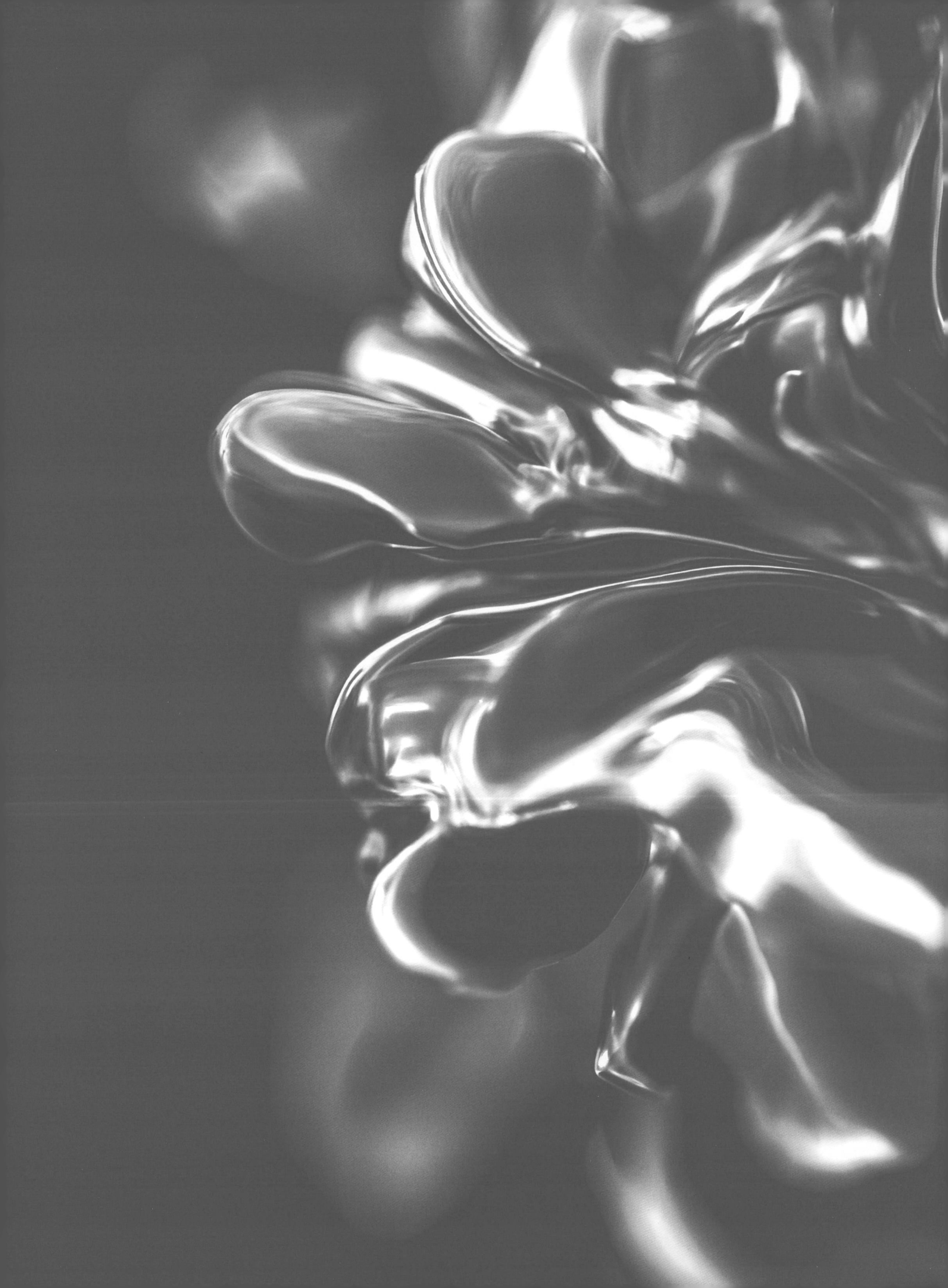

2.2

Cyclicity: Natural Rhythms

The succeeding seasons are reflected in the aspect of the river, with changes on the surface depending on the condition of its water: the density, transparency and effects of the light. The Arno reacts to the natural weather patterns, changing gradually in a subtle equilibrium between apparent tranquility and continuous movement.

Autumn opens the sequence with a current that accelerates gradually; leaves fall lightly, dancing in the air before they come to rest on the water like bits of gold. They float for some distance before sinking, along an uncertain trajectory, like fleeting memories. Winter arrives with a more determined mindset: the wind is harsh and ruffles the surface, waves break on broken branches lying in the river bed. The landscape turns darker, the days are shorter and the water is charged with a visceral, almost tempestuous force. With the arrival of spring, the flow lightens: petals and flowers drift in the current, light glitters and is refracted, vegetation revives. Everywhere there is germination, even in the river, and when summer comes, it spreads its calm over the landscape, the water sparkles; reflections lengthen; the current slows. This cycle, both natural and perceptive, does not merely follow the altering climate: it is the liquid alphabet that the river uses to describe the ways in which it inhabits the world.

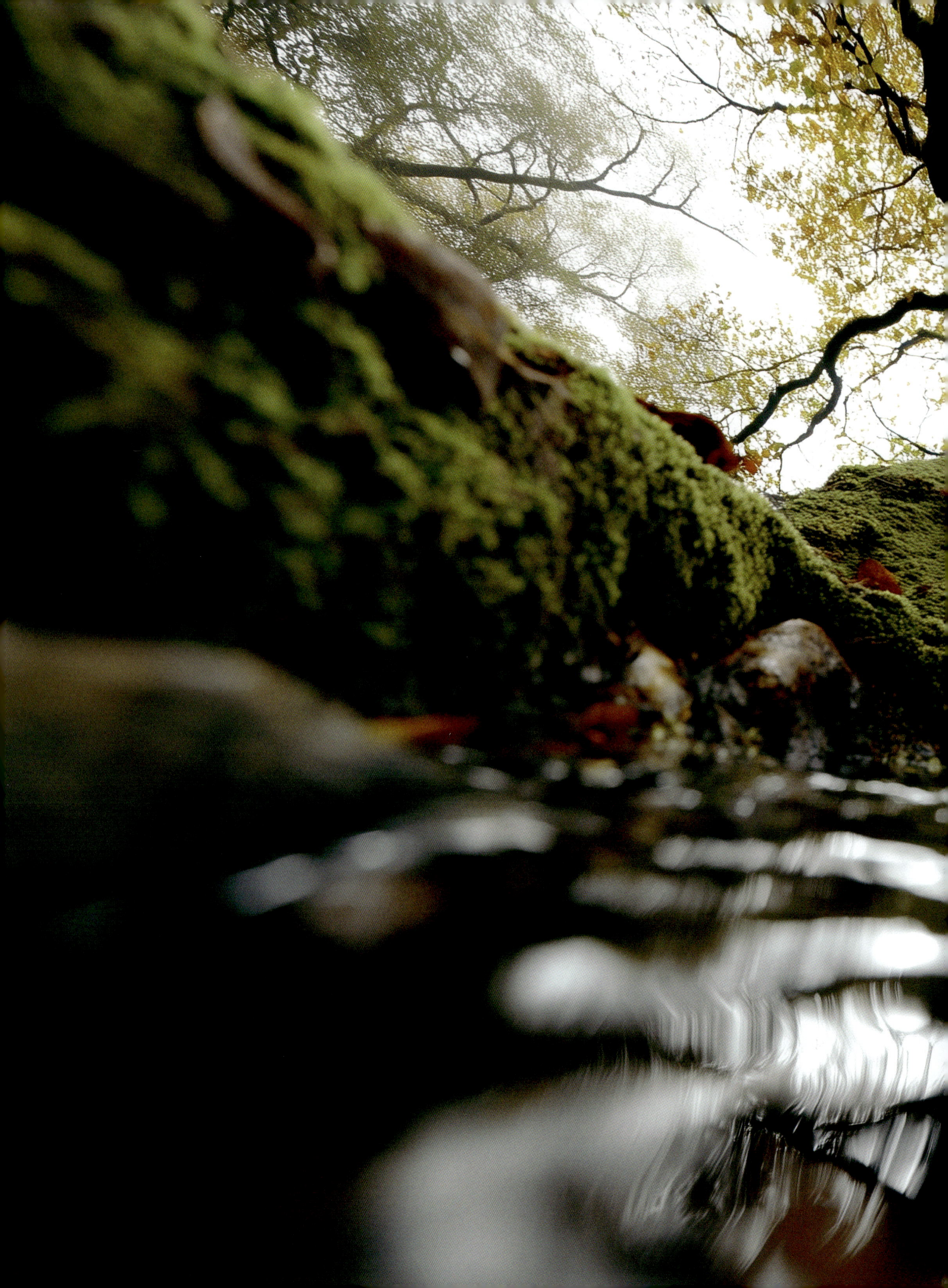

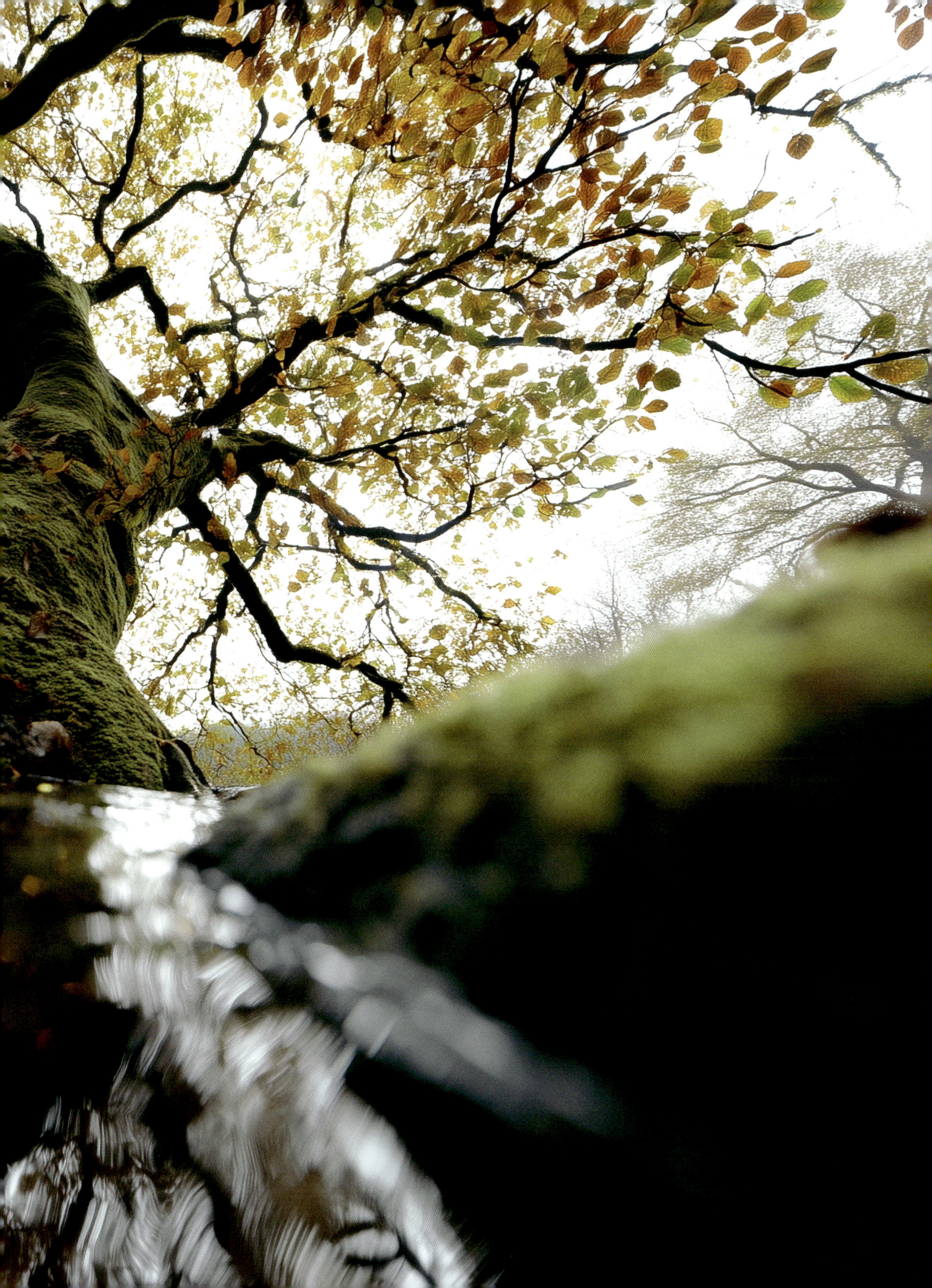

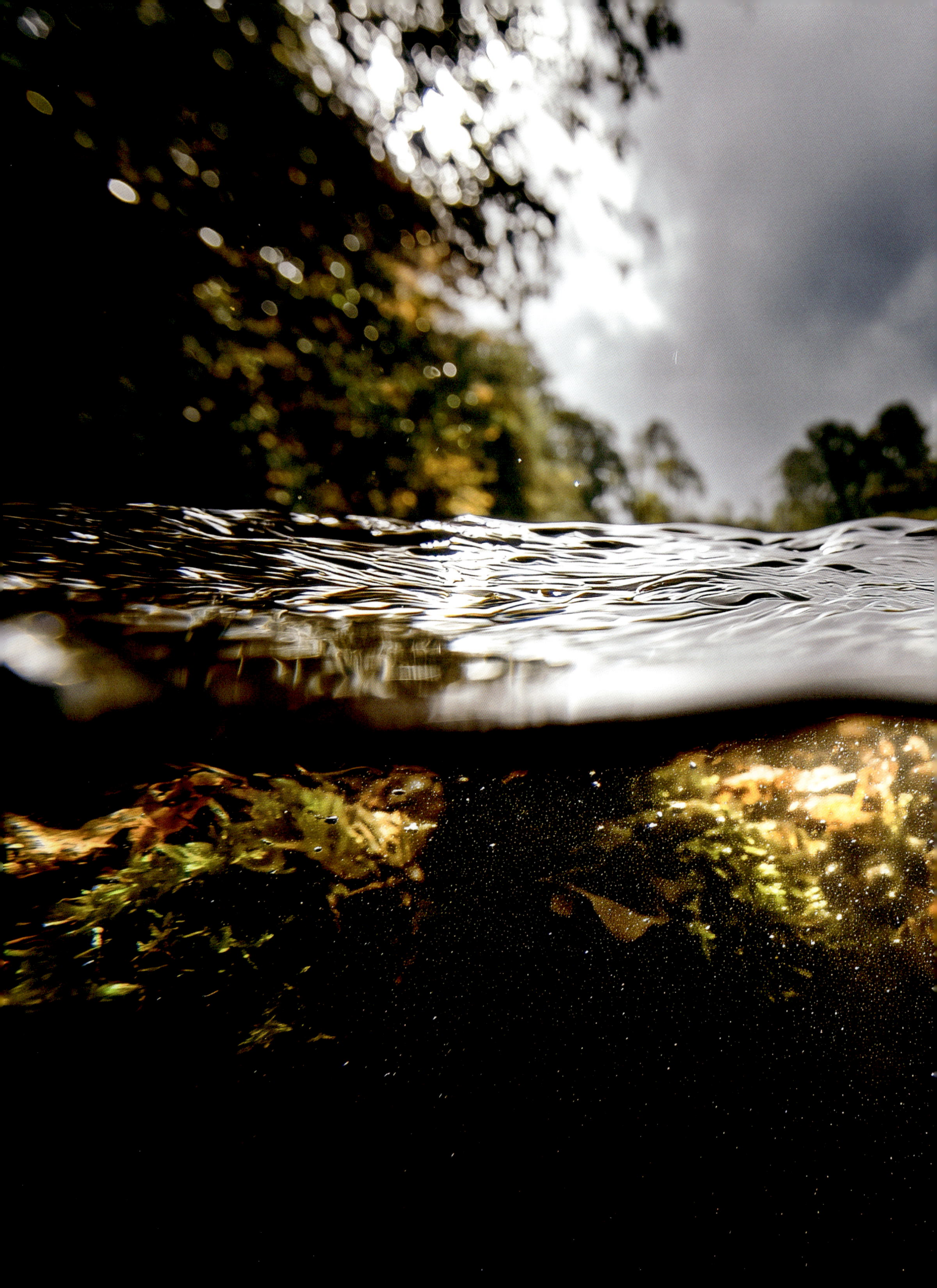

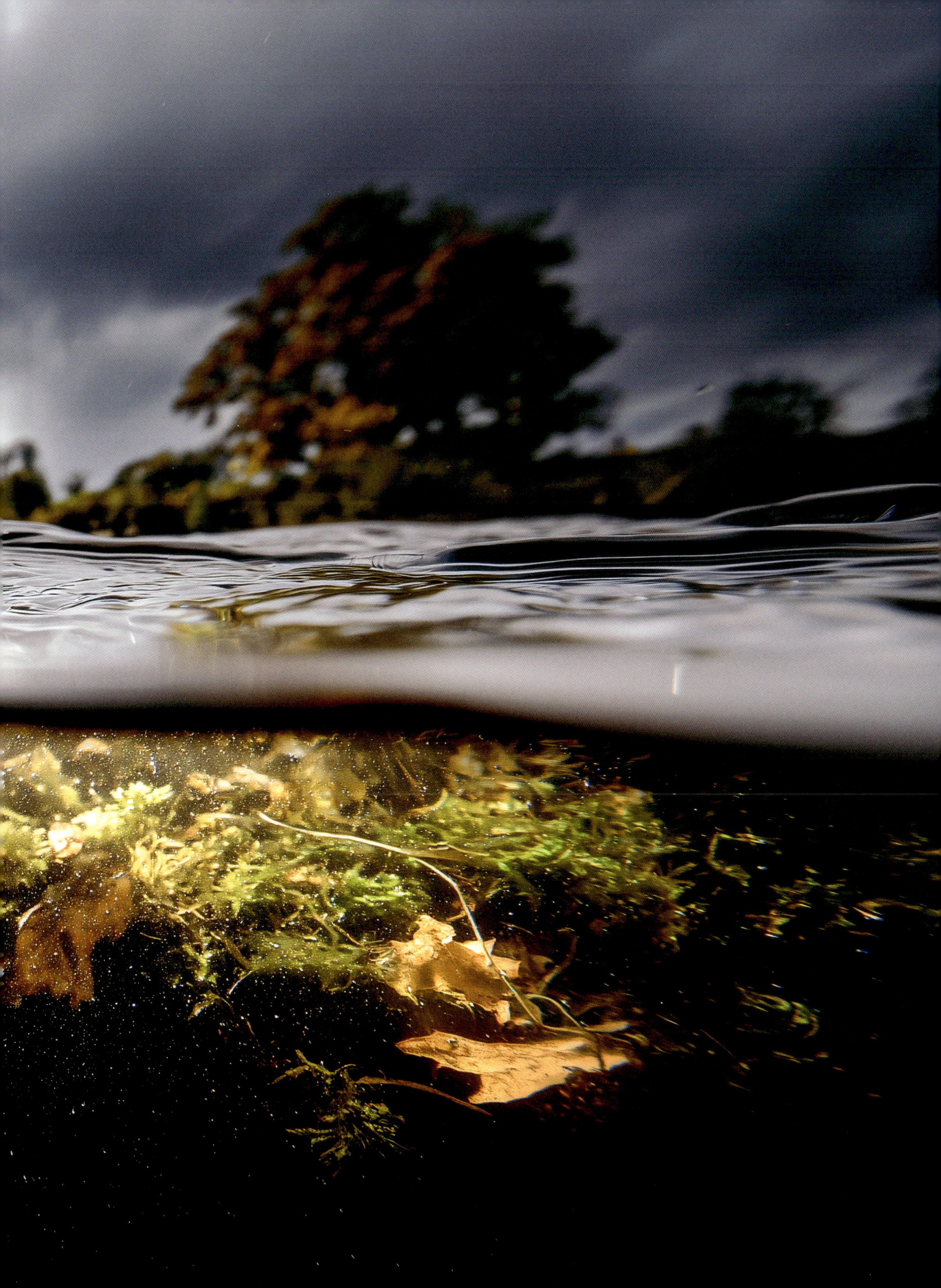

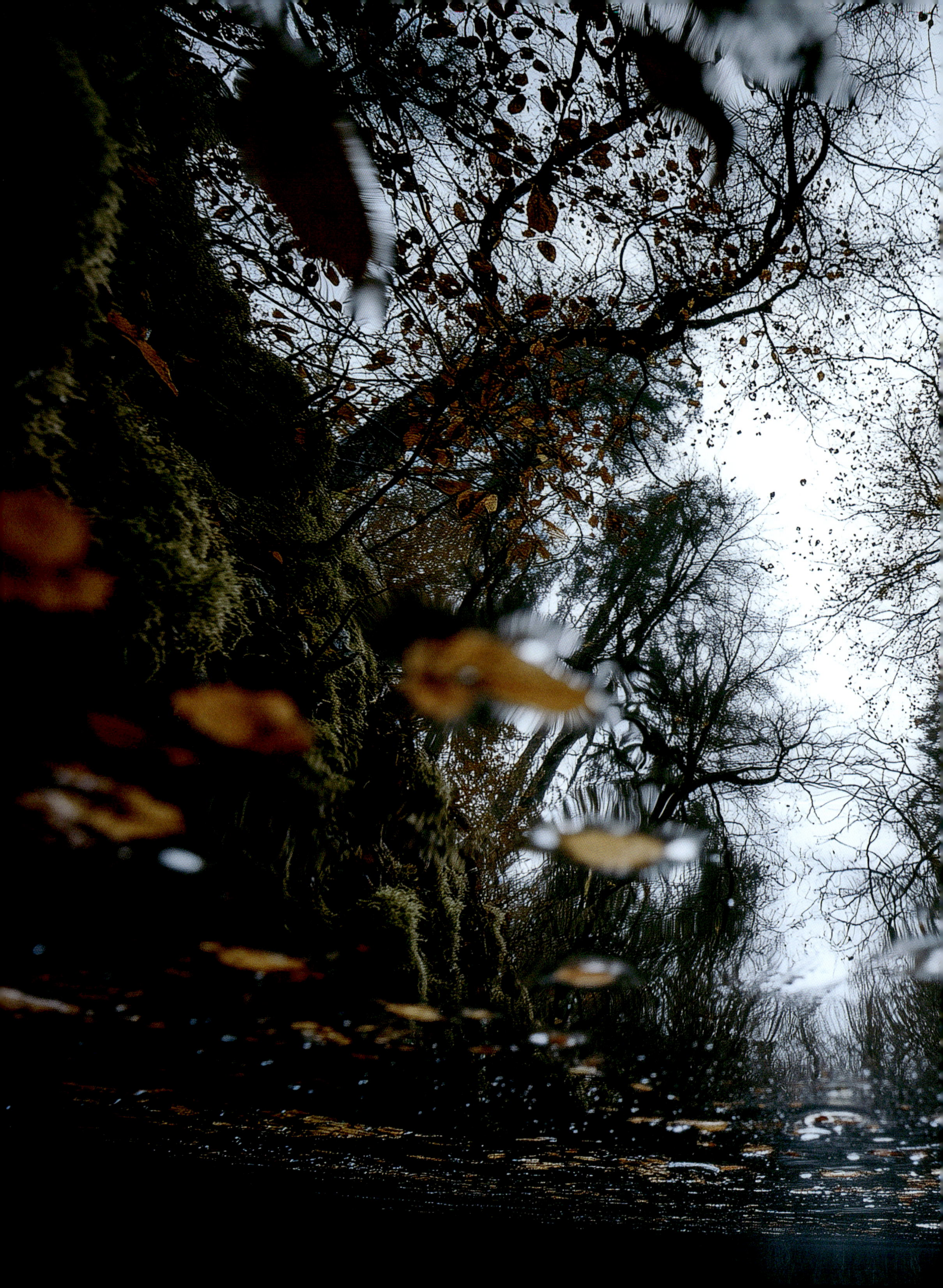

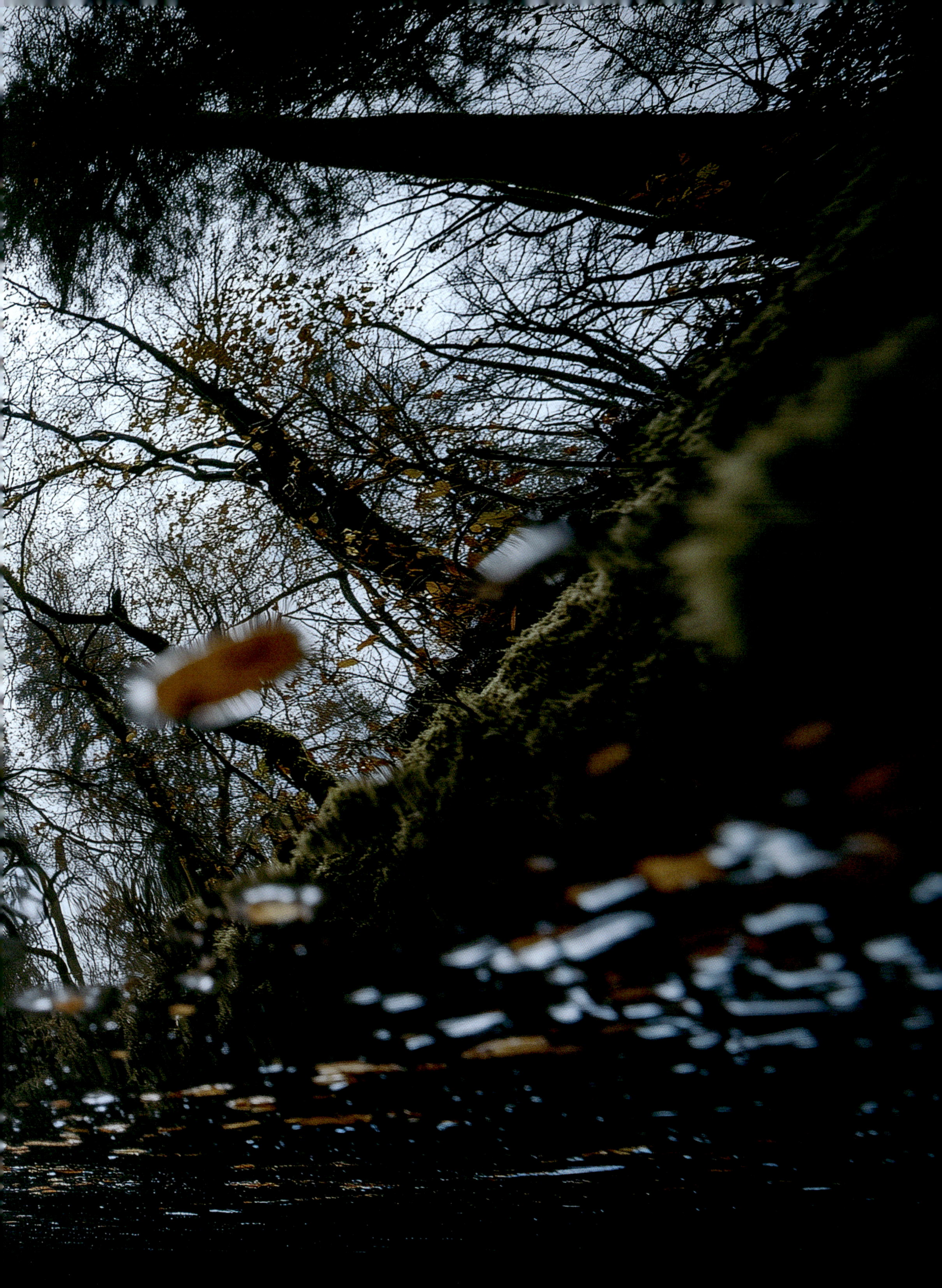

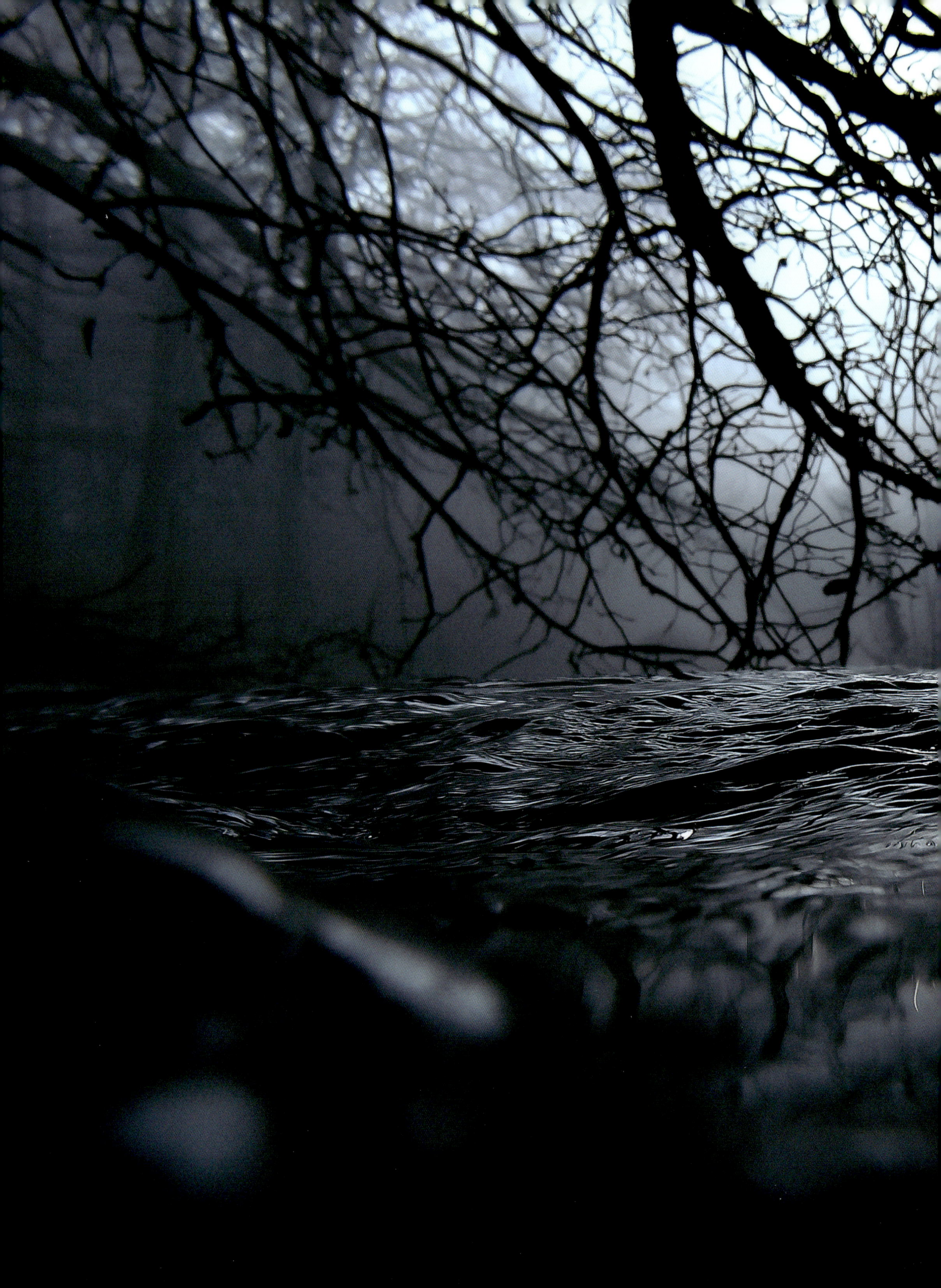

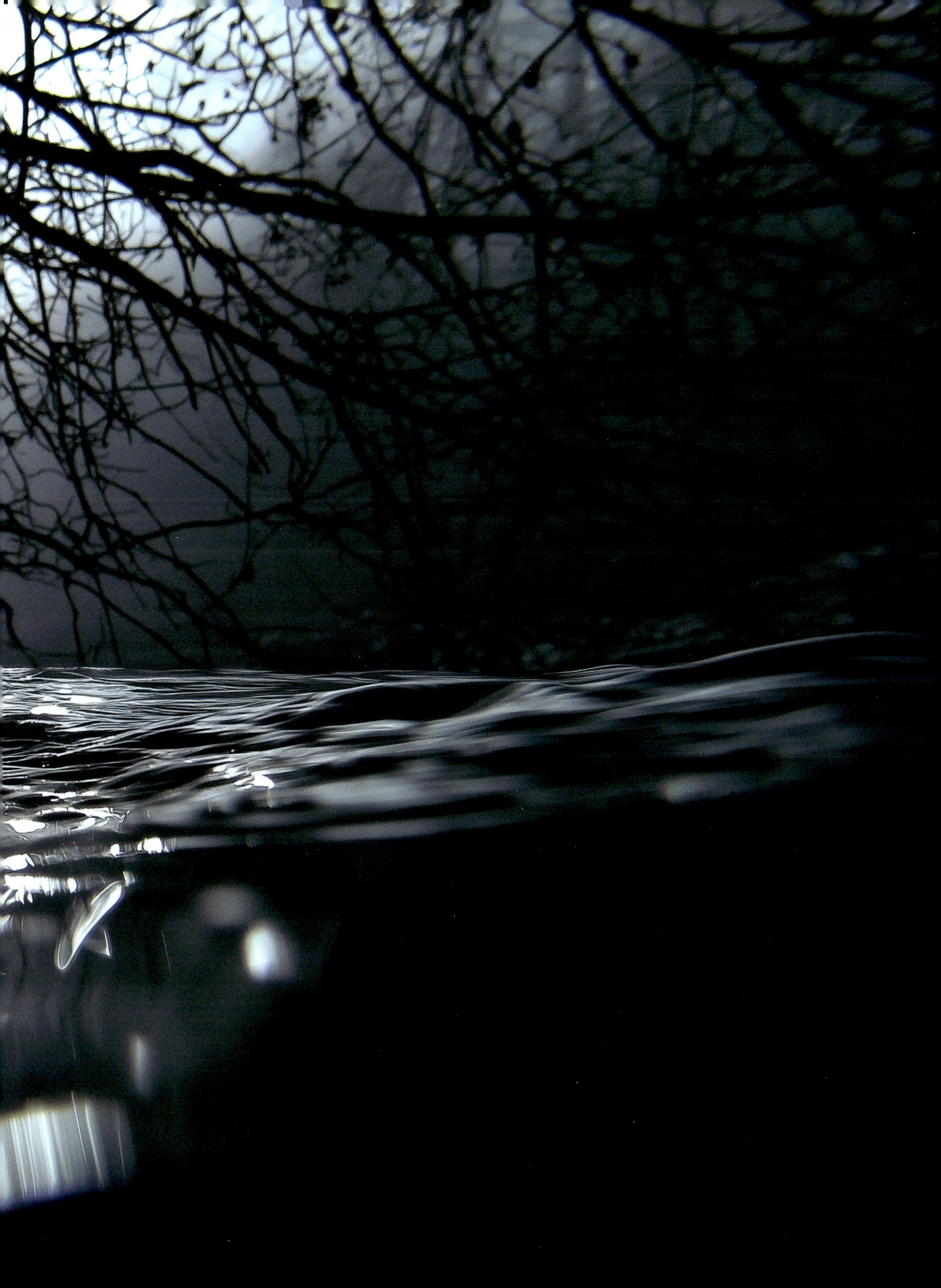

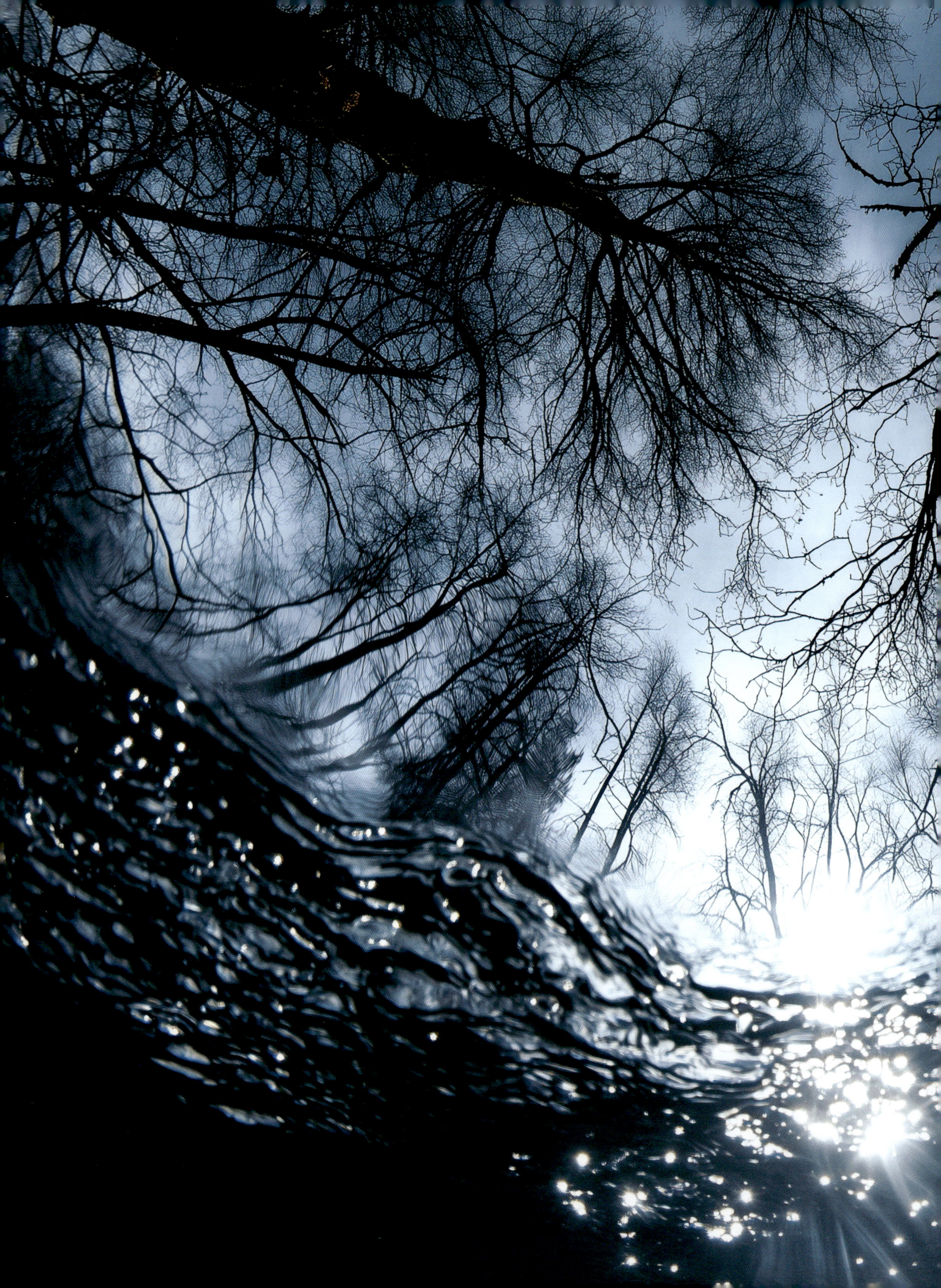

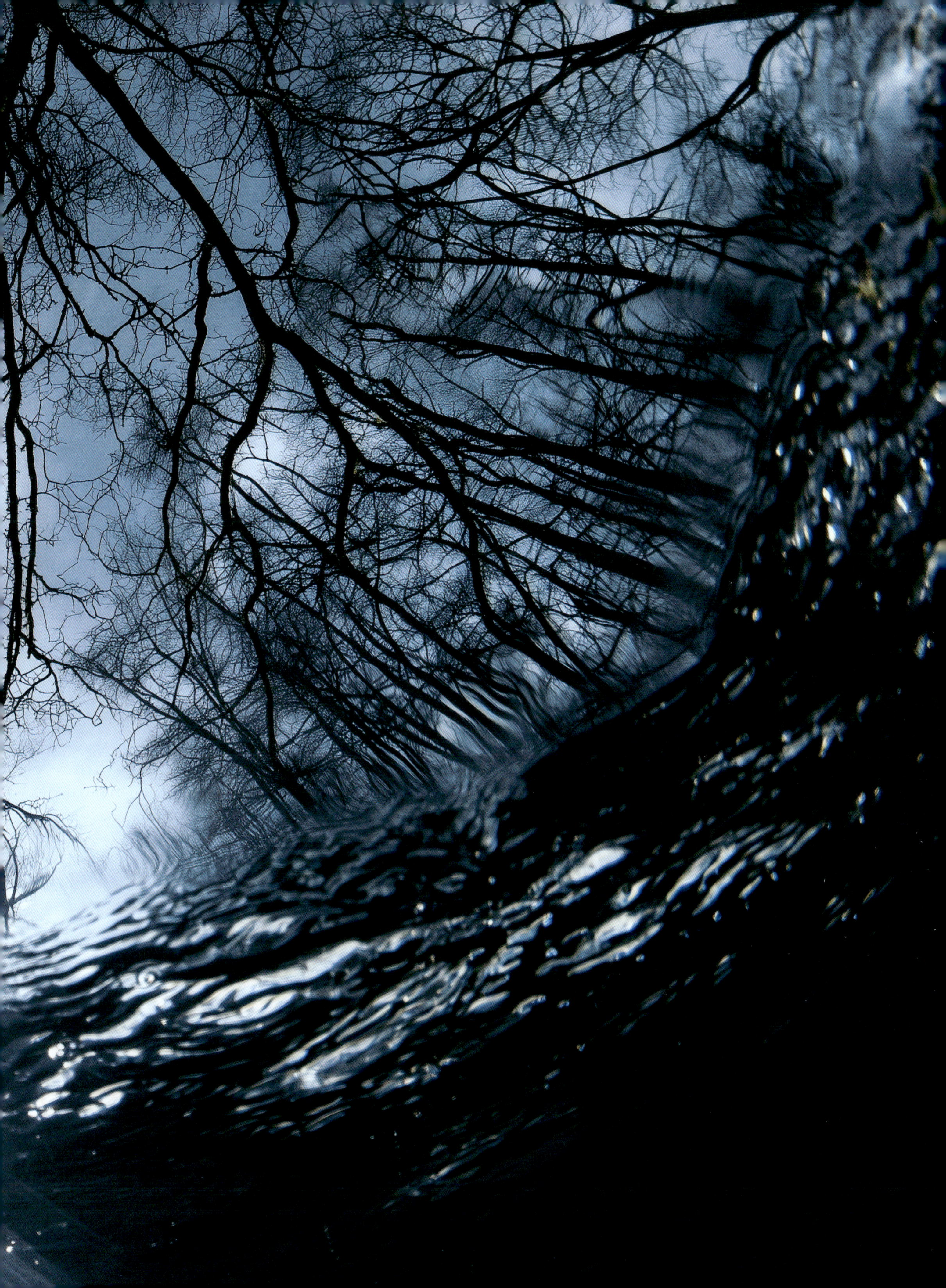

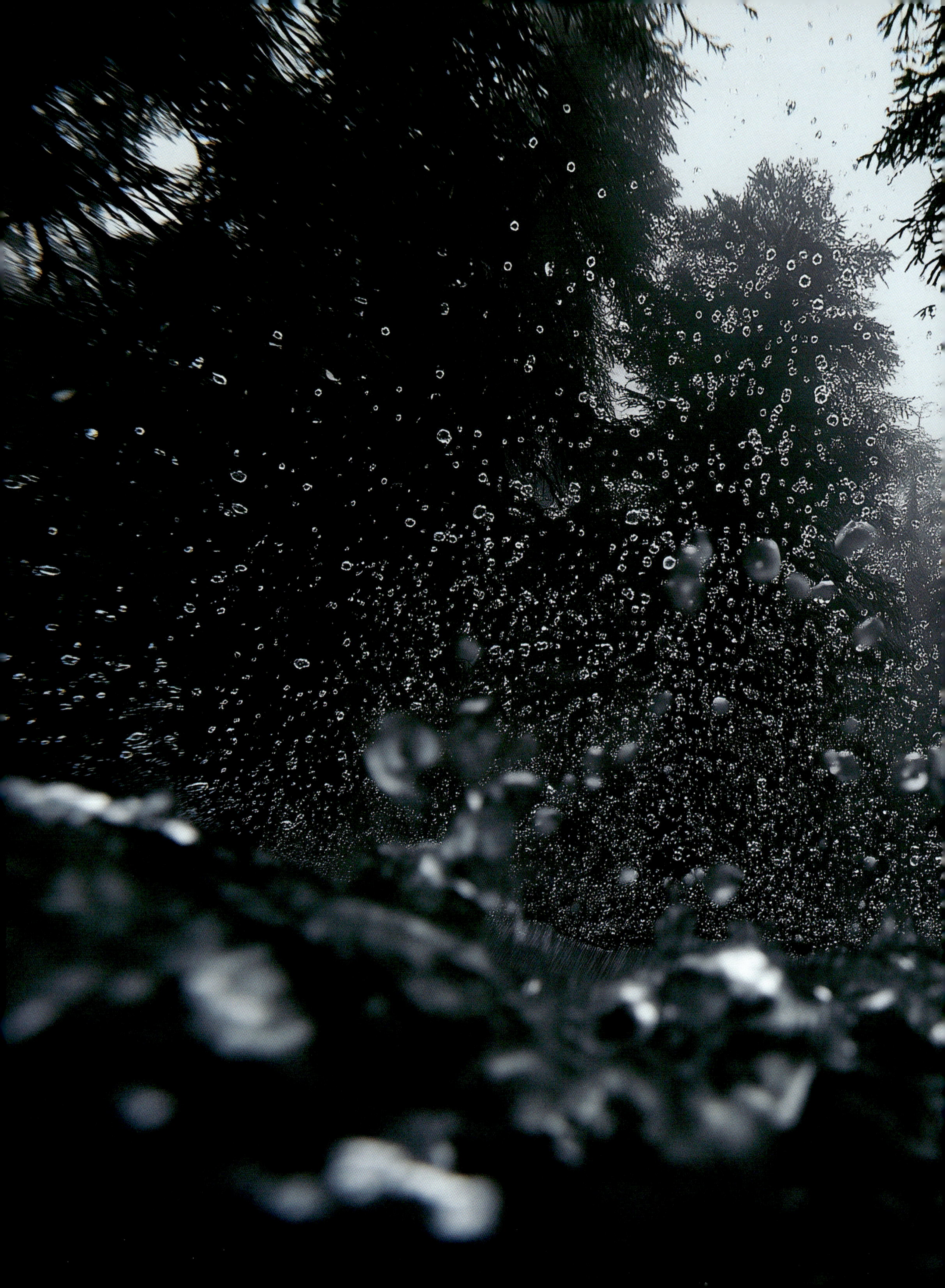

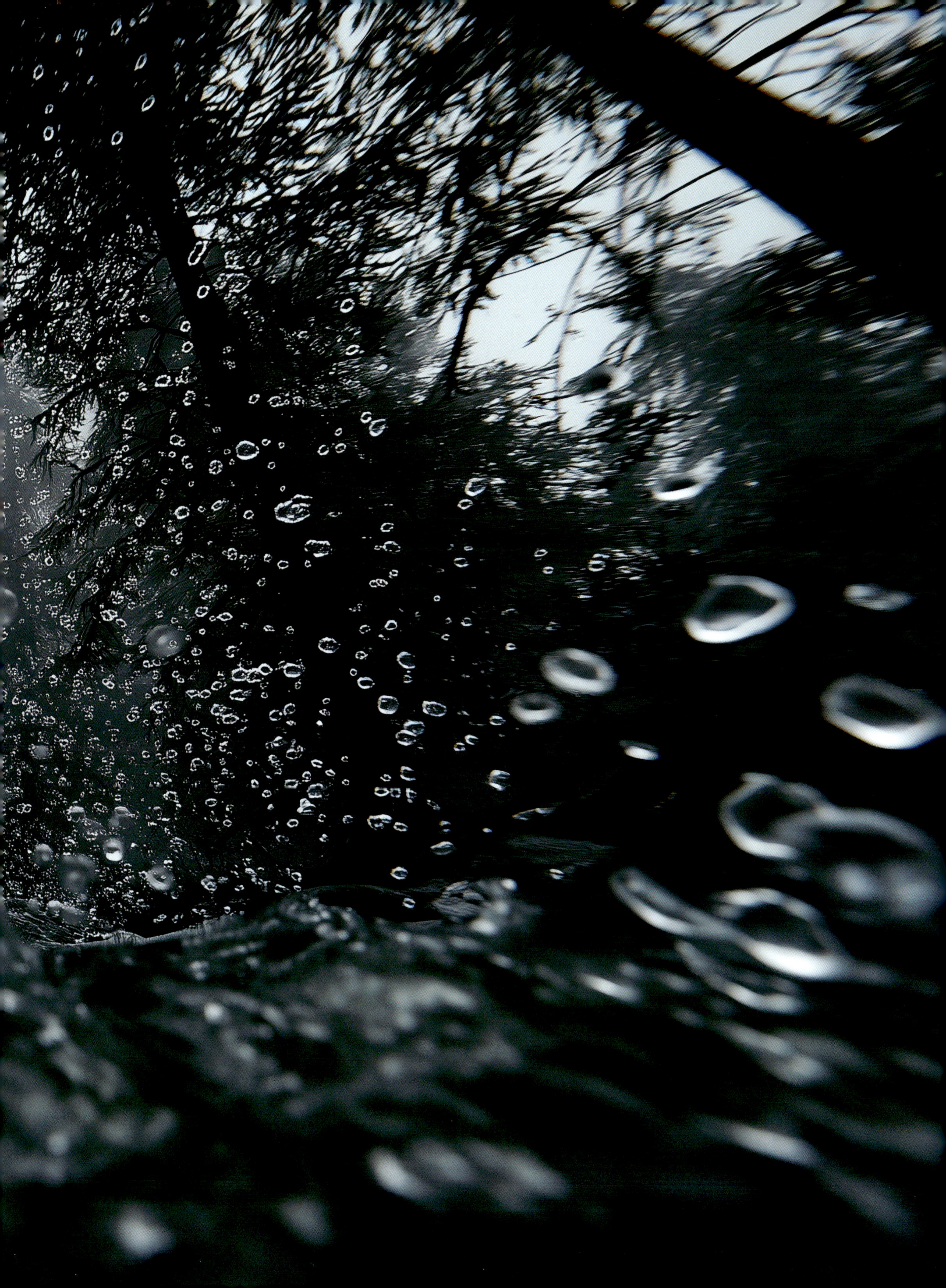

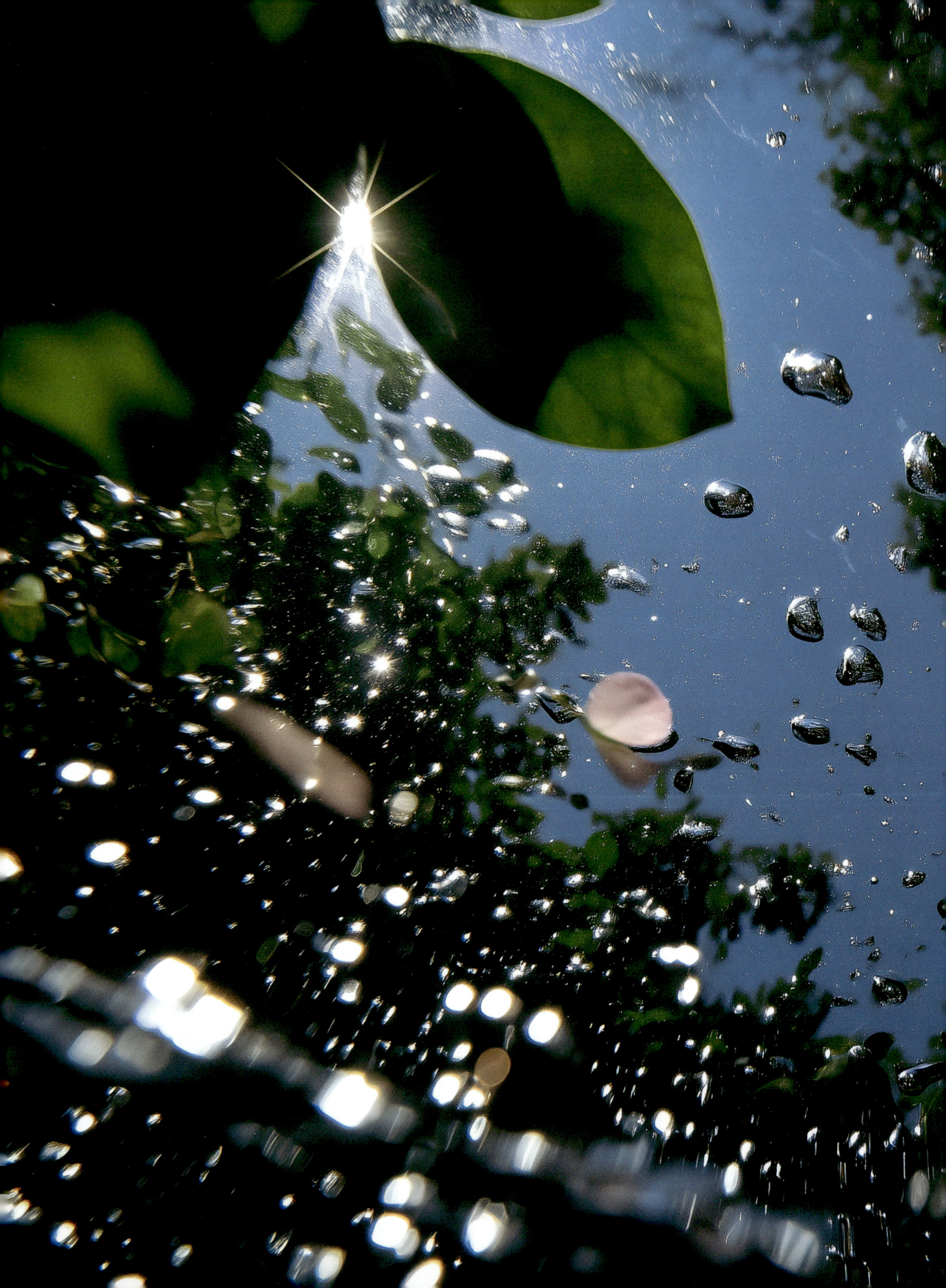

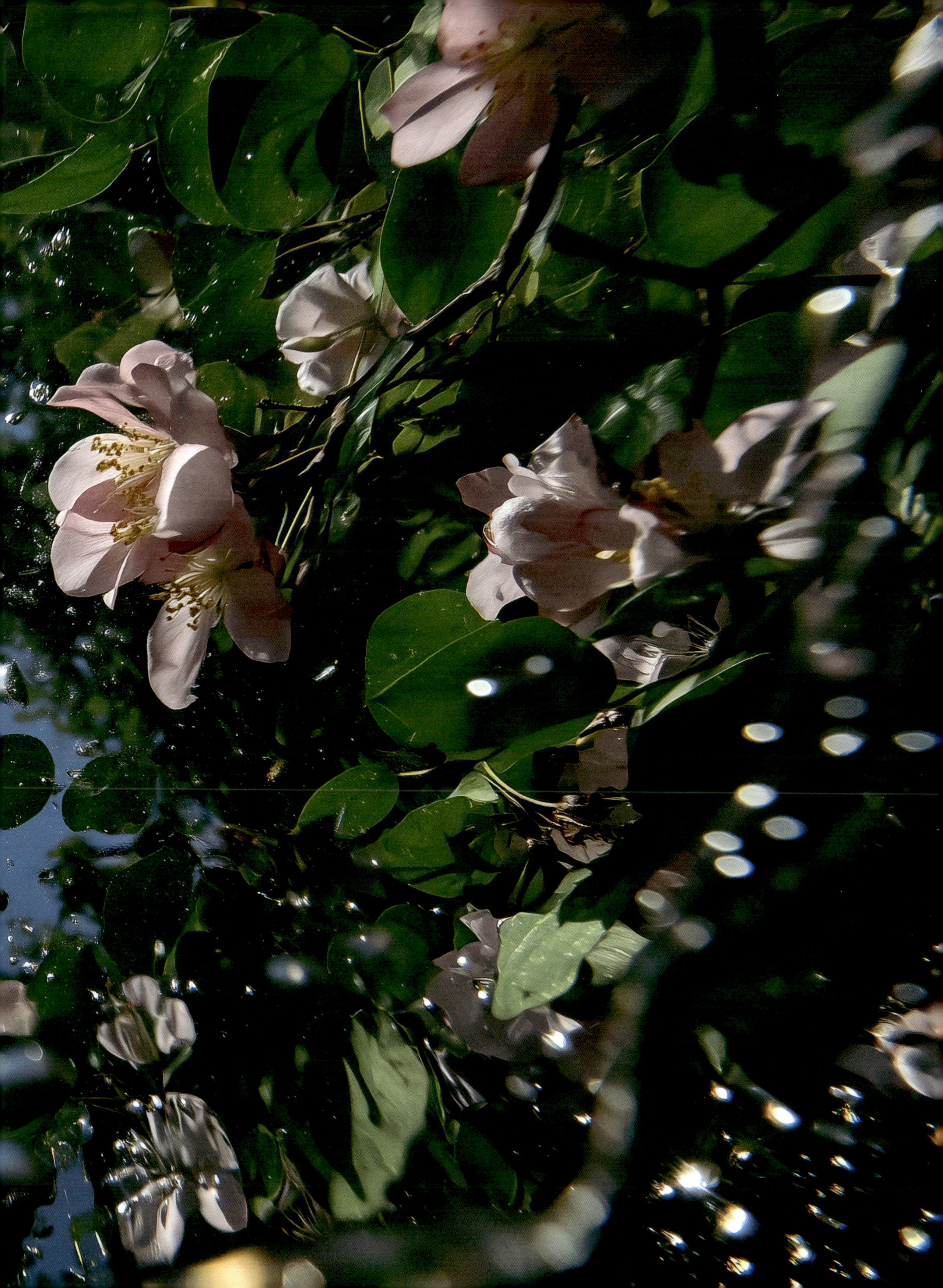

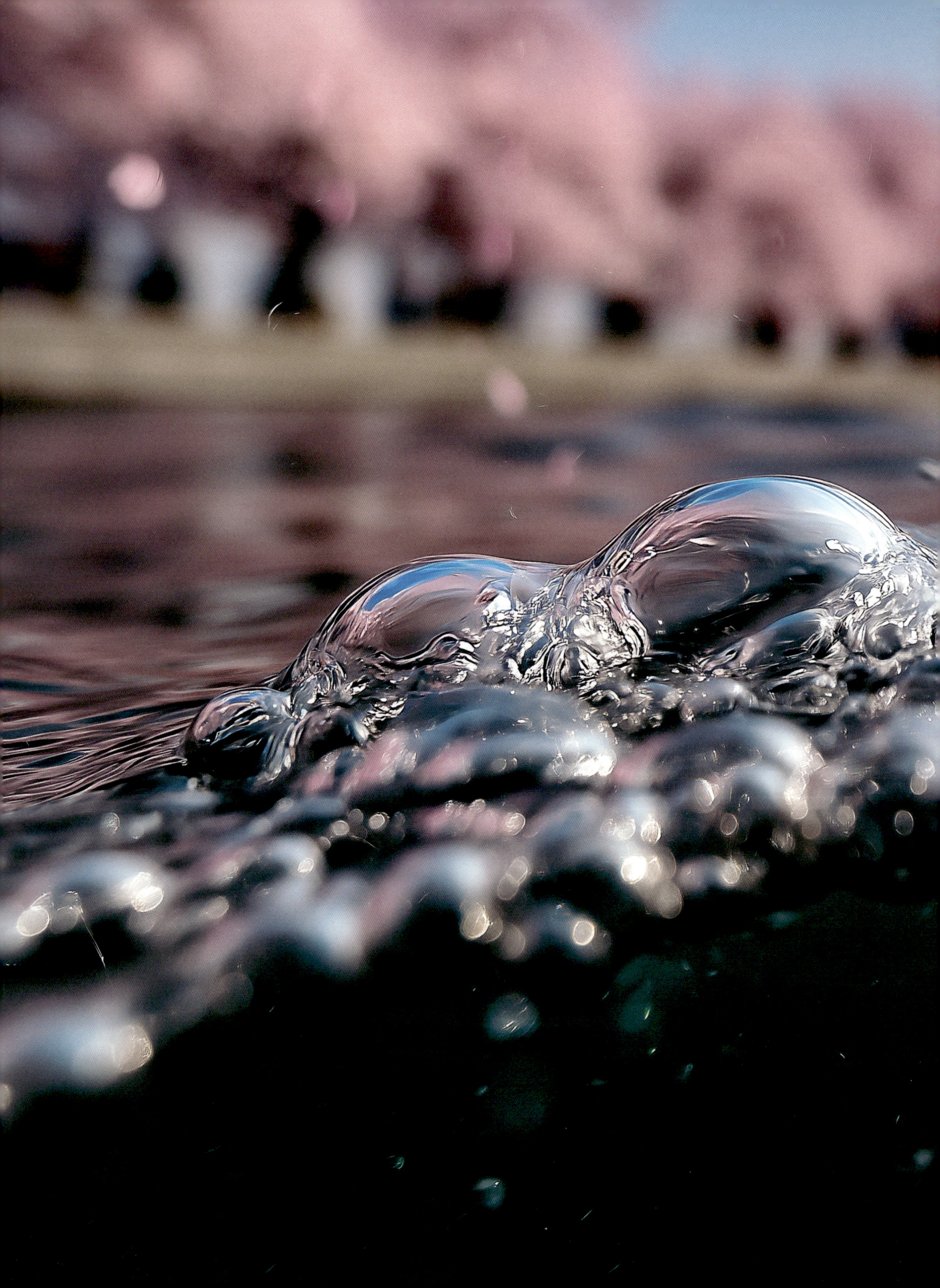

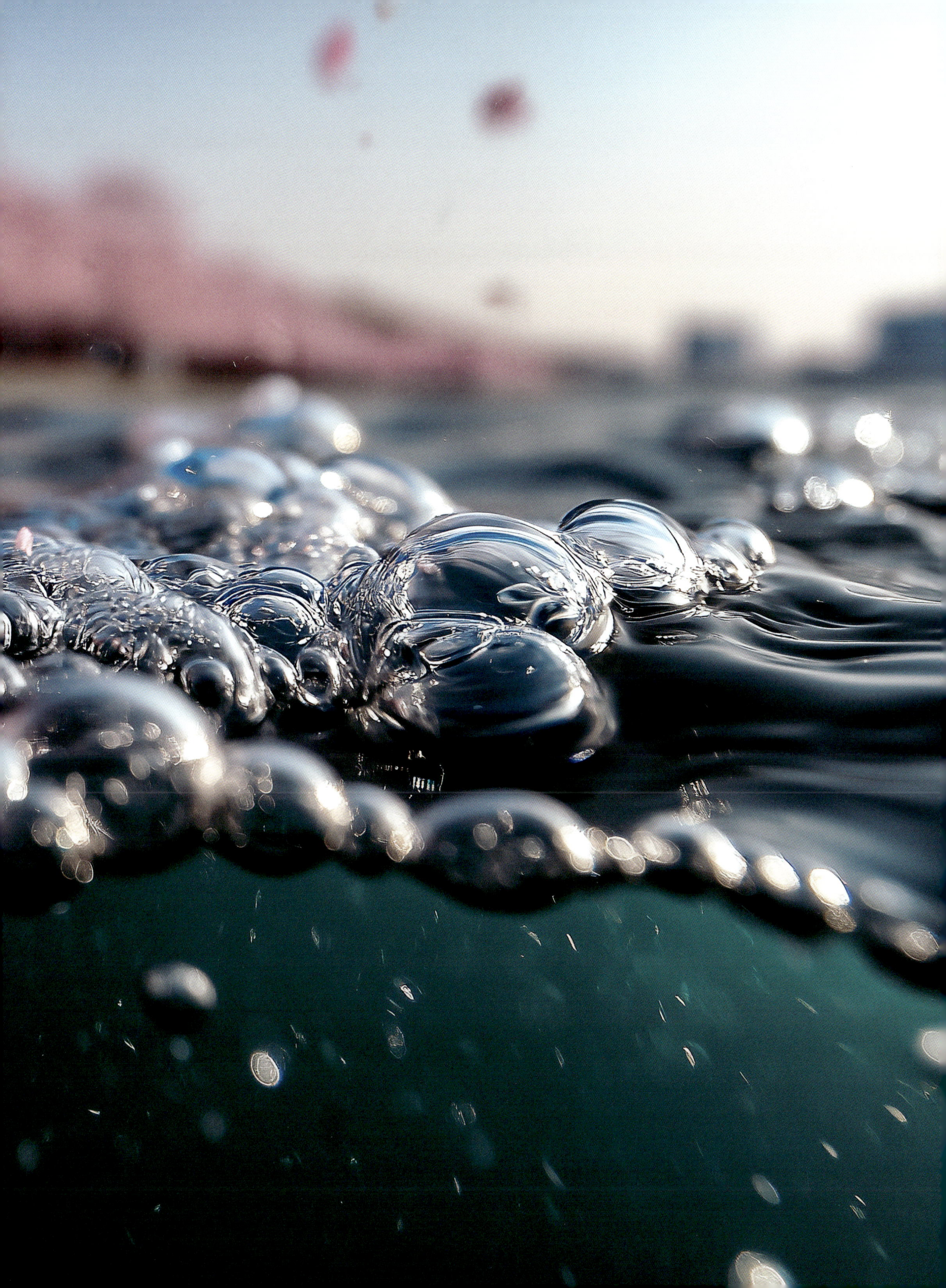

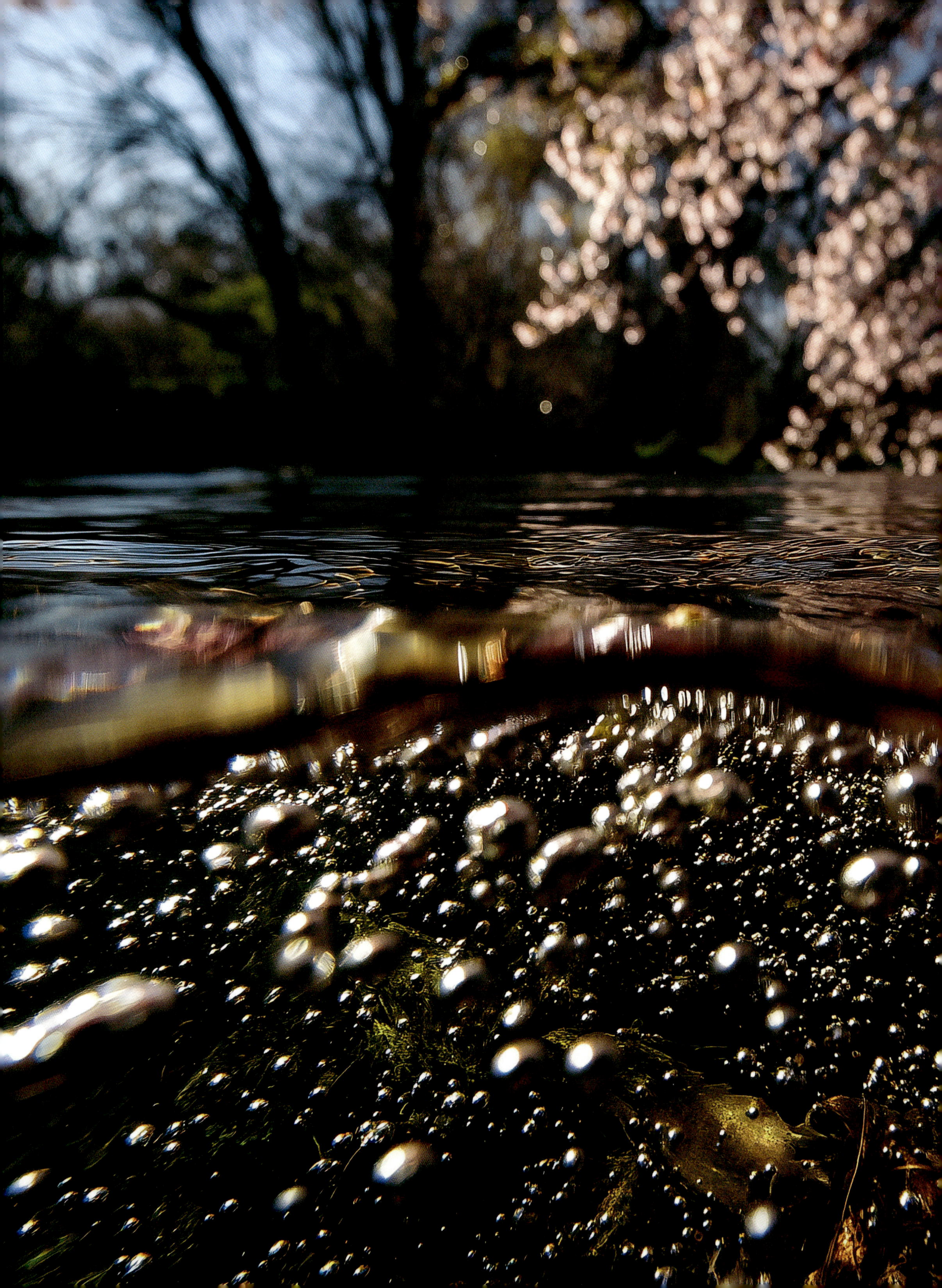

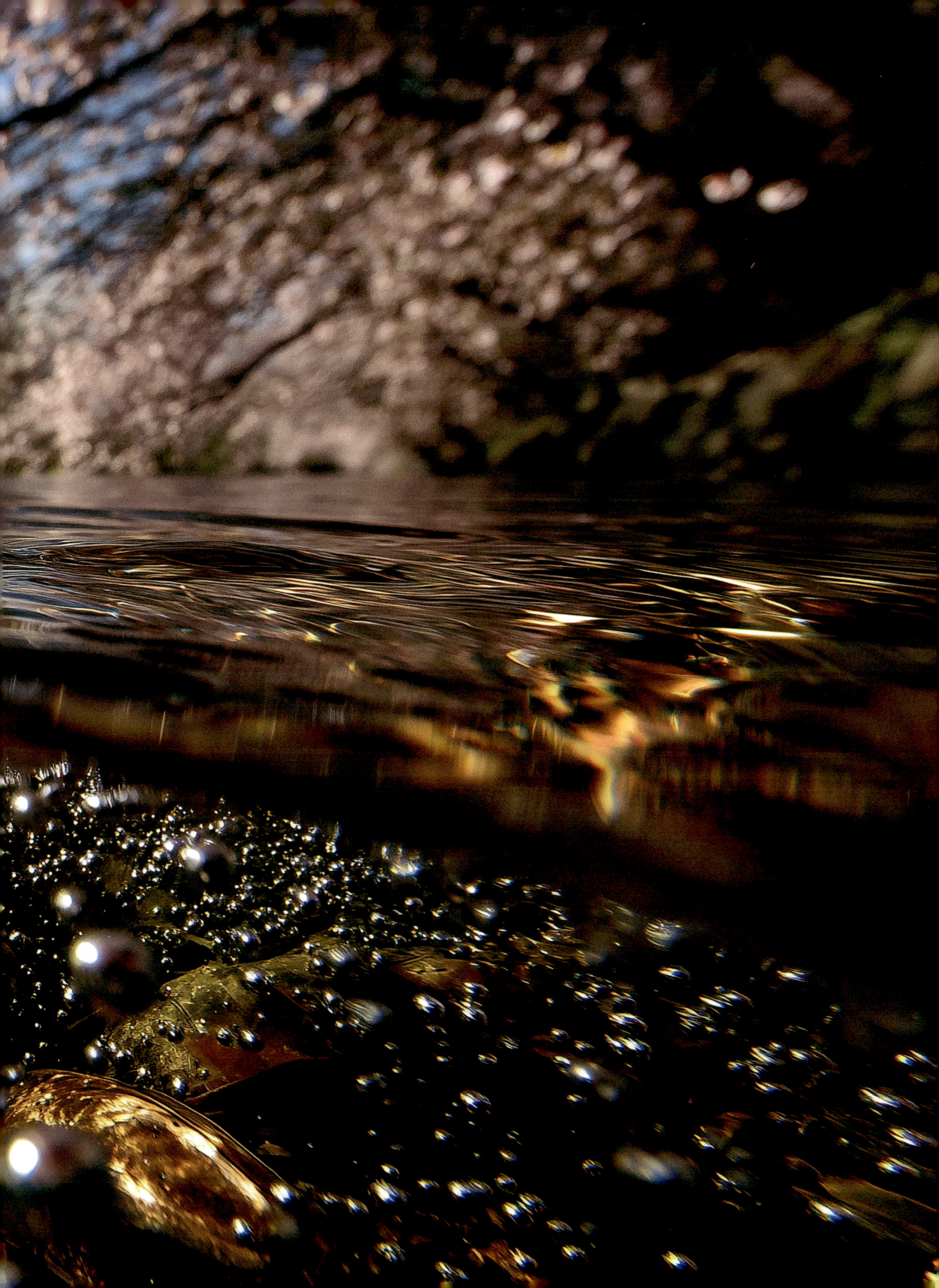

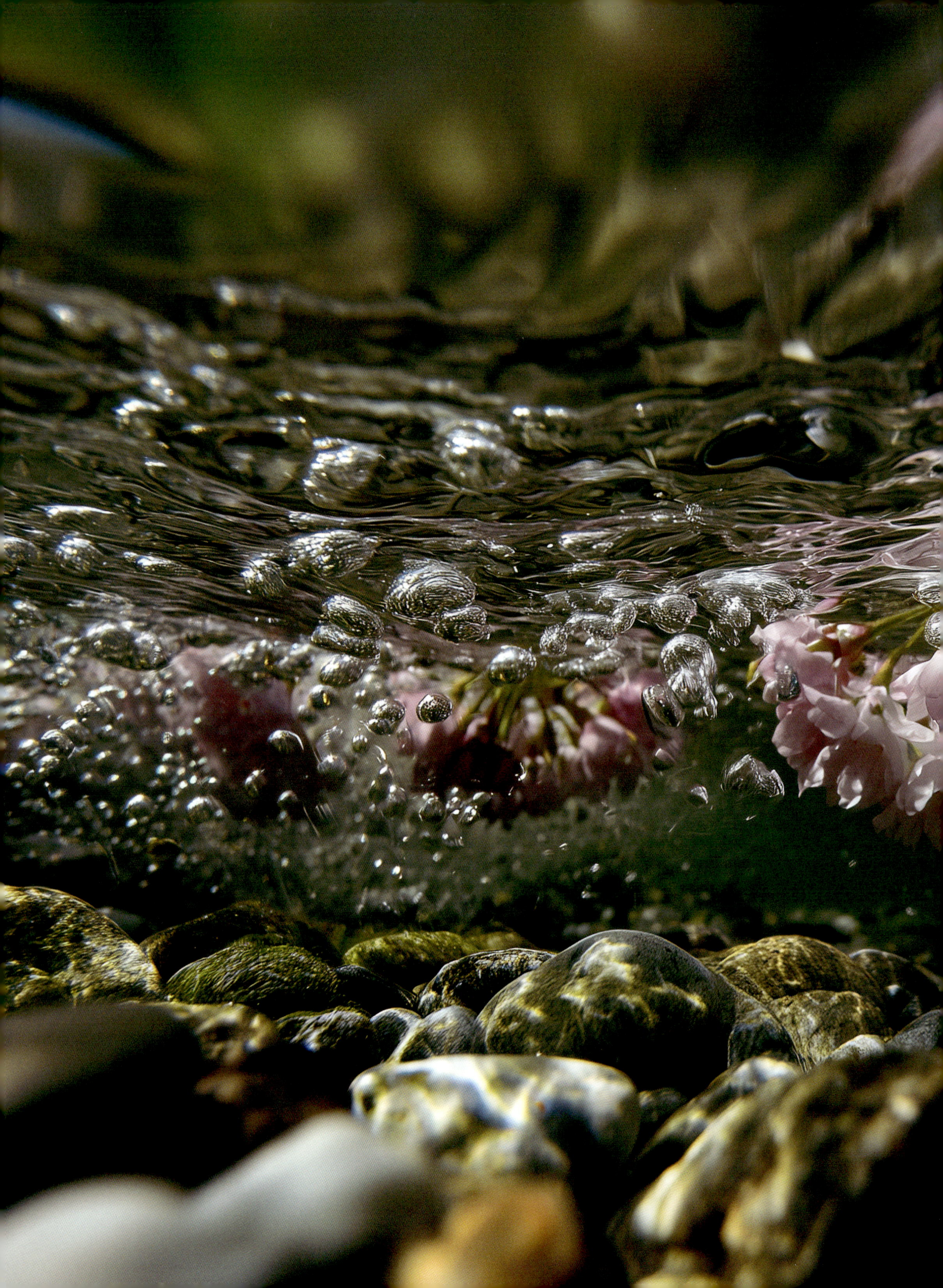

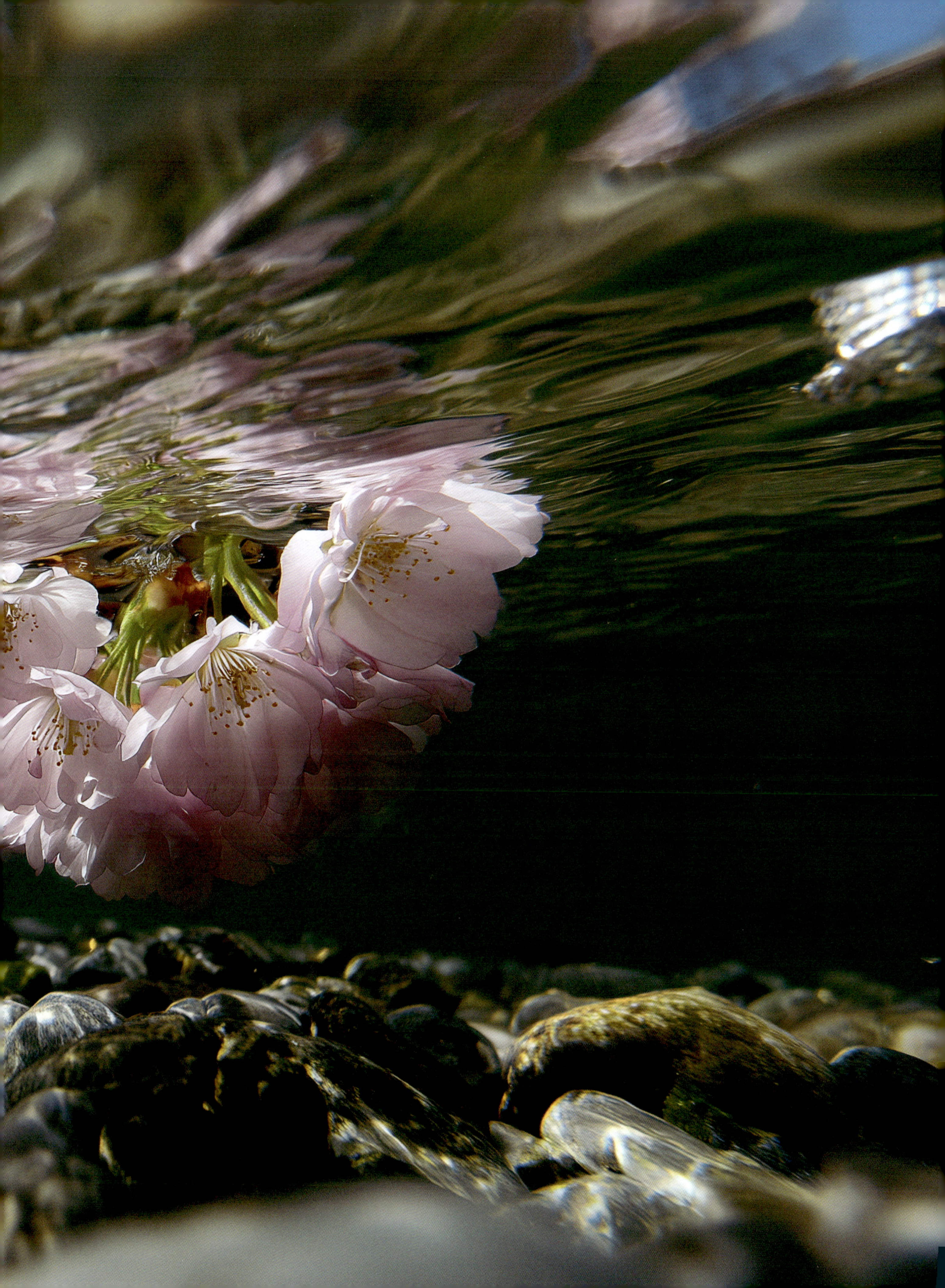

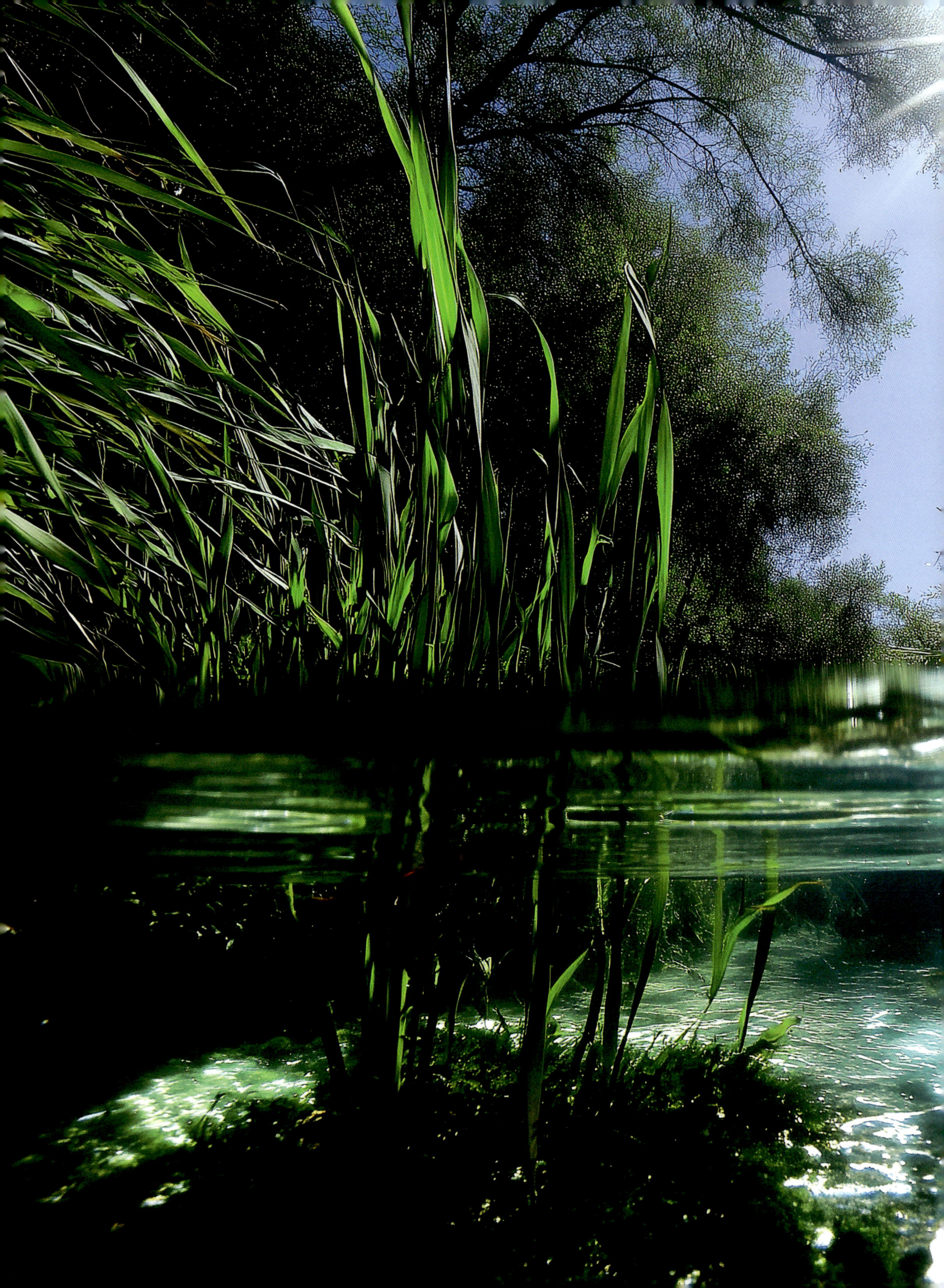

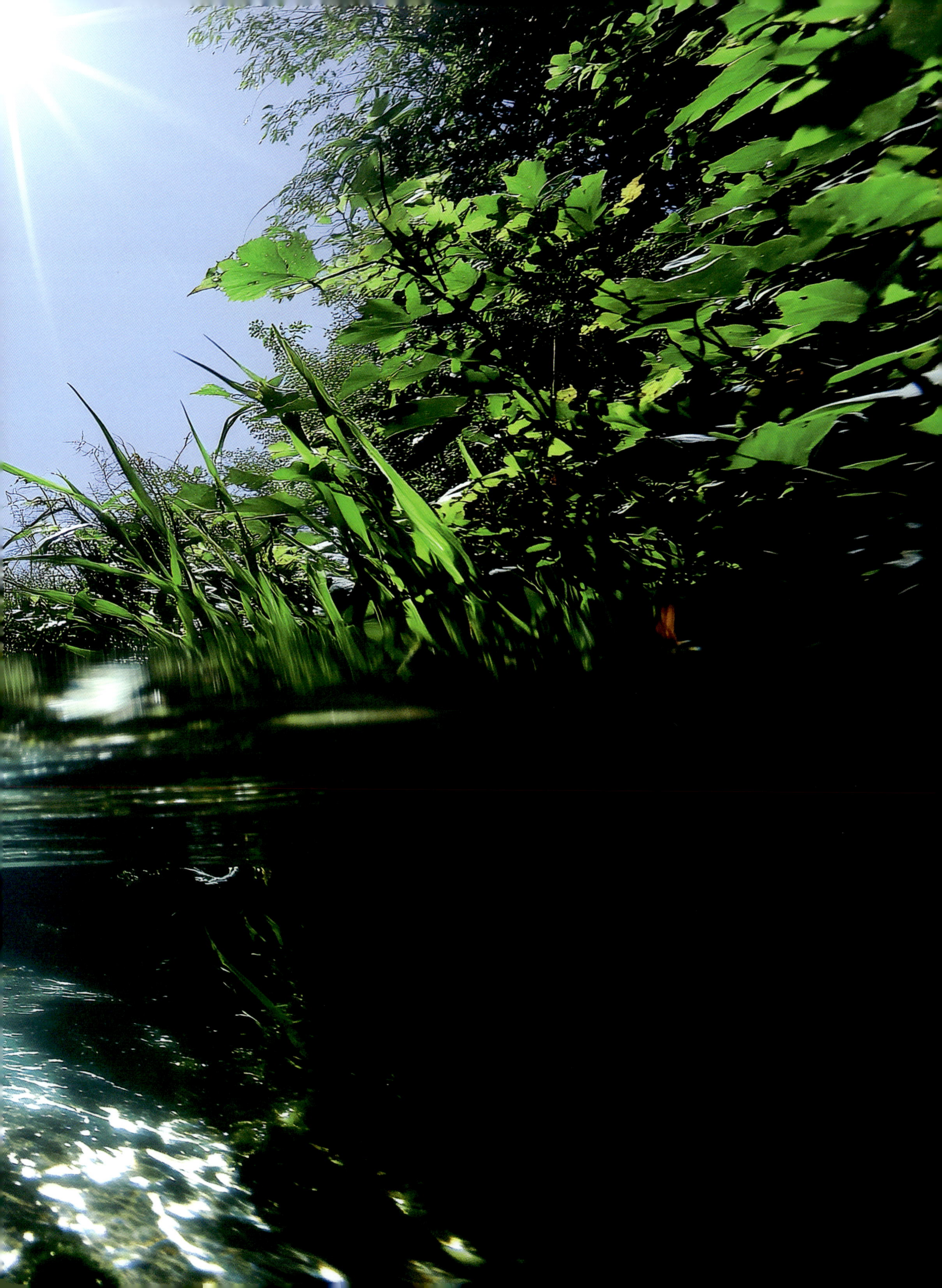

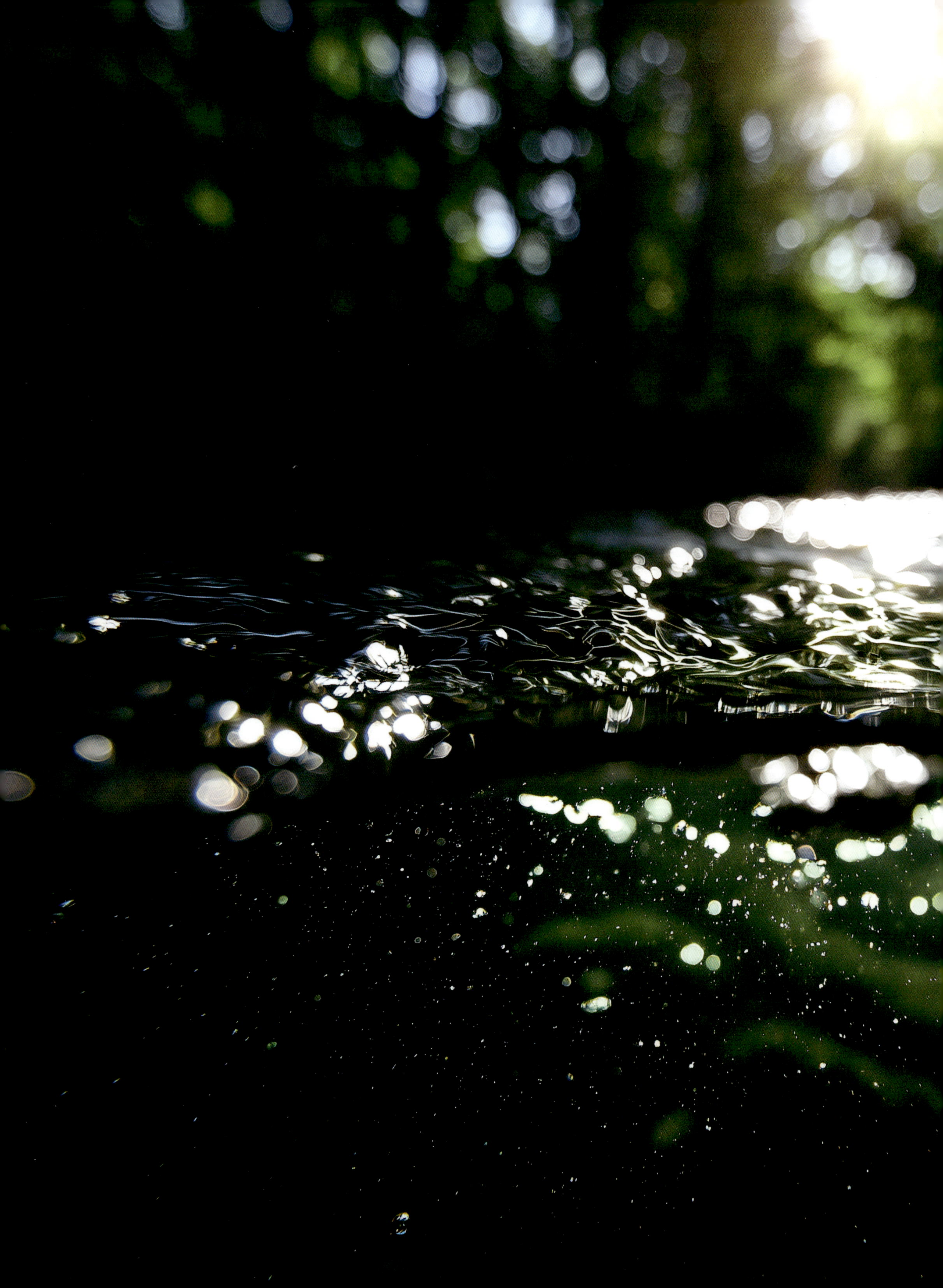

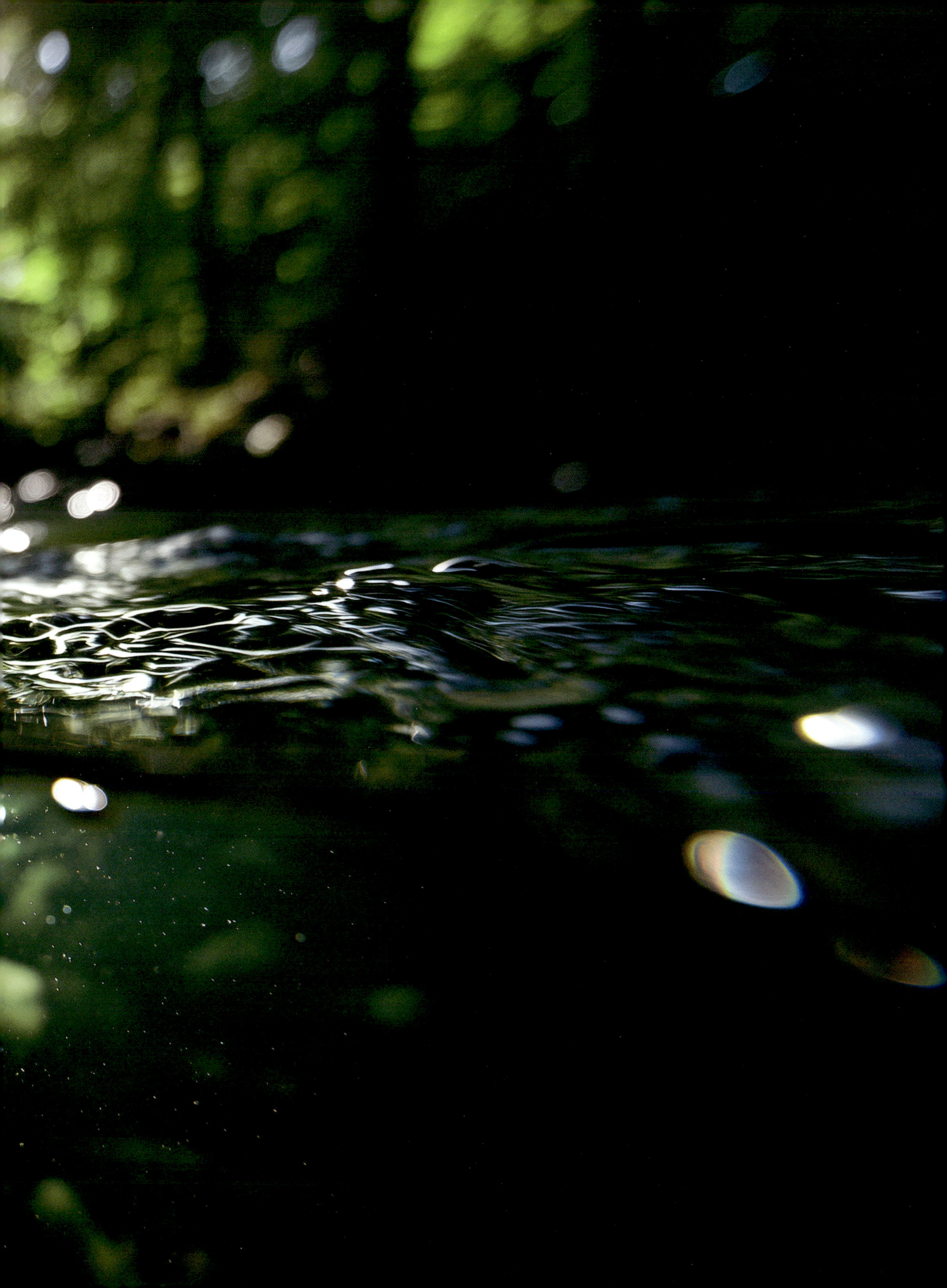

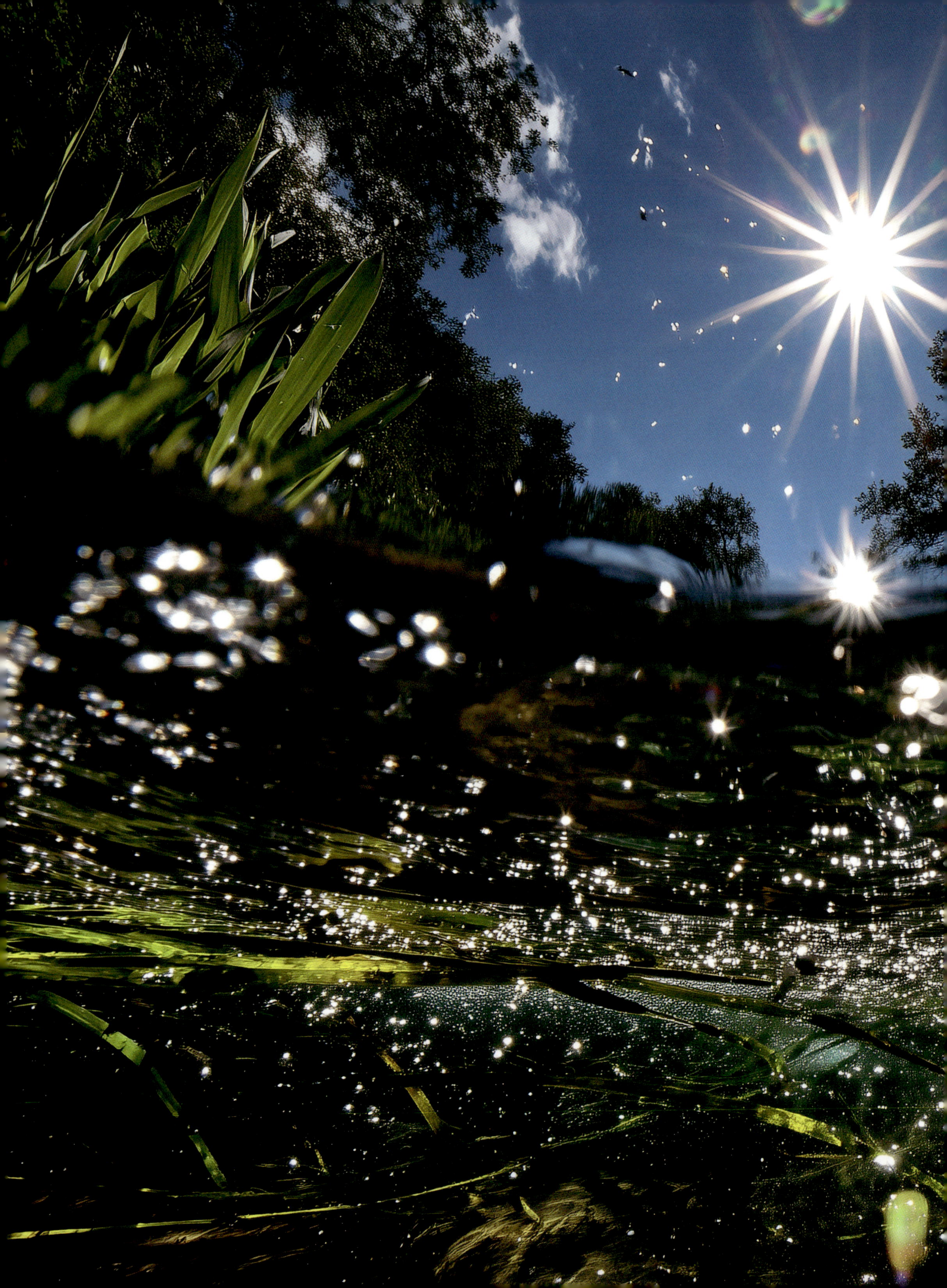

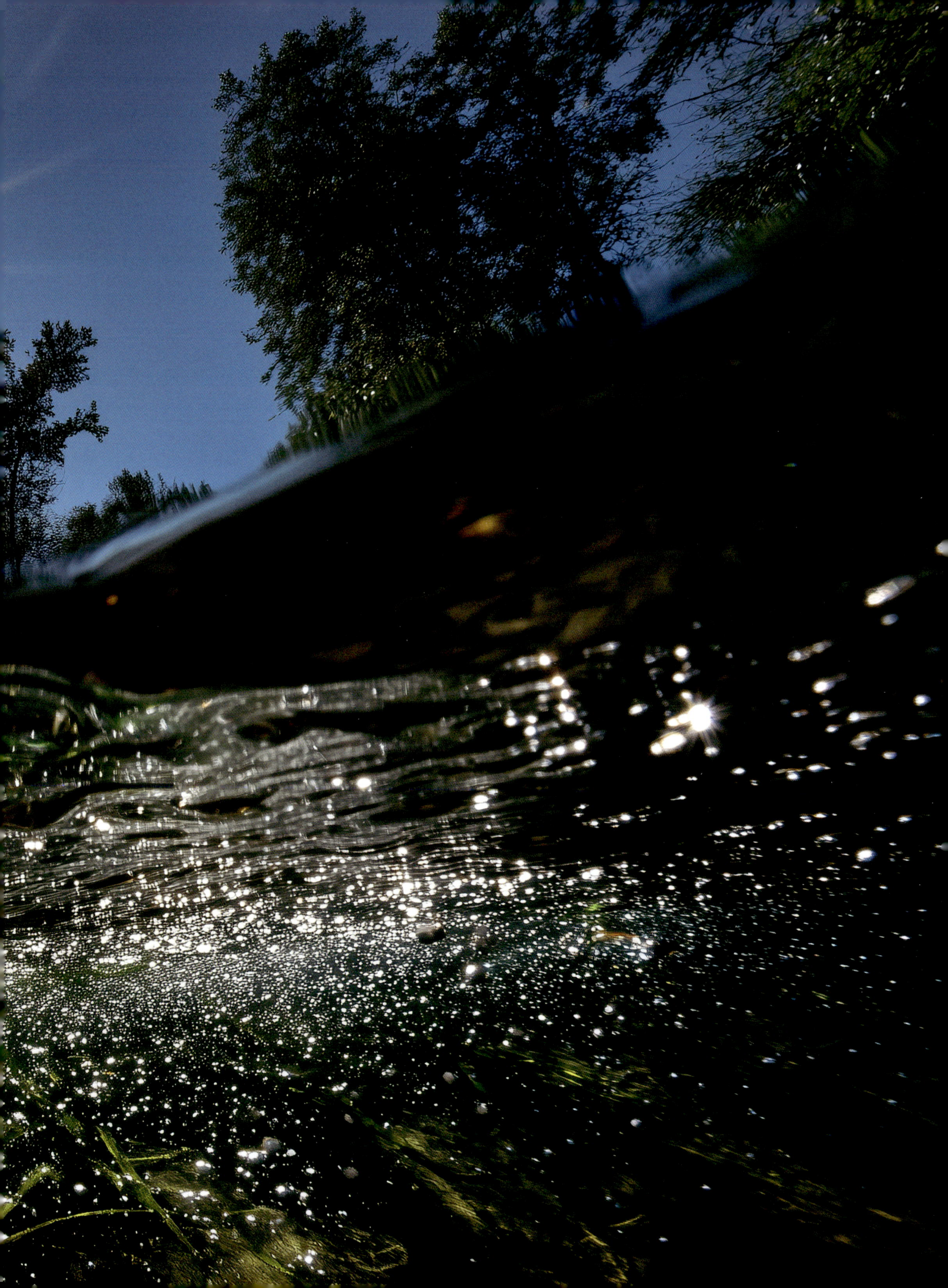

PROMPT_02 [springtime split shot from river surface, cherry blossoms falling from above, bubbles and soft light below the surface, everything glowing with early sun, vibrant colors and clean atmosphere, poetic renewal feel. --chaos 15 --ar 16:9 --raw --stylize 50]

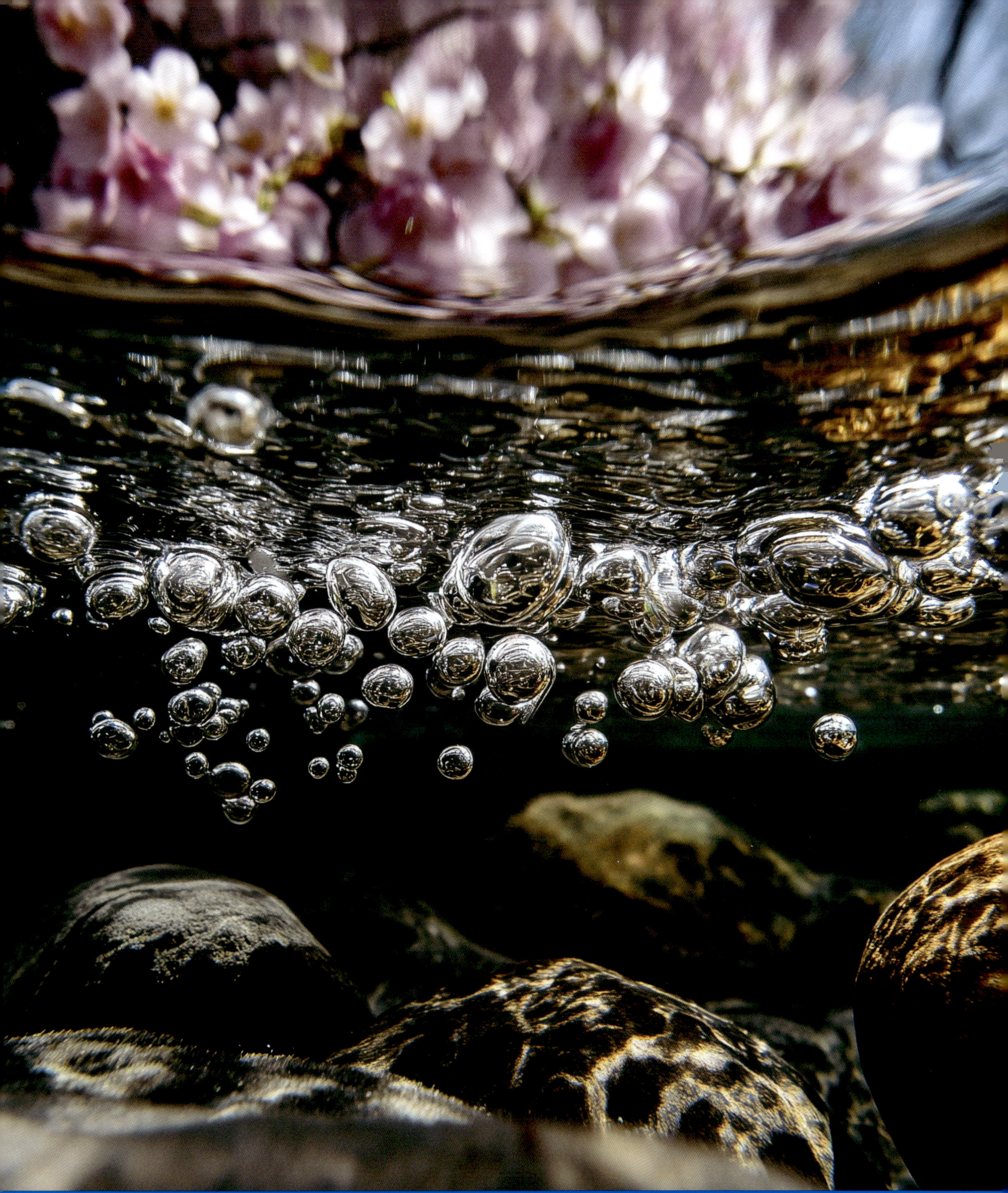

IMG_02

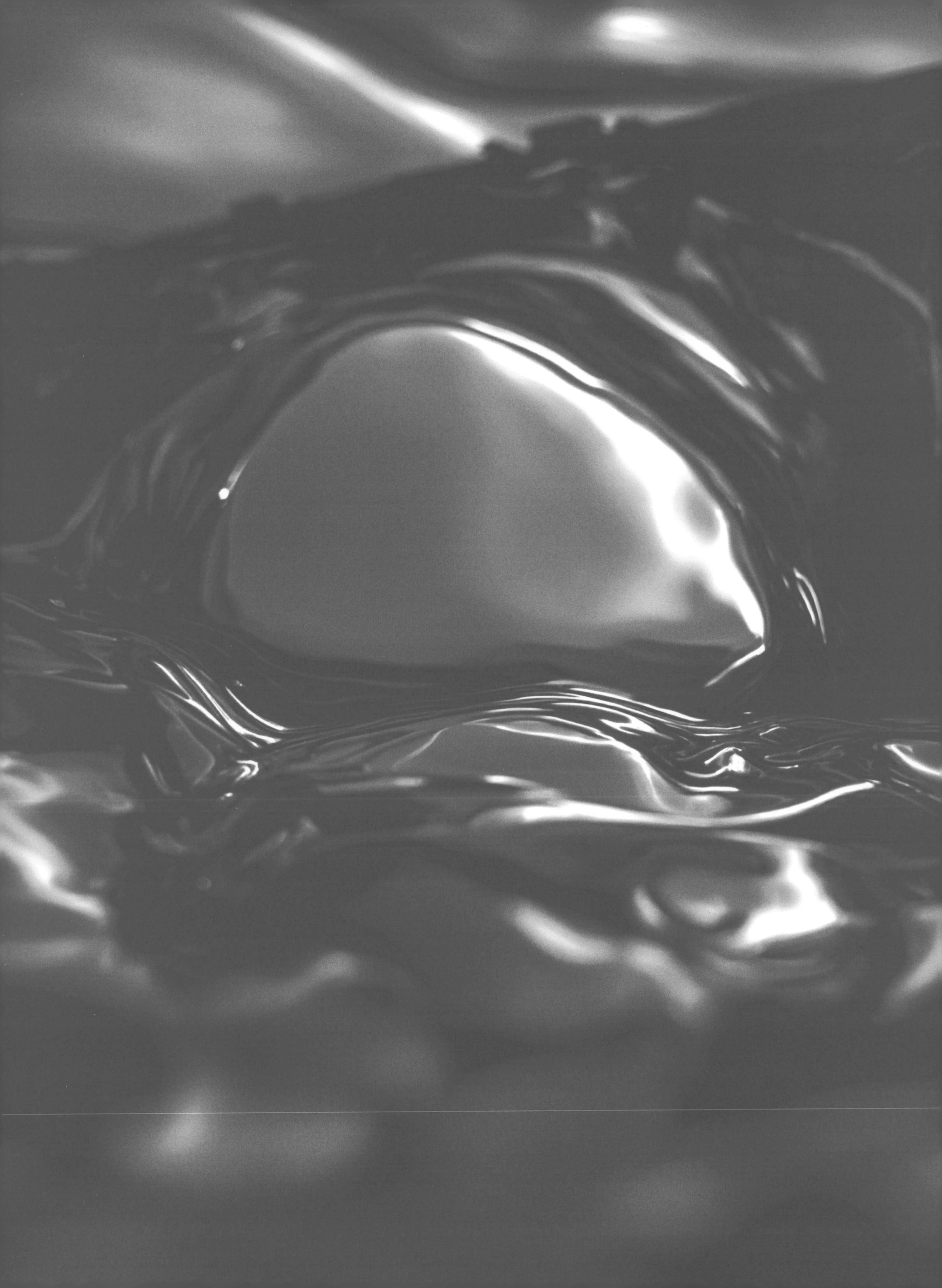

2.3

Time: Architectural Transformations

The passage of time is revealed in the incessant transformation of matter and of the urban landscape, beyond simple chronological sequentiality. The evolution of architecture along the Arno is illustrated in a continuous visual sequence, generated by digital AI models and systems, which reconstruct the evolving shapes of the city of Florence according to the style and philological rigor of the period, from the architecture of the 13th century, through the Renaissance and high Renaissance periods to the 17th century – when Florence became the Capital of Italy. Emblematic buildings like the Mint Tower, Palazzo Capponi delle Rovinate, the Vasarian Corridor, Ponte Santa Trinita and Palazzo Serristori appear in a sequence like nocturnal visions, reflected on the water, illuminated by a warm, dramatic light that emphasizes the historic stratifications.

The changes occur smoothly, the materials change, the lights move, while the passing time flows on, marking the sequence of epochs. Every work of architecture becomes a narrative threshold, evoking different urban atmospheres and cultural contexts. In its uninterrupted flow, the Arno accompanies the city through its changes, gently inviting us to follow it with our eyes as it takes us deep into the many strata of its splendid history.

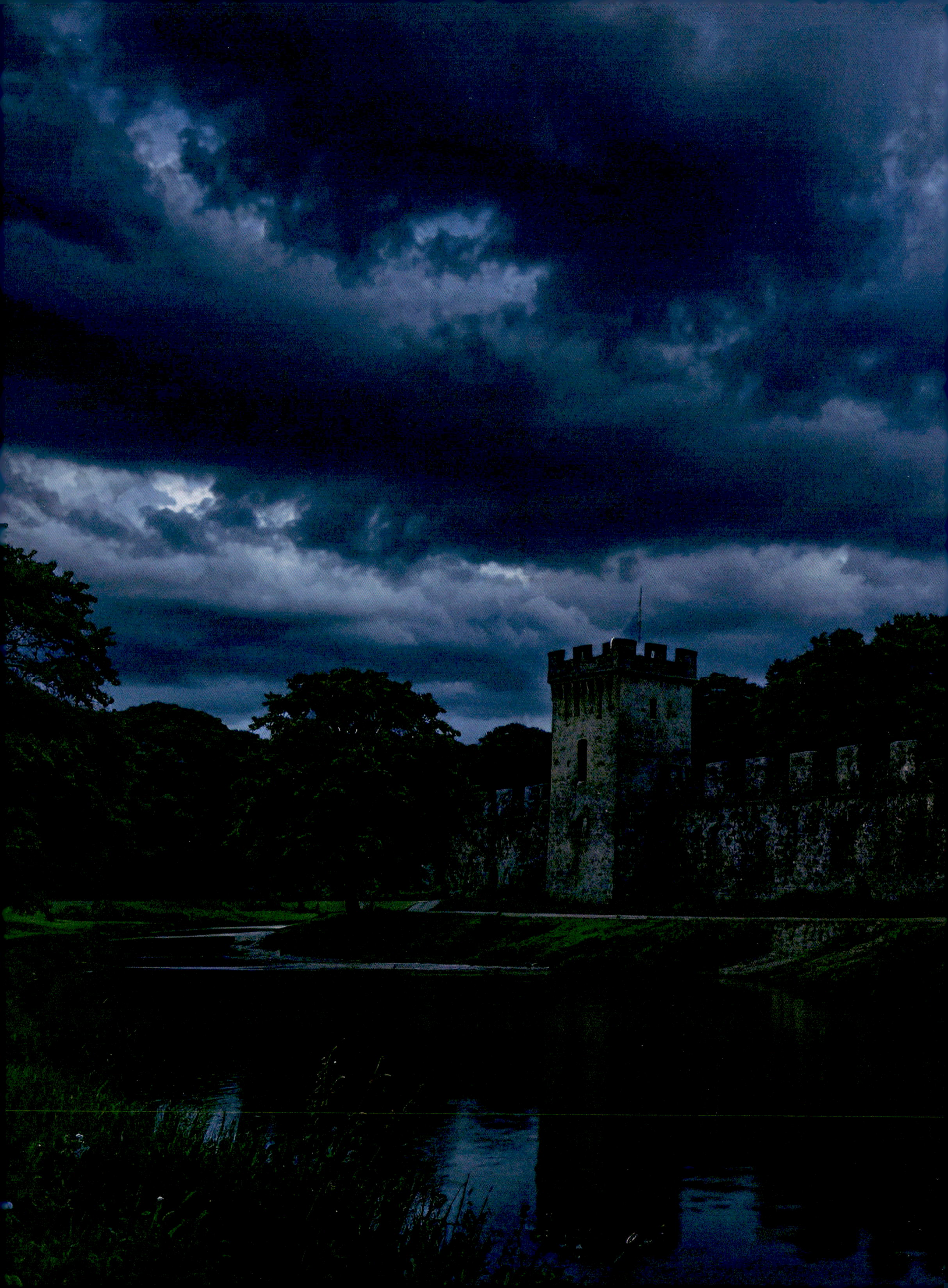

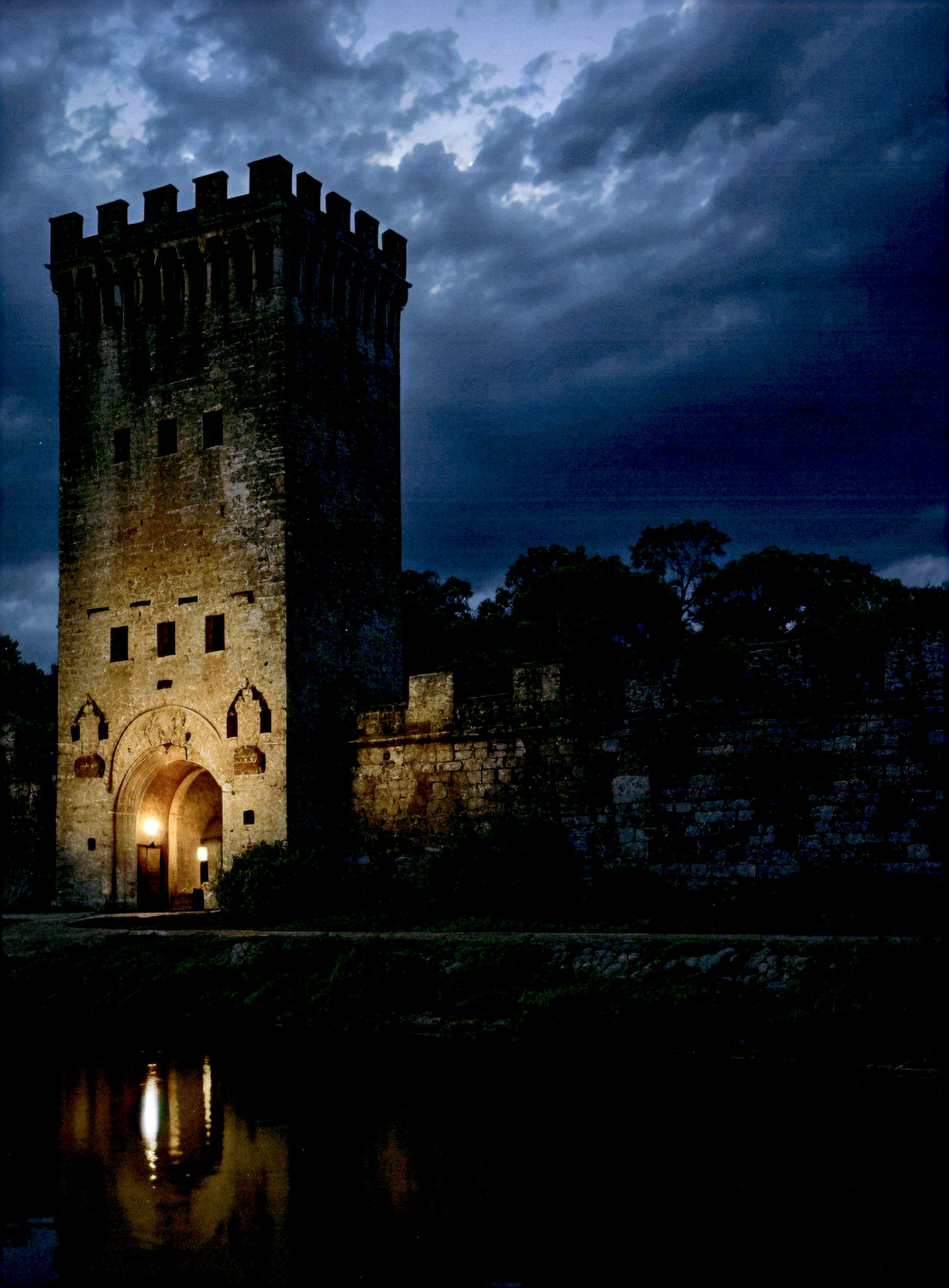

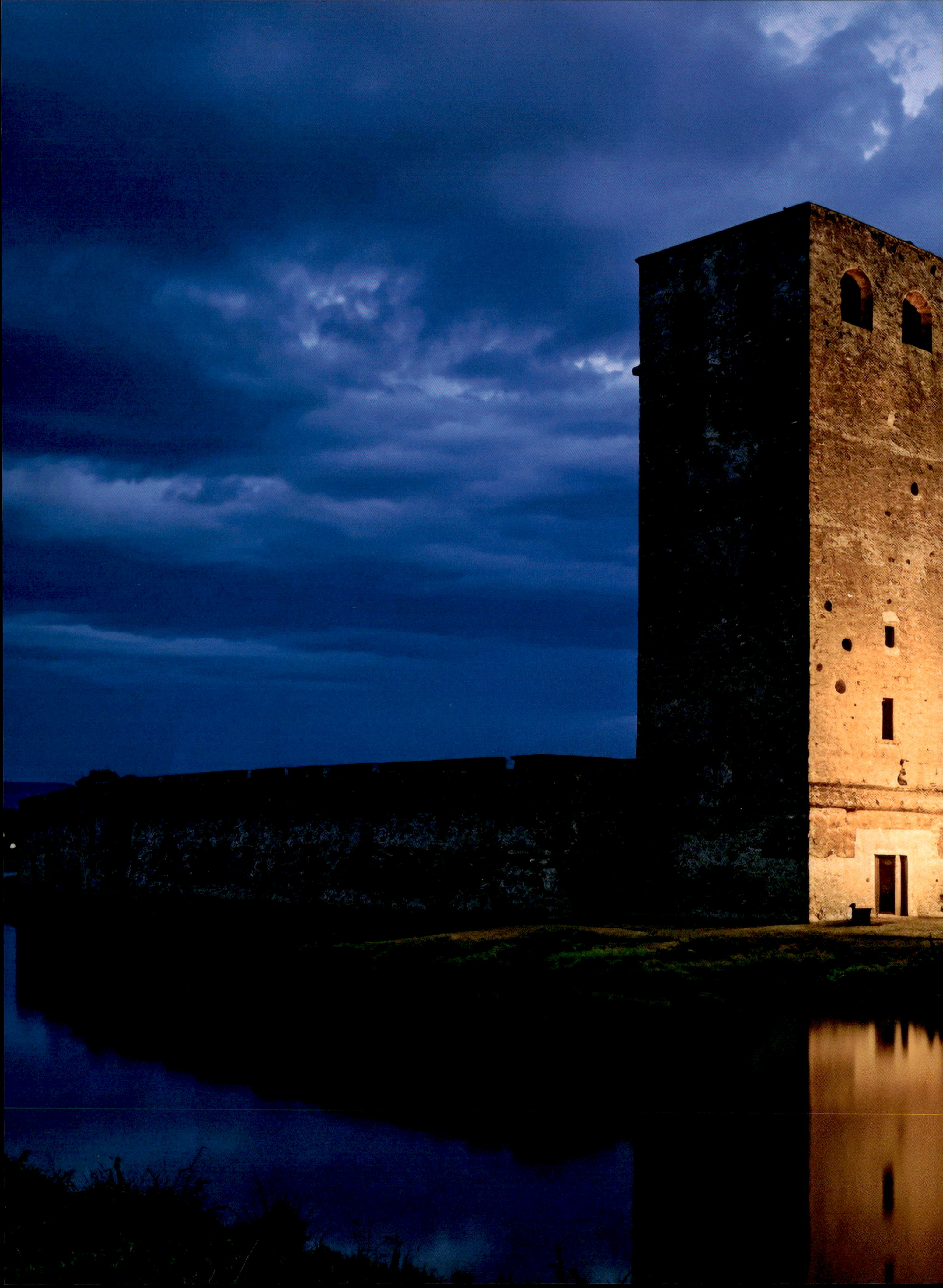

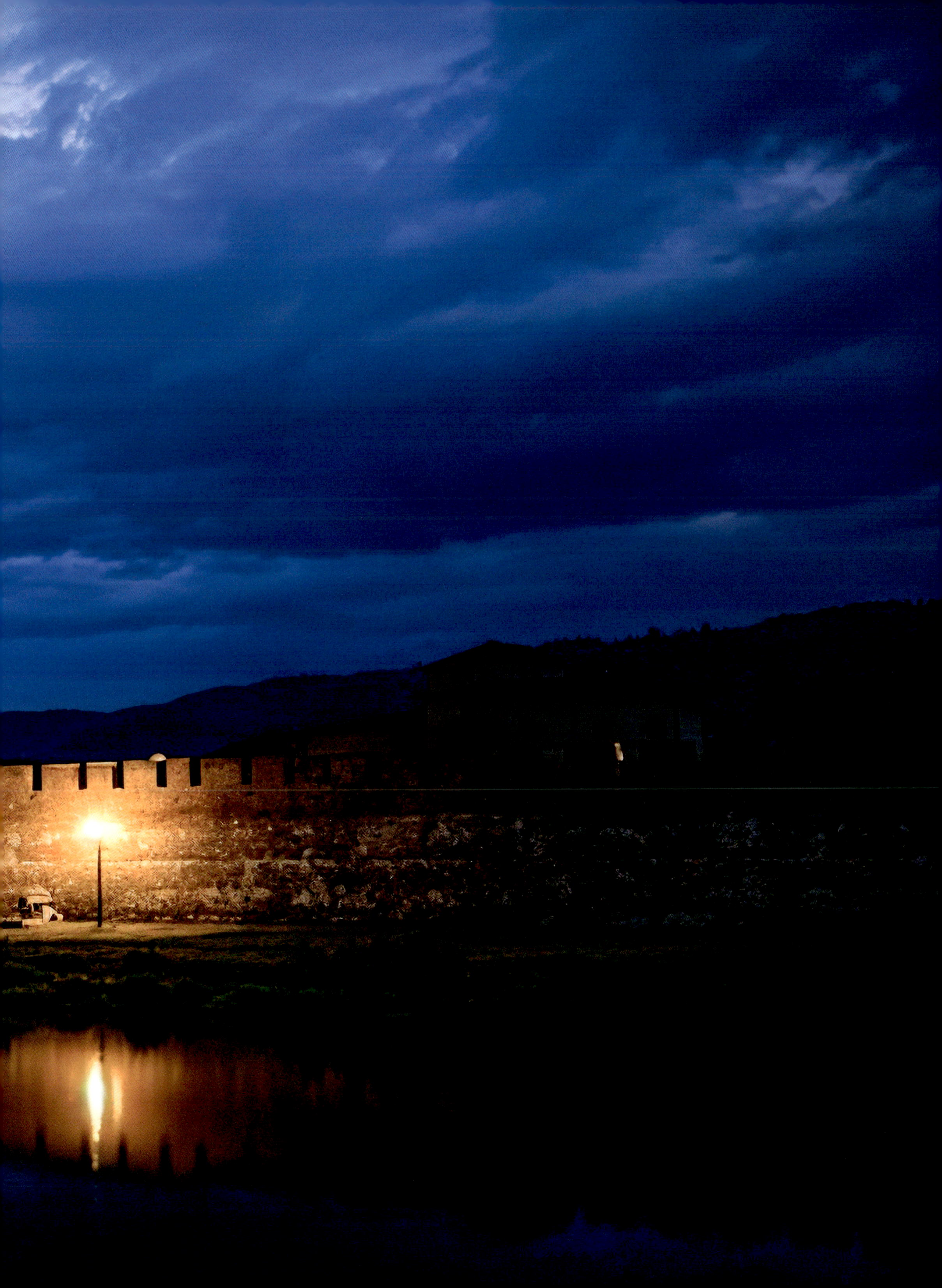

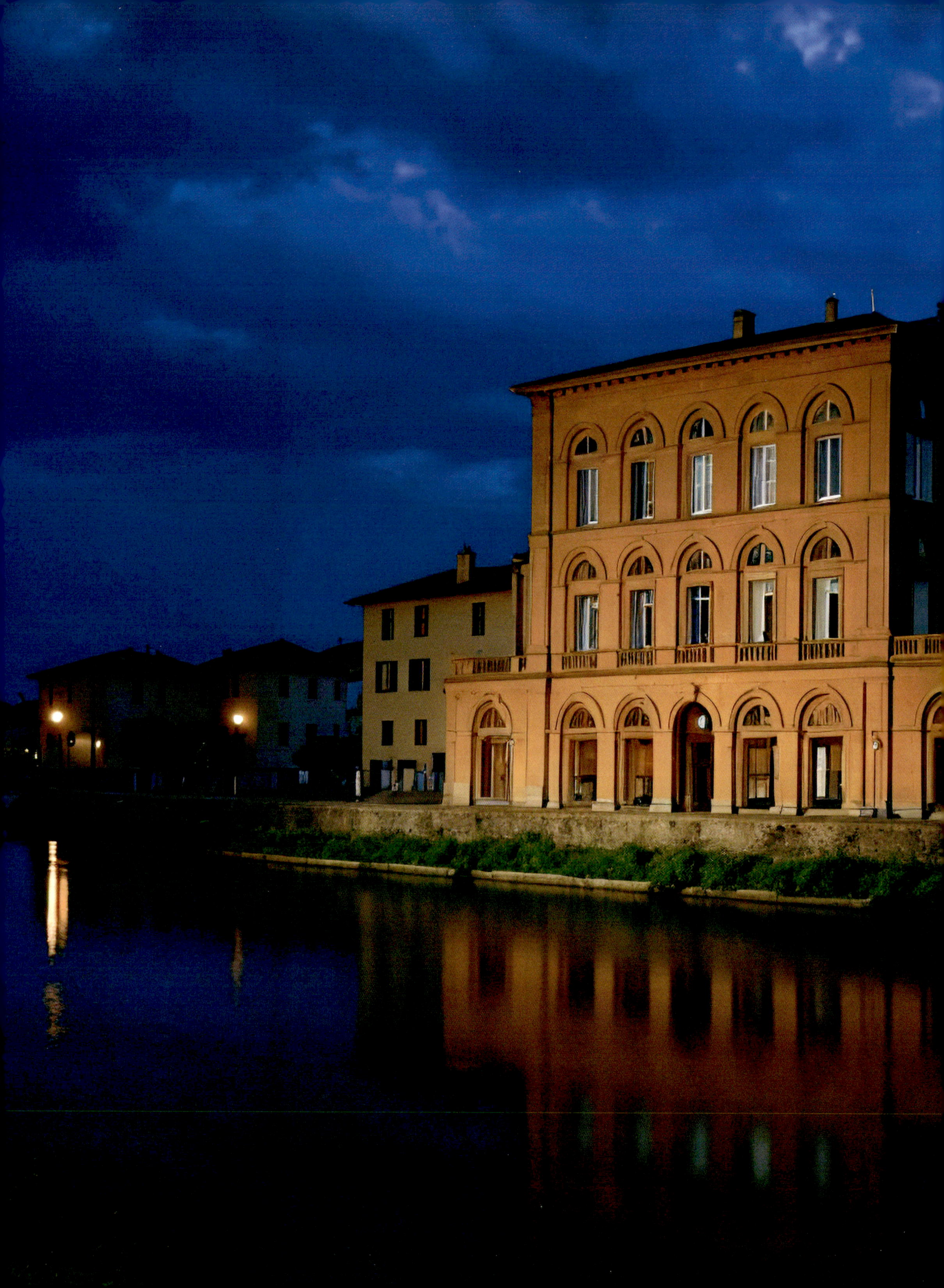

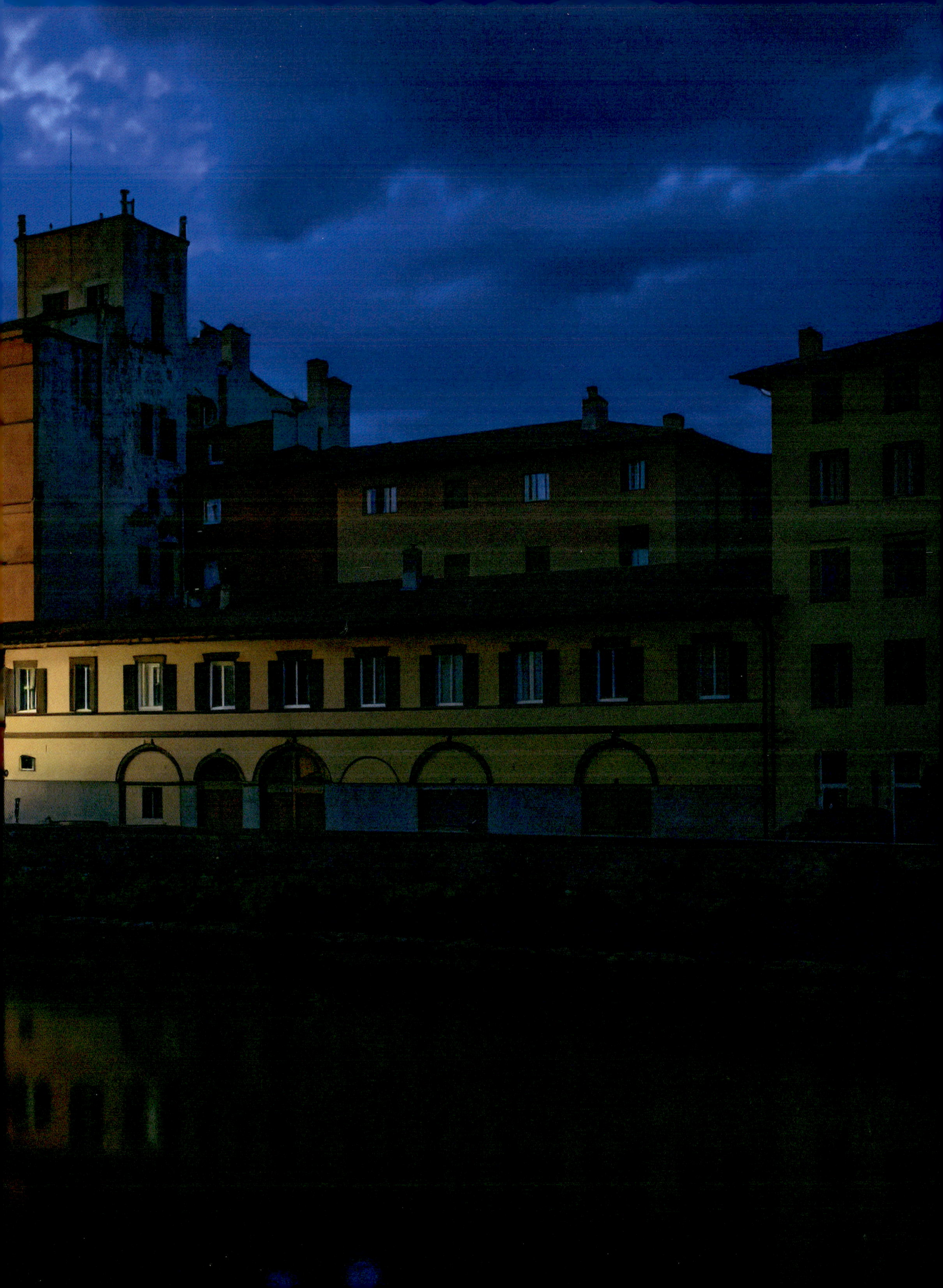

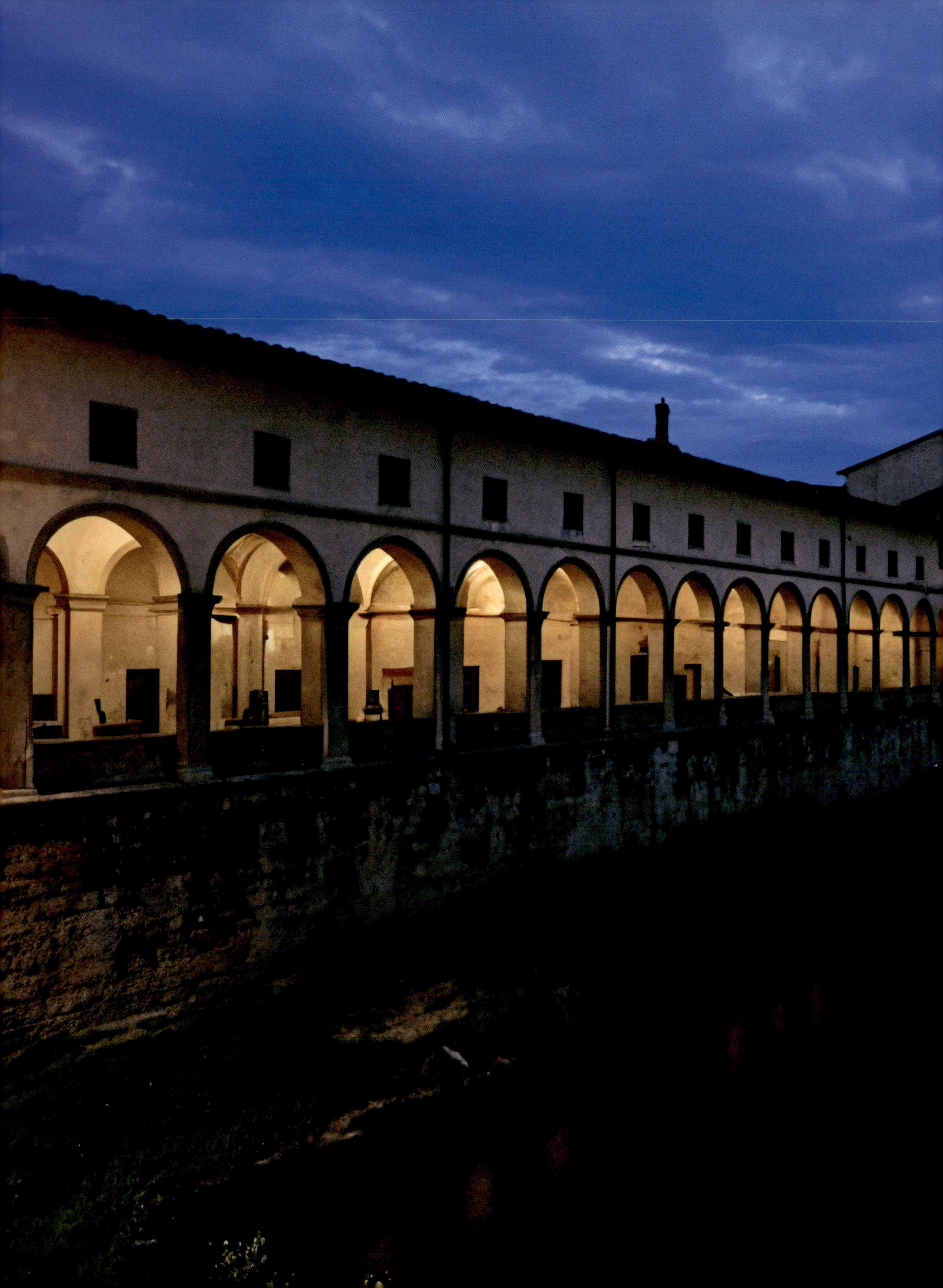

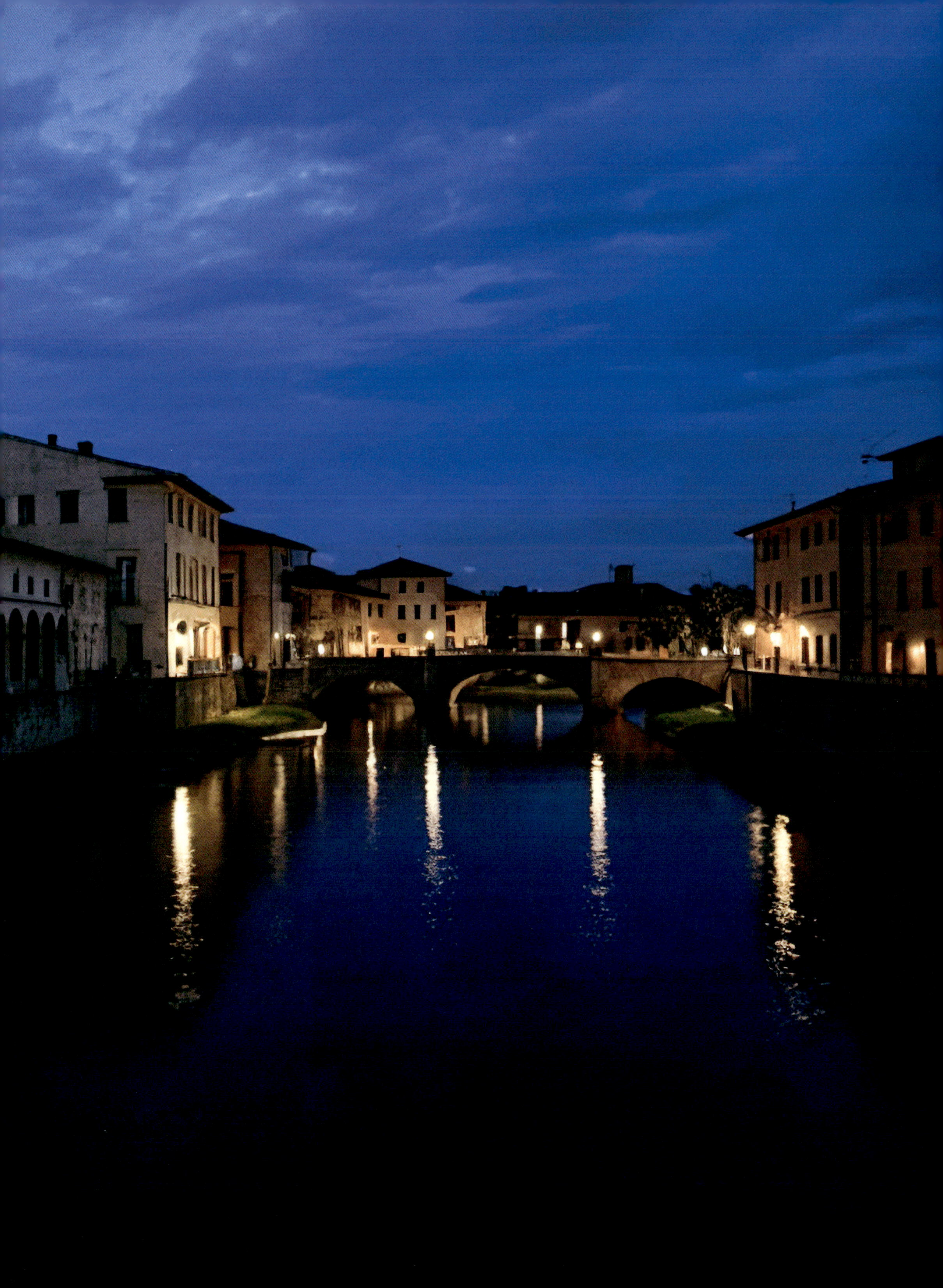

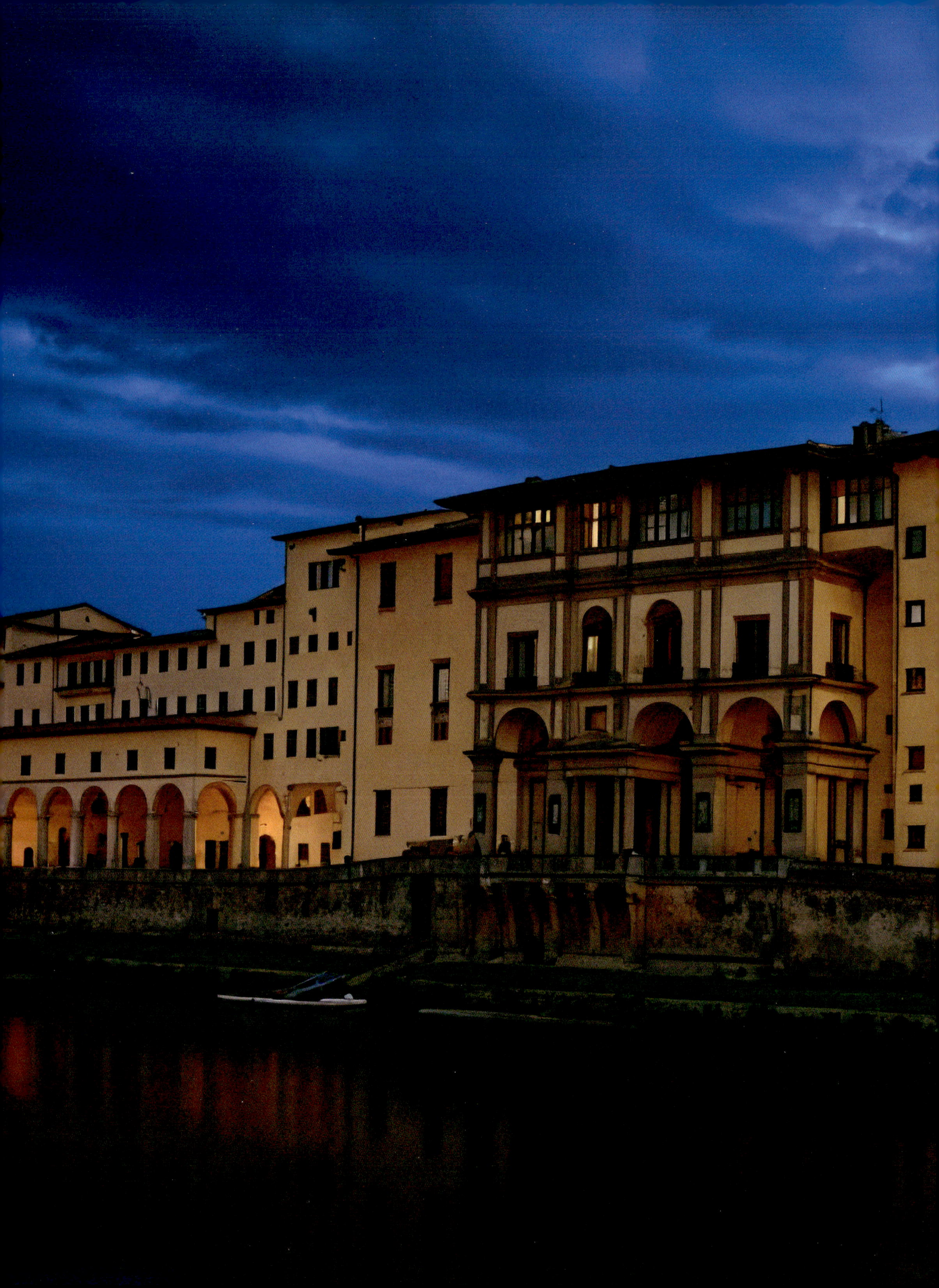

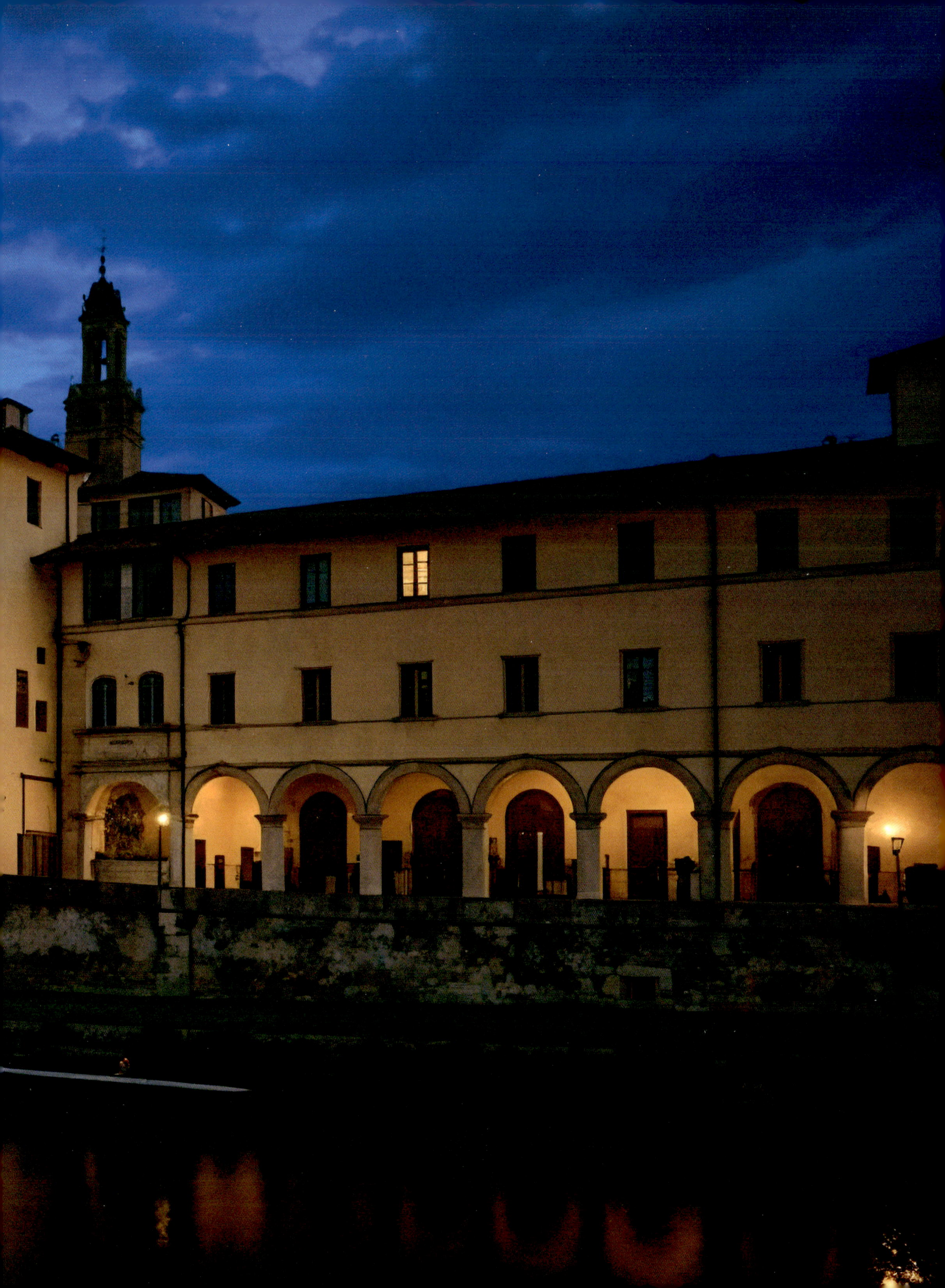

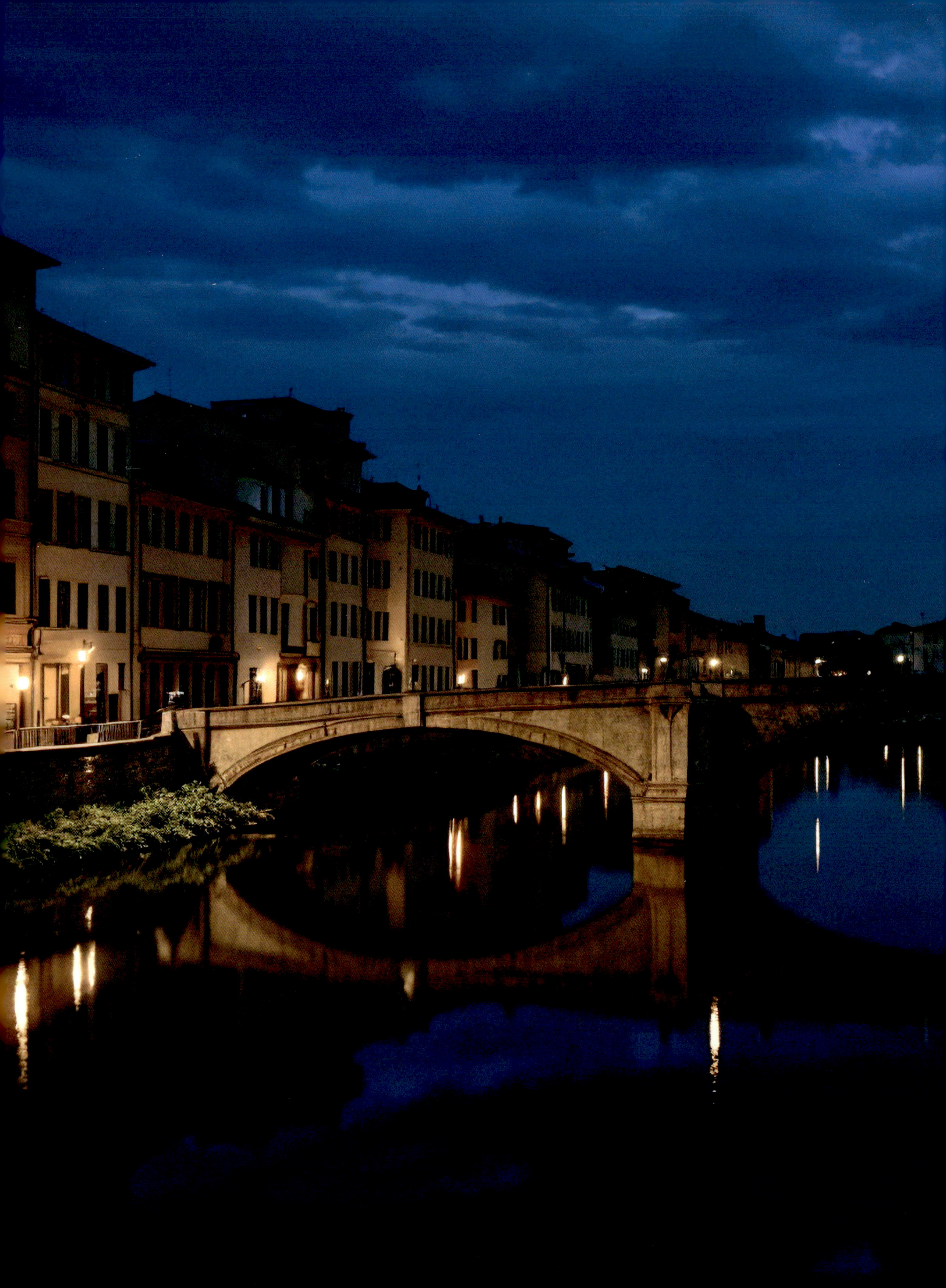

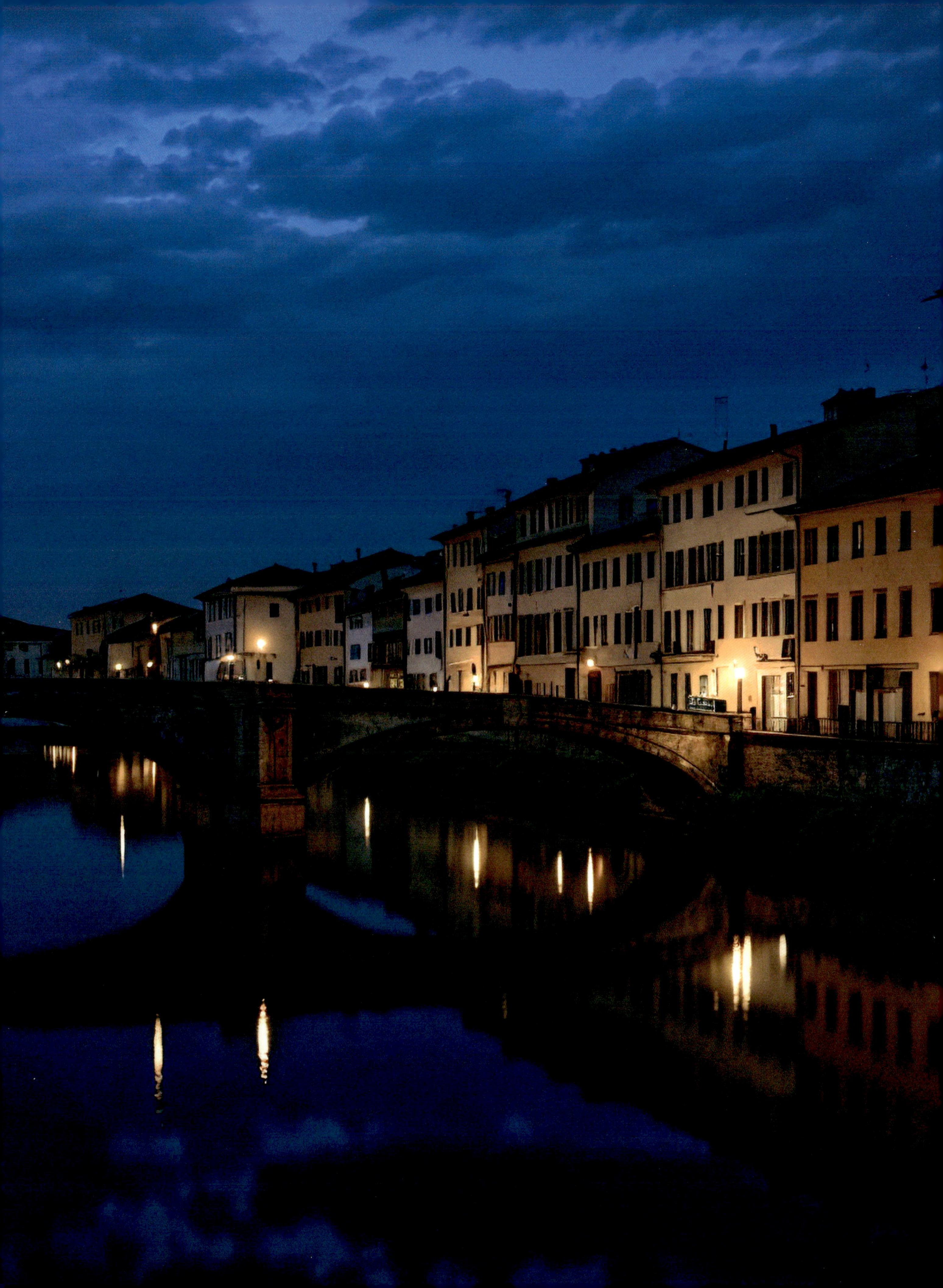

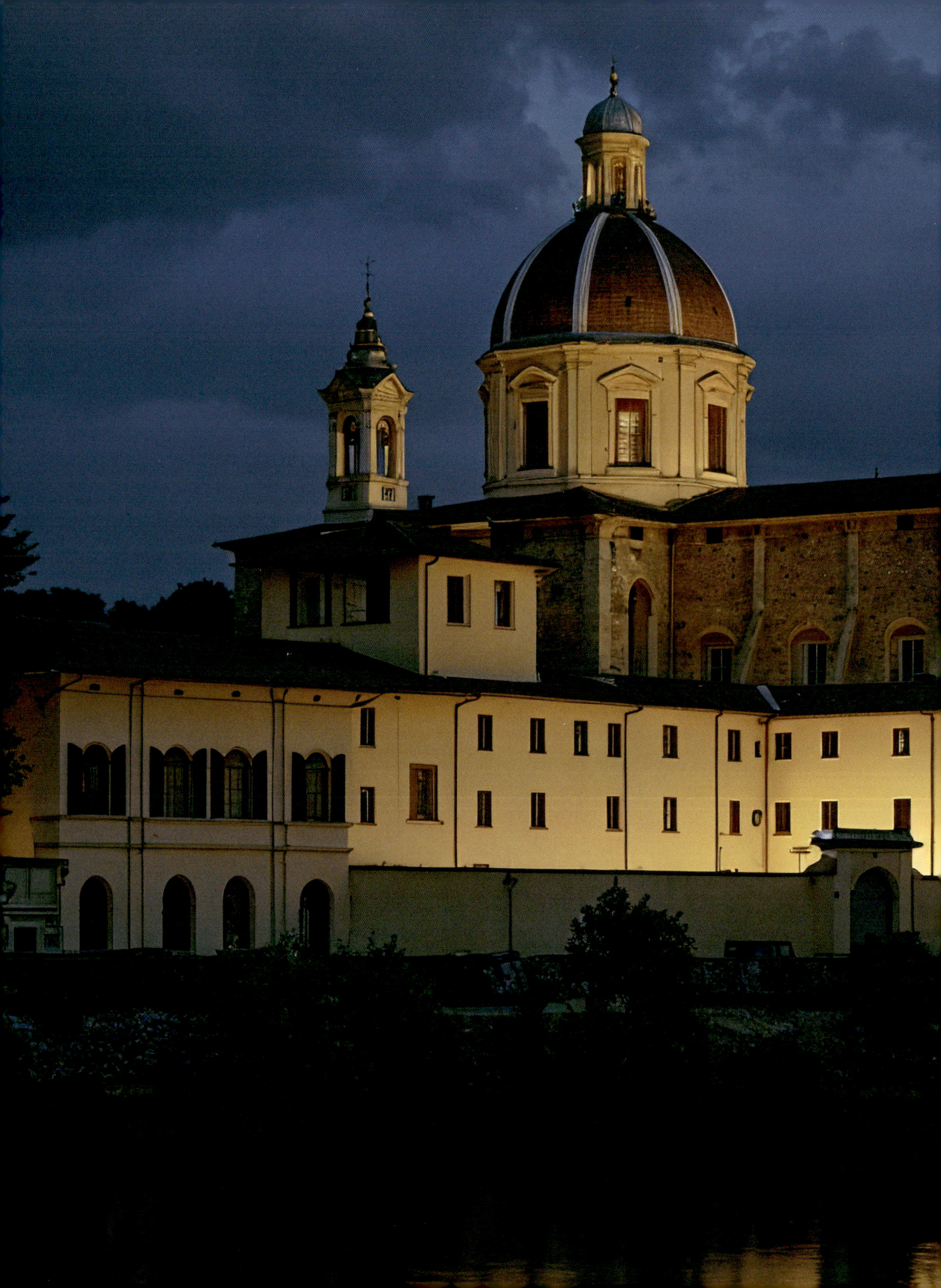

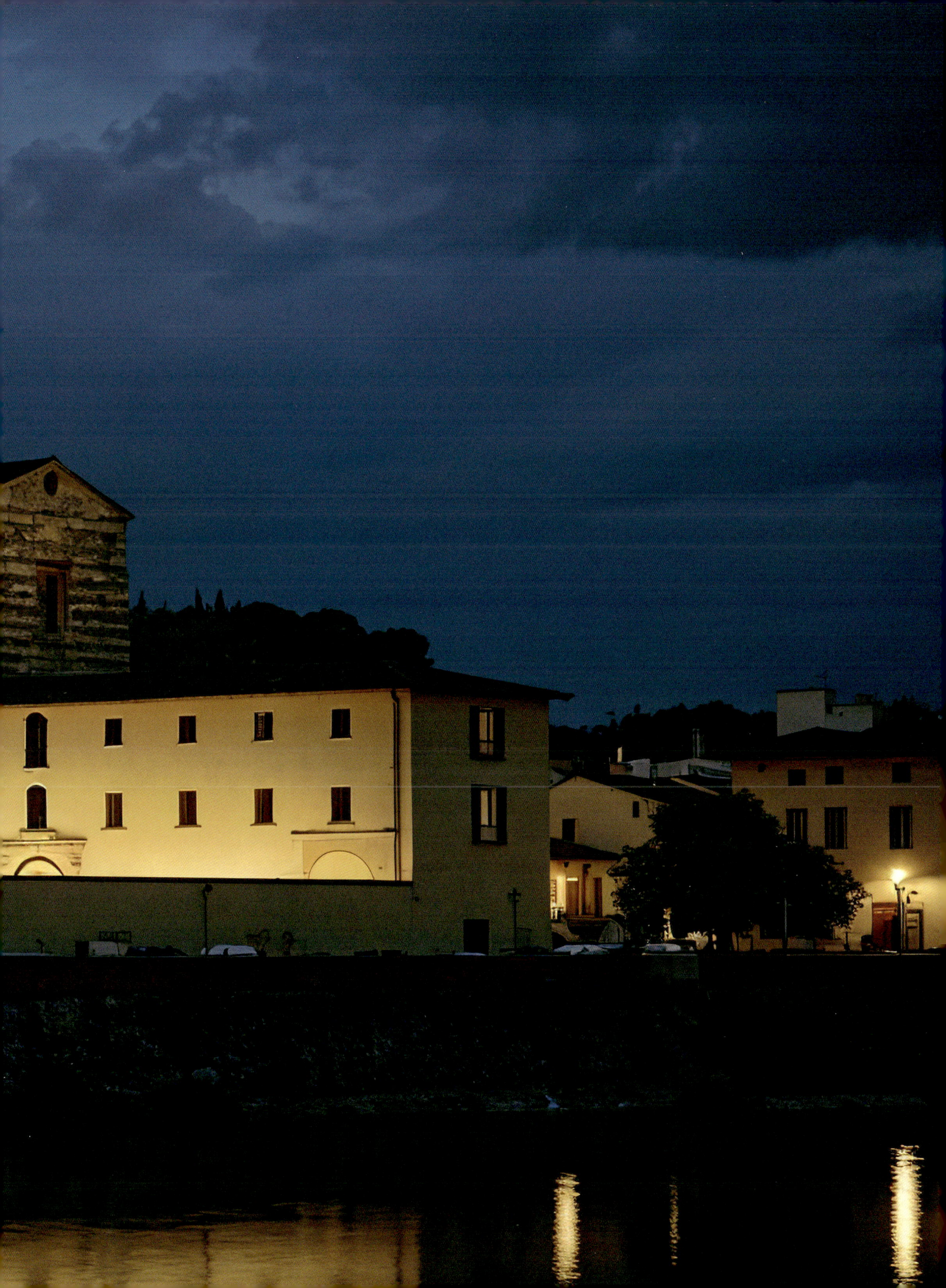

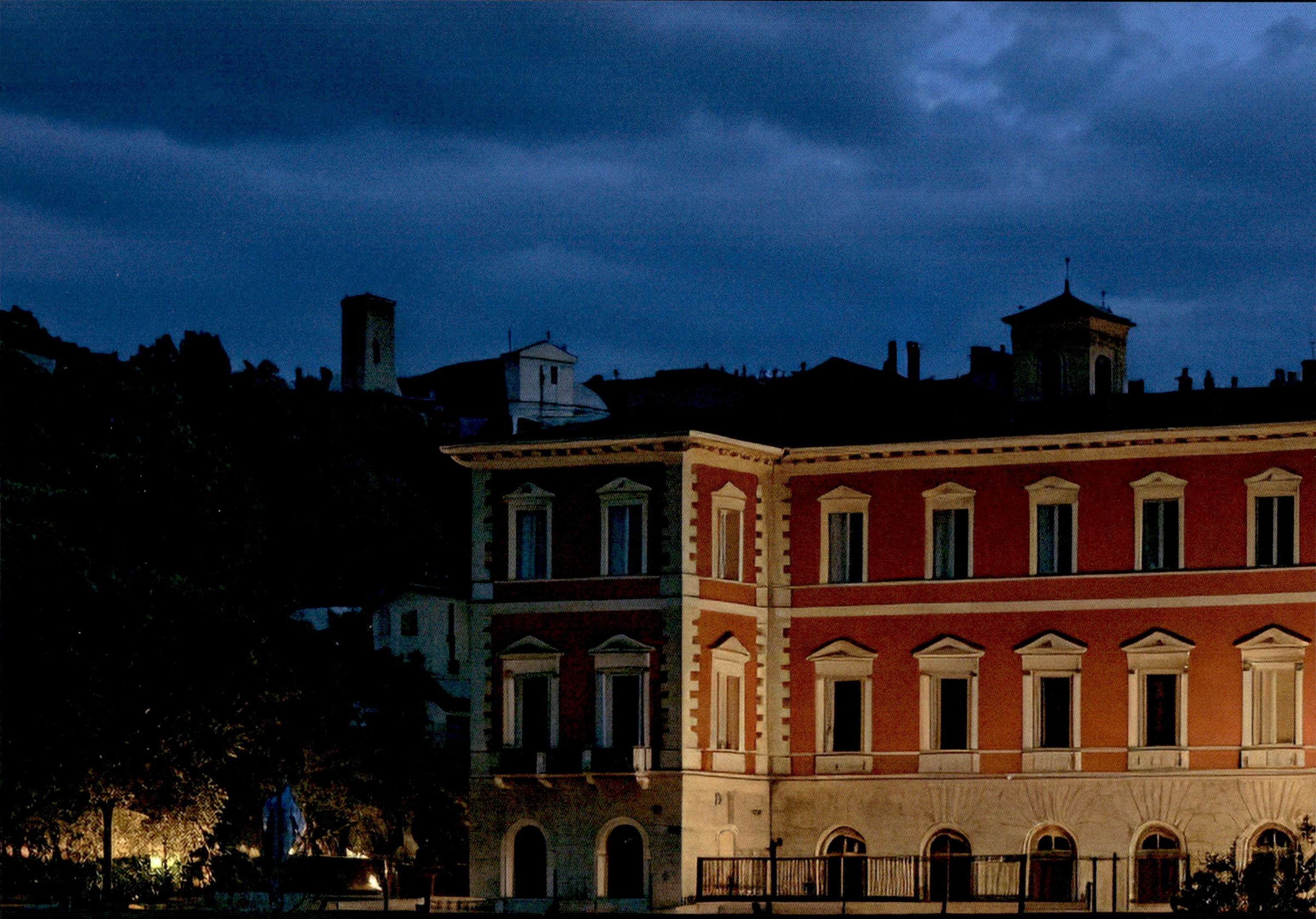

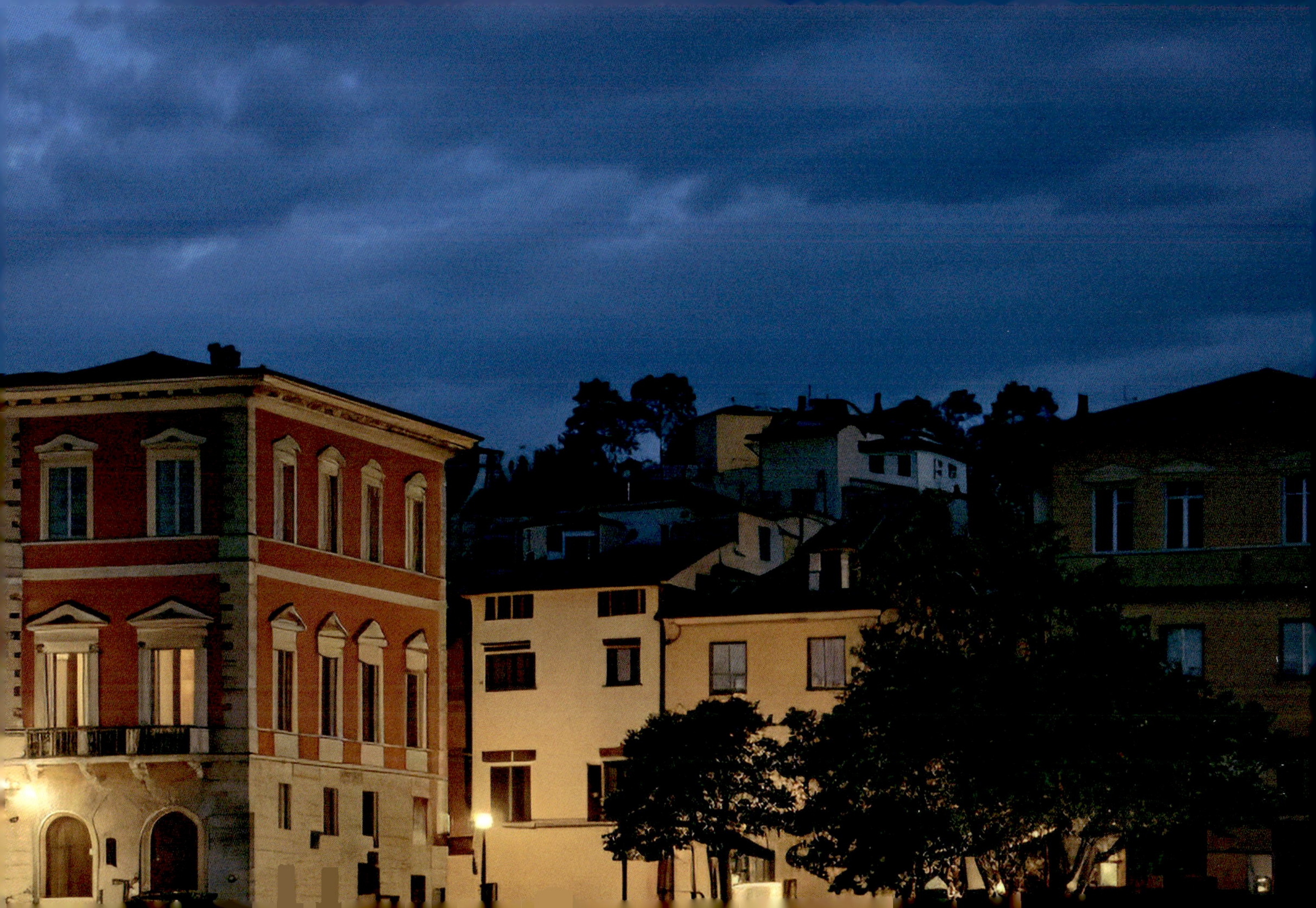

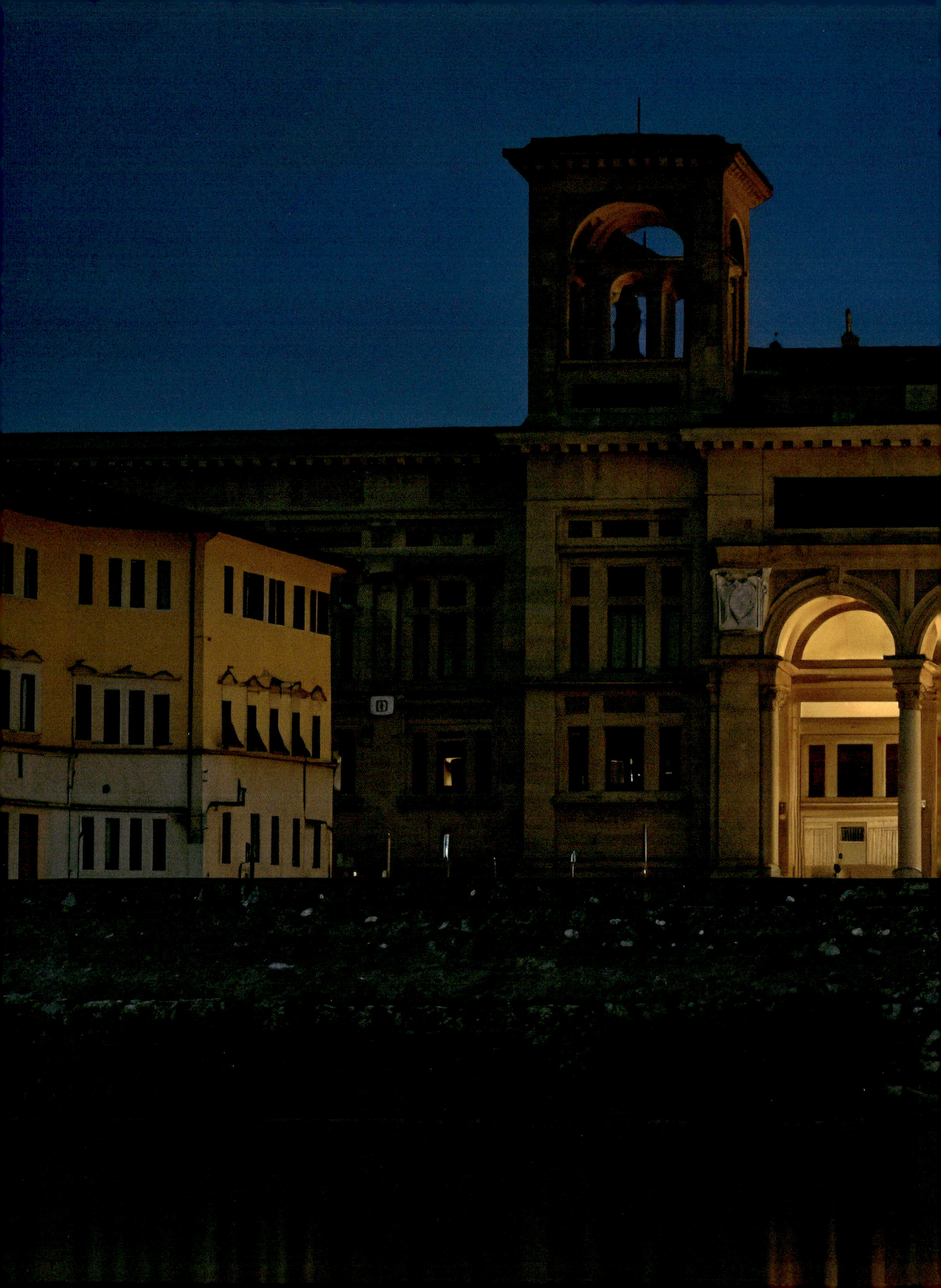

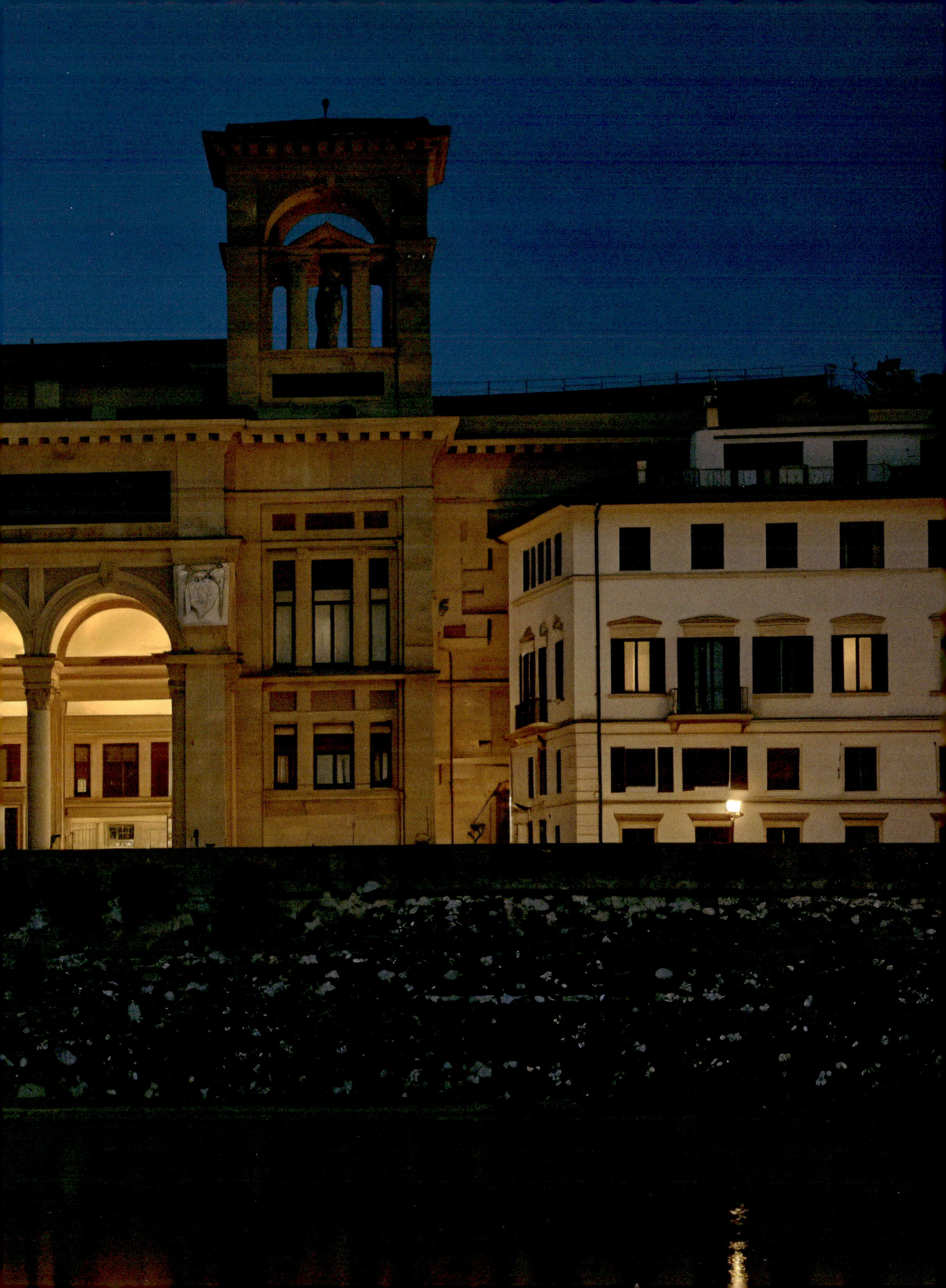

PROMPT_03 [late 16th-century Florence under Medici rule; the Corridoio Vasariano appears in its original context as an elevated, enclosed walkway along the Arno.

subject / main architecture: the Corridoio Vasariano's arches and stone structure are faithfully preserved, running partially elevated along the riverbank.

visual style: hyperrealistic nighttime scene; twilight blues and purples in the sky, ambient natural light reveals details. The Arno reflects the Corridoio Vasariano's arches and sky with mirror-like clarity; vivid accents on stone and grass.

atmosphere & light: the atmosphere is surreal and poetic; lingering light softly reveals structure and landscape. The still river enhances the Corridoio Vasariano's rhythm through reflection.]

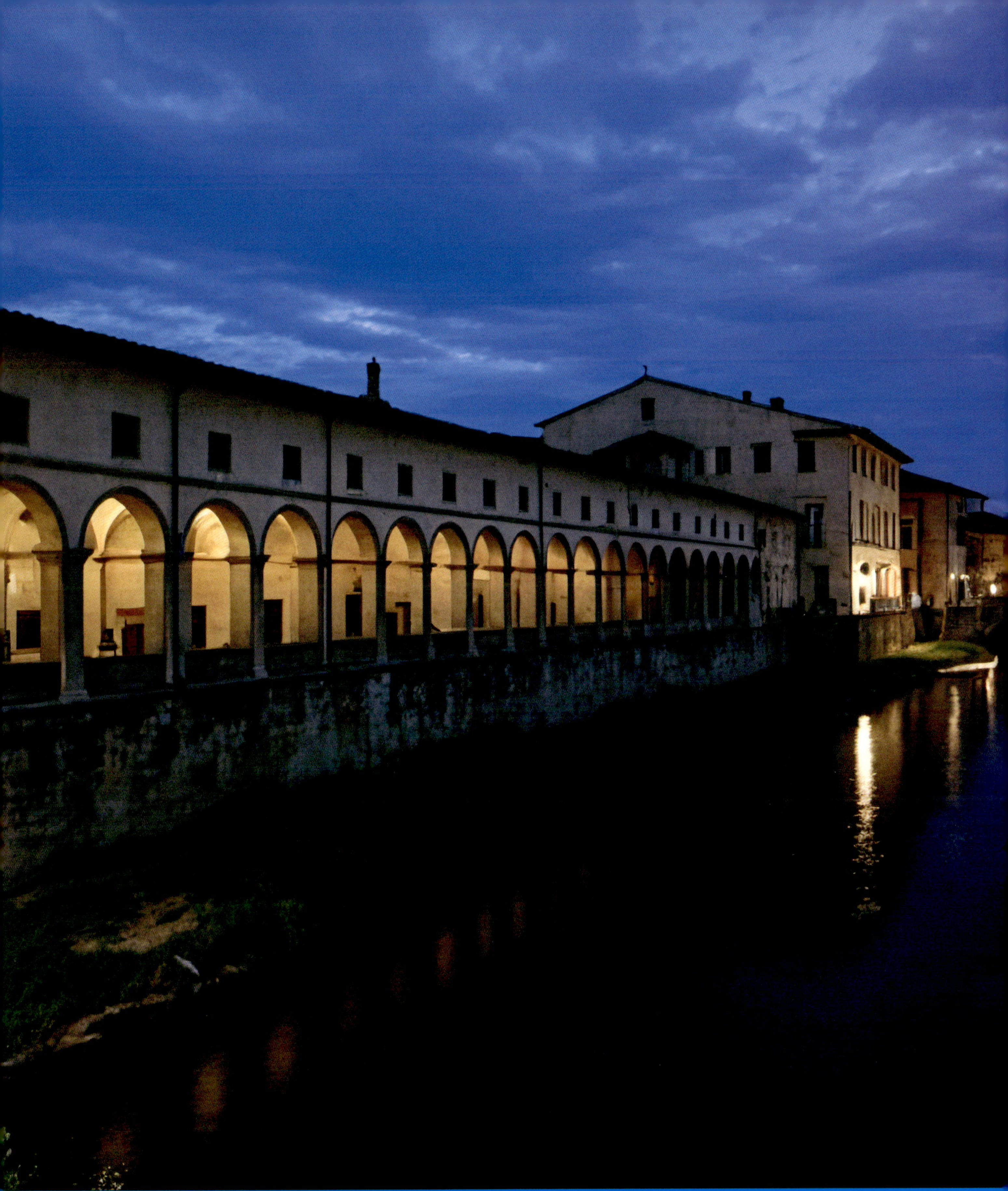

 IMG_03

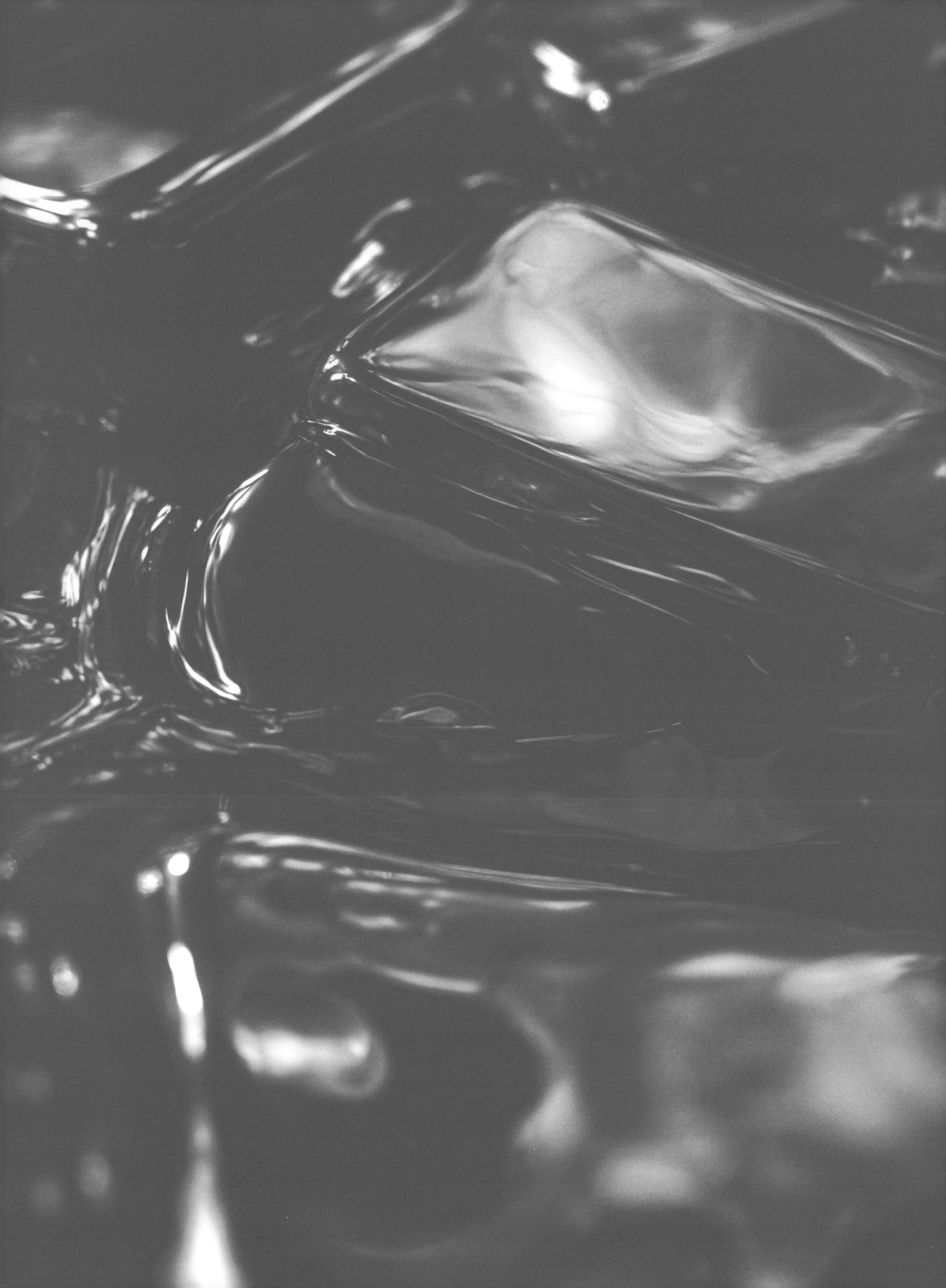

2.4

Findings: Submerged Objects

Abandoned objects, things lost and forgotten: all that the river has collected in time rises to the surface in a suspended space, where the objects tell their stories. In a slow, hypnotic orbital motion, fragments of an unexpected archeological treasure trove emerge: Etruscan vases, rusty bracelets, coins worm smooth, a typewriter, old radios, all the way to the modern cellular telephones of our own time.

They revolve around each other, immersed in liquid time, corroded by the water and the length of their immersion. The faint light reveals the damage: every detail is a fissure in time. It is not a simple collection of objects, but a legible archive that illustrates the material memory of an entire civilization. Every finding brings the memory of a use, a setting, a function: technologies of the past, ritual objects or everyday tools, accumulated on the bottom as cultural sediment. The river never forgets what it receives: it preserves some things, transforms others, and holds on possessively to everything. Every object that enters its domain becomes part of its fluid body, incorporated into its geological memory. In this submerged landscape, the Arno becomes library and historian, preserving fragments of our evolution in its quiet depths, in the knowledge that everything passes and nothing is lost.

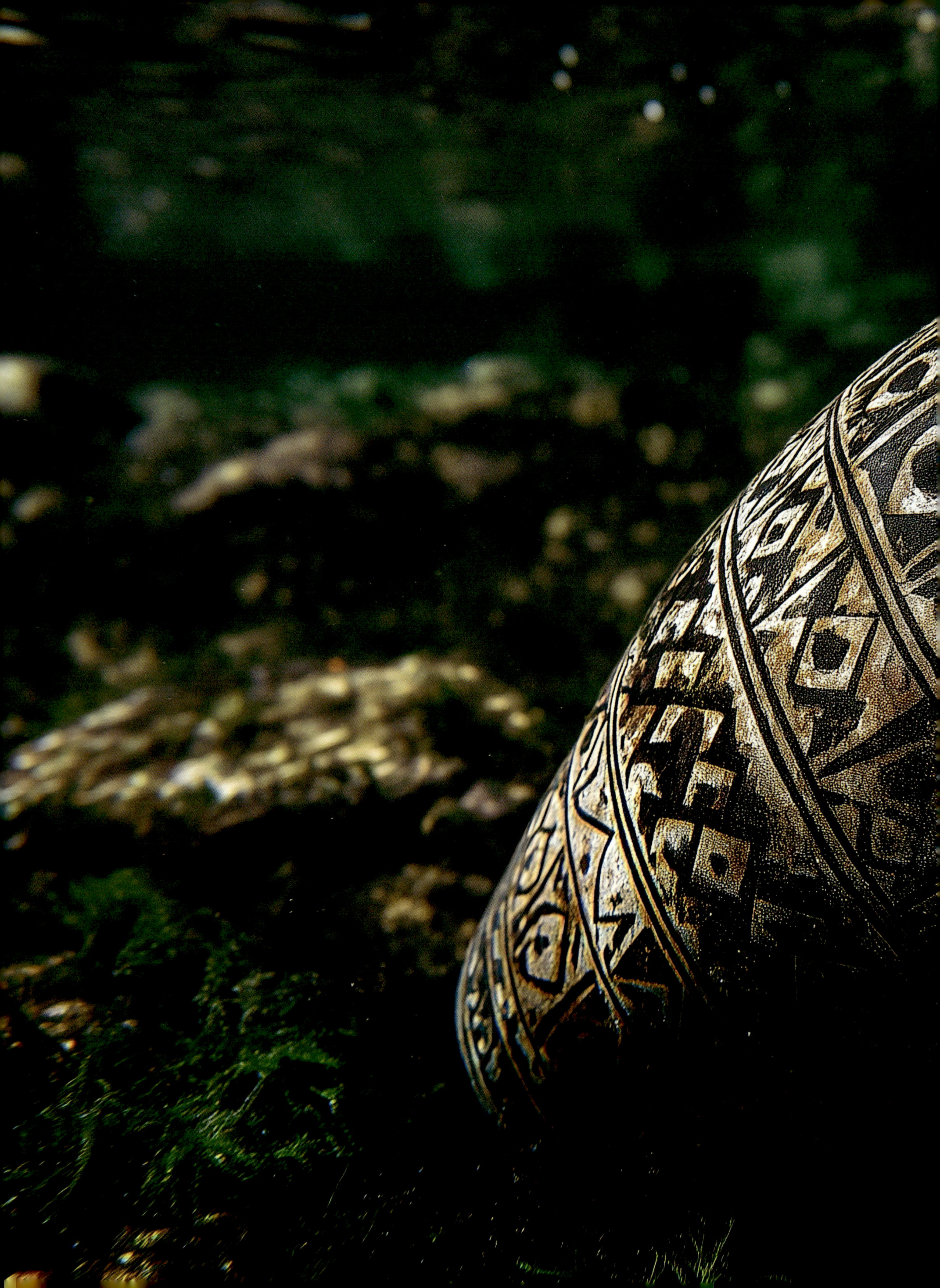

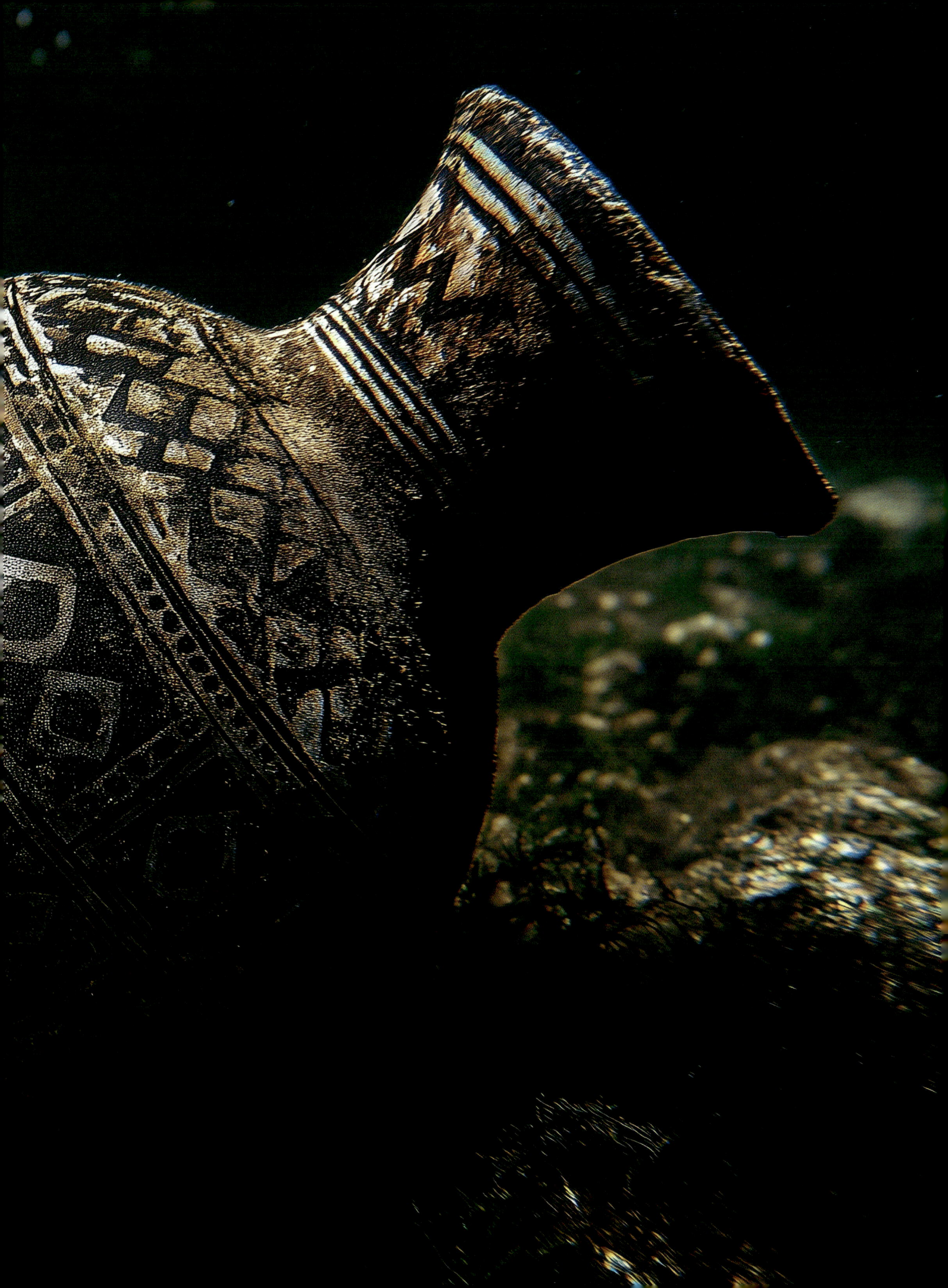

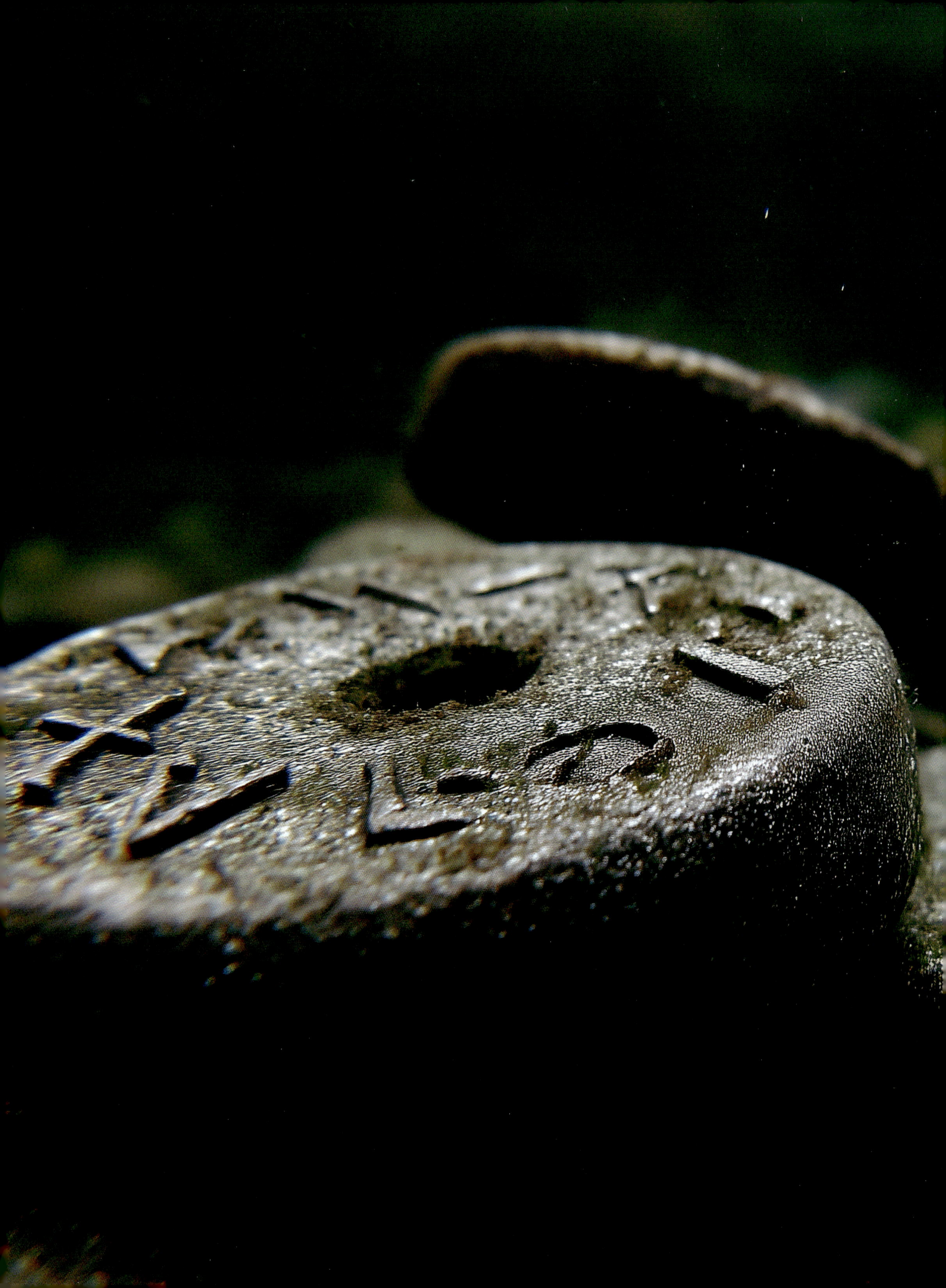

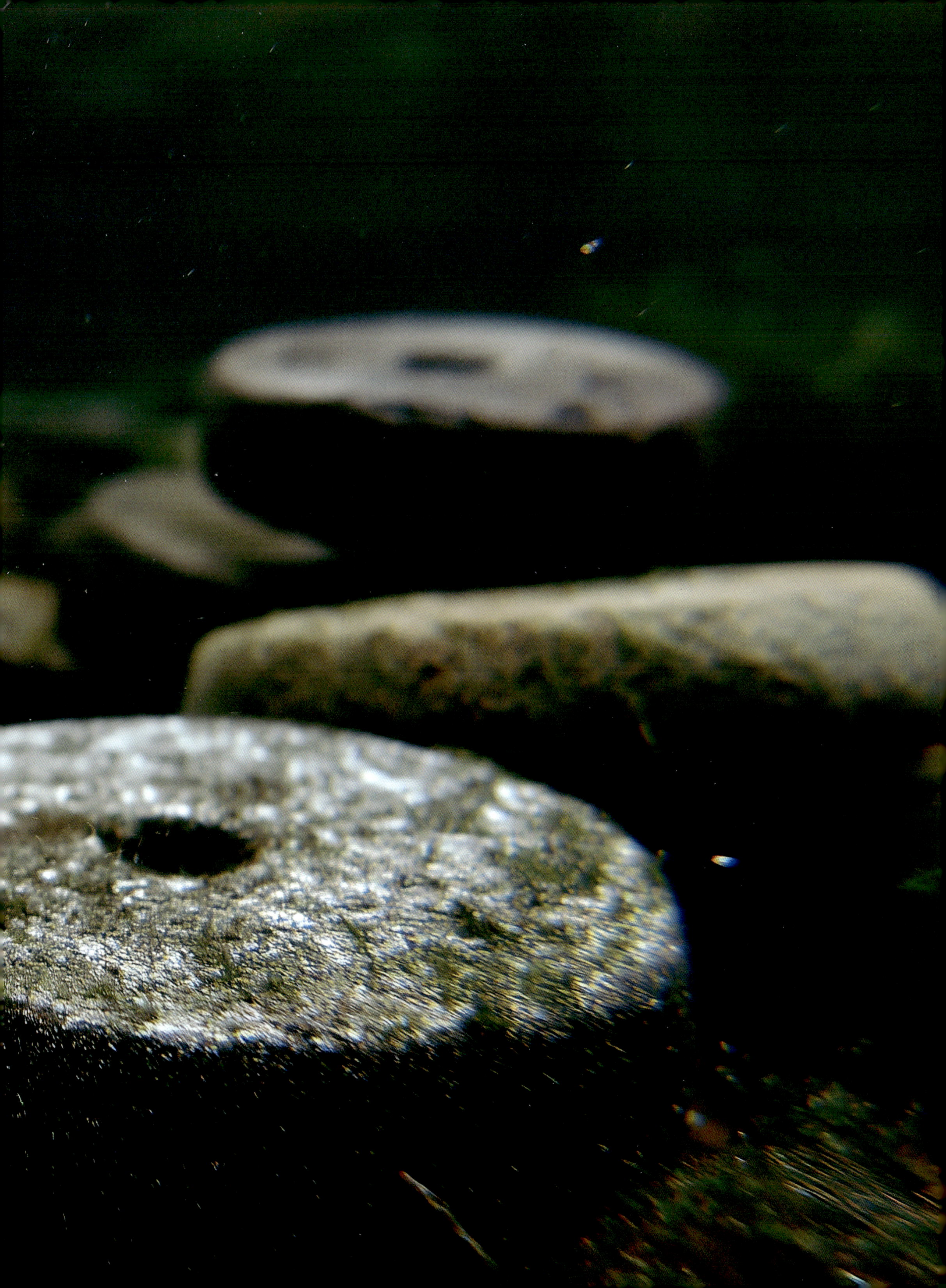

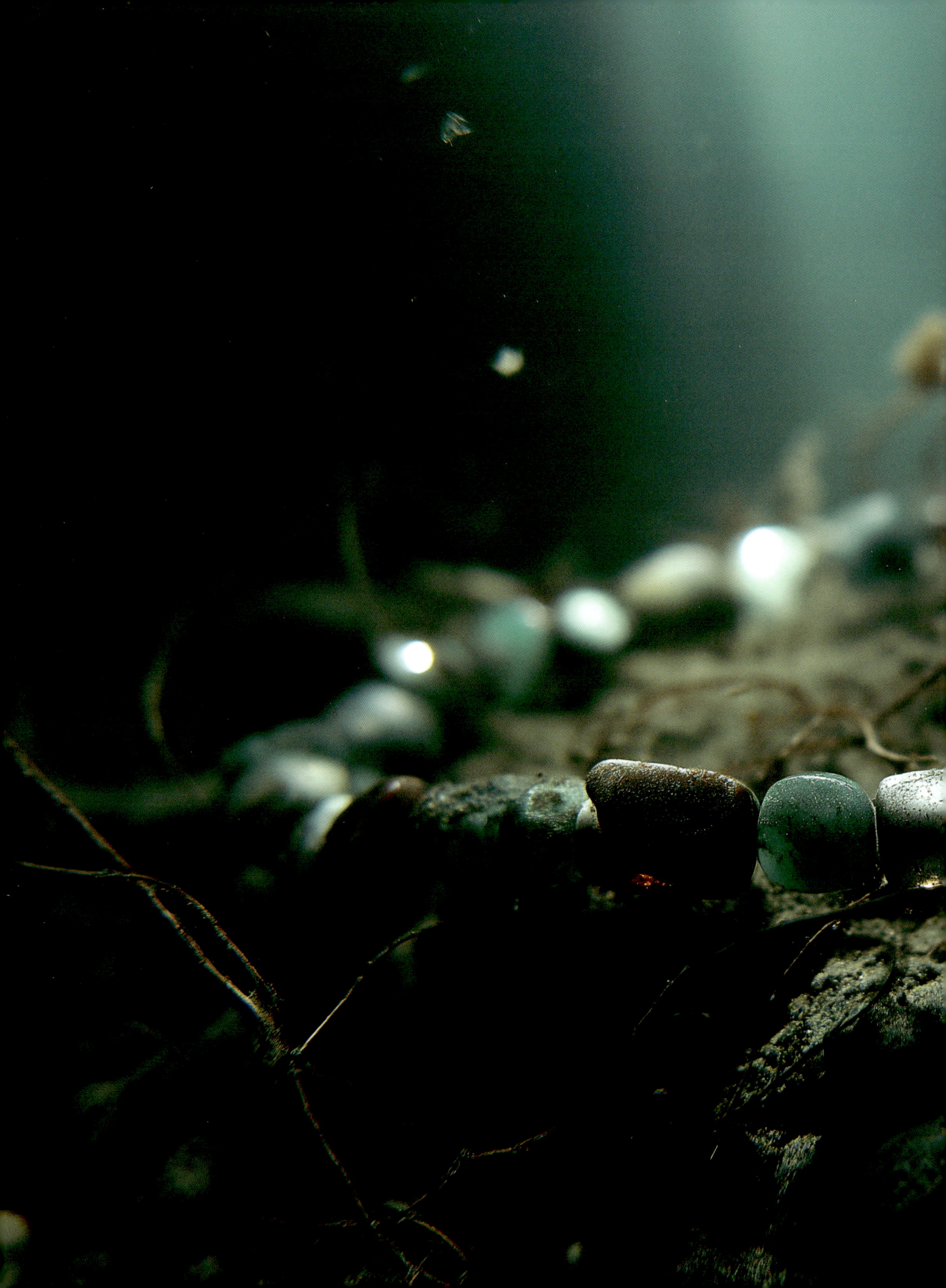

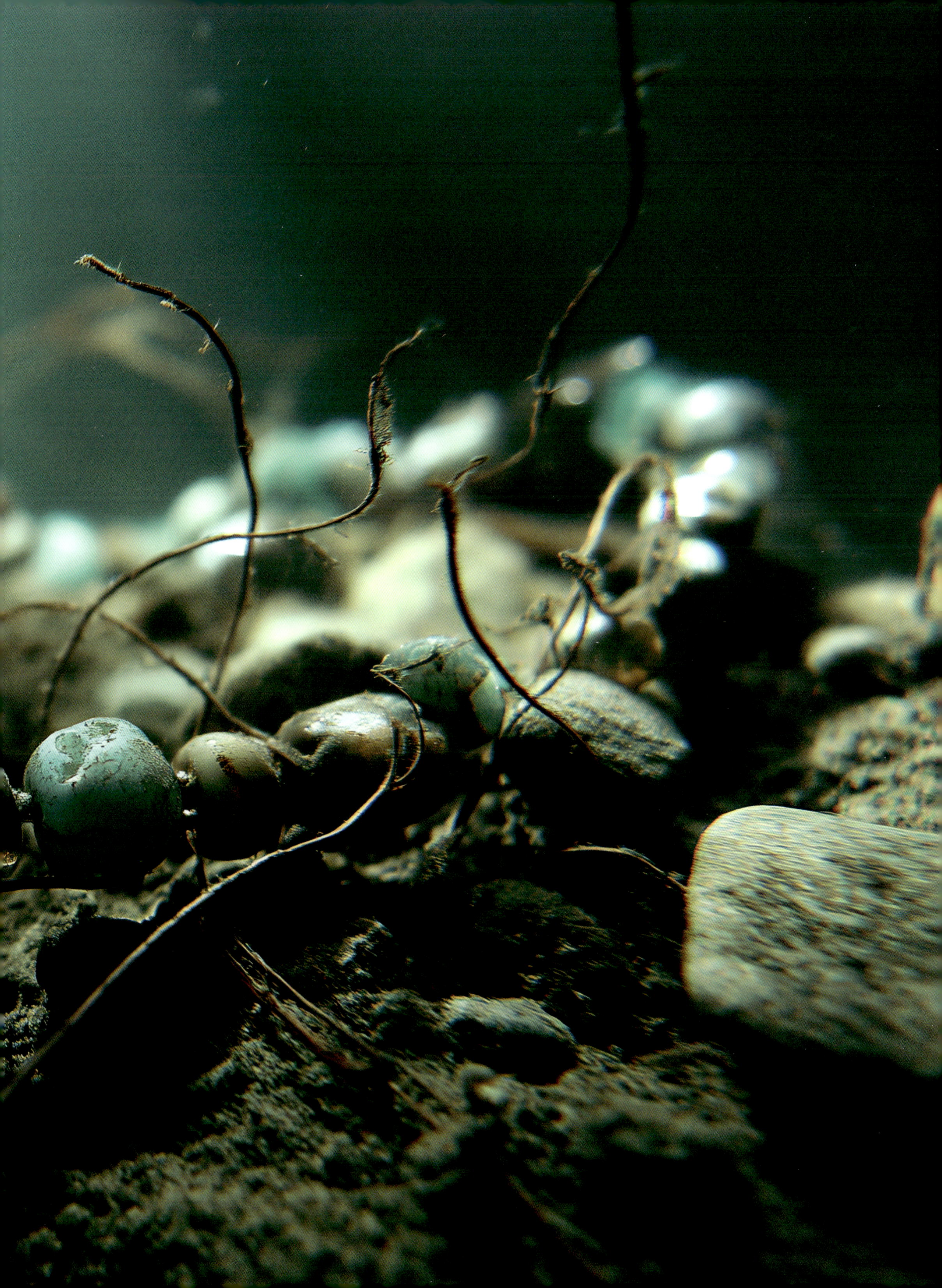

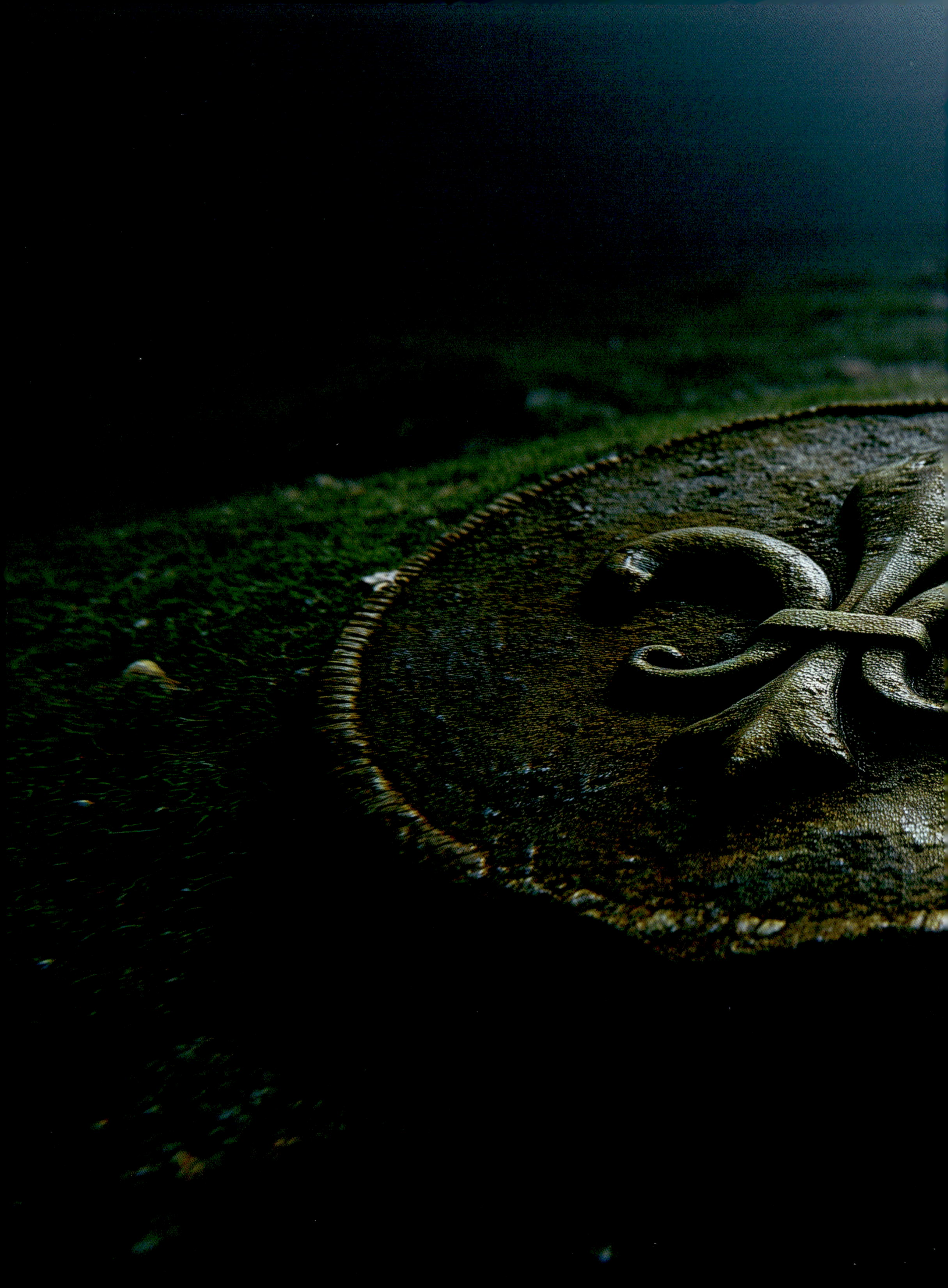

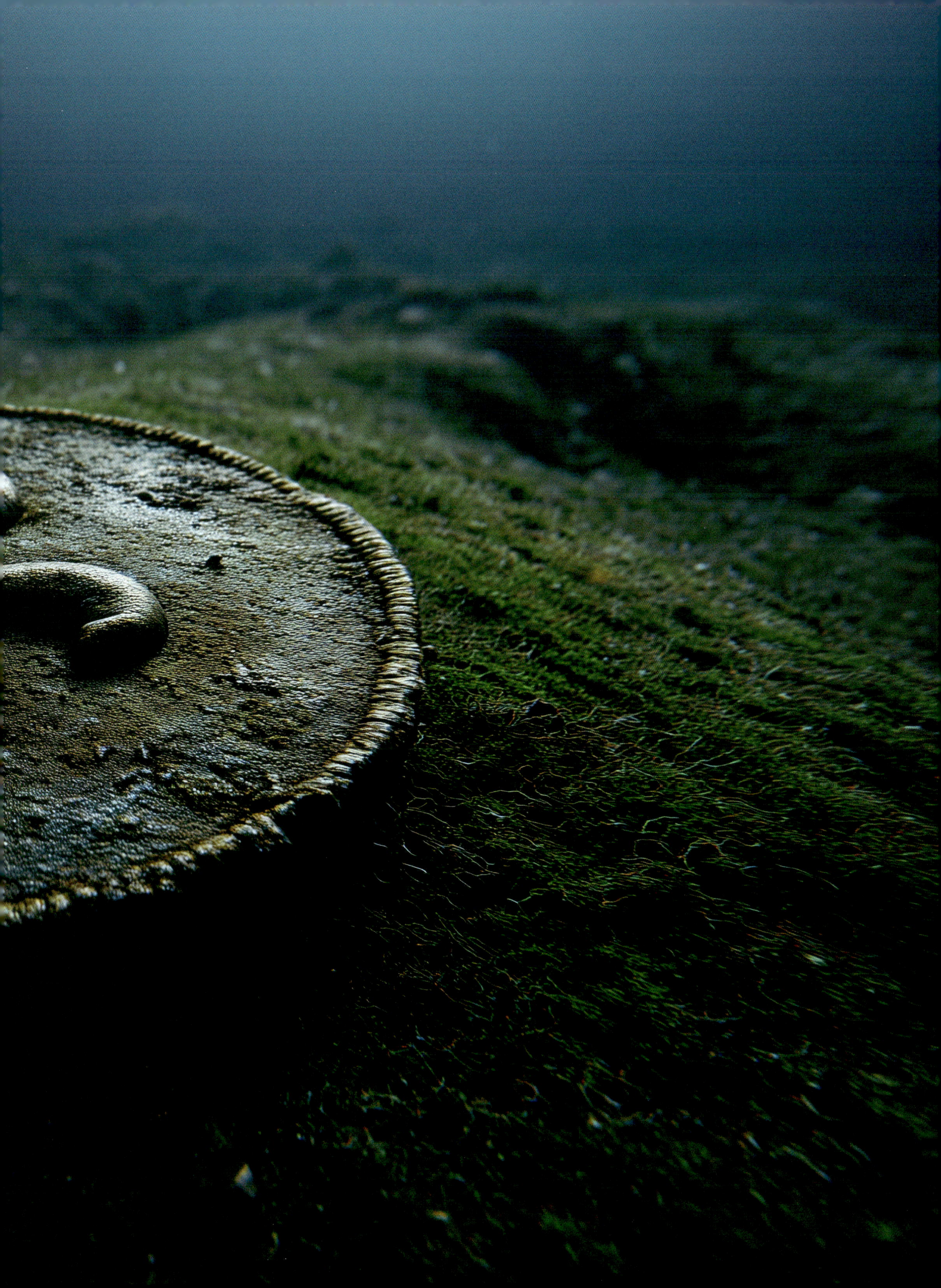

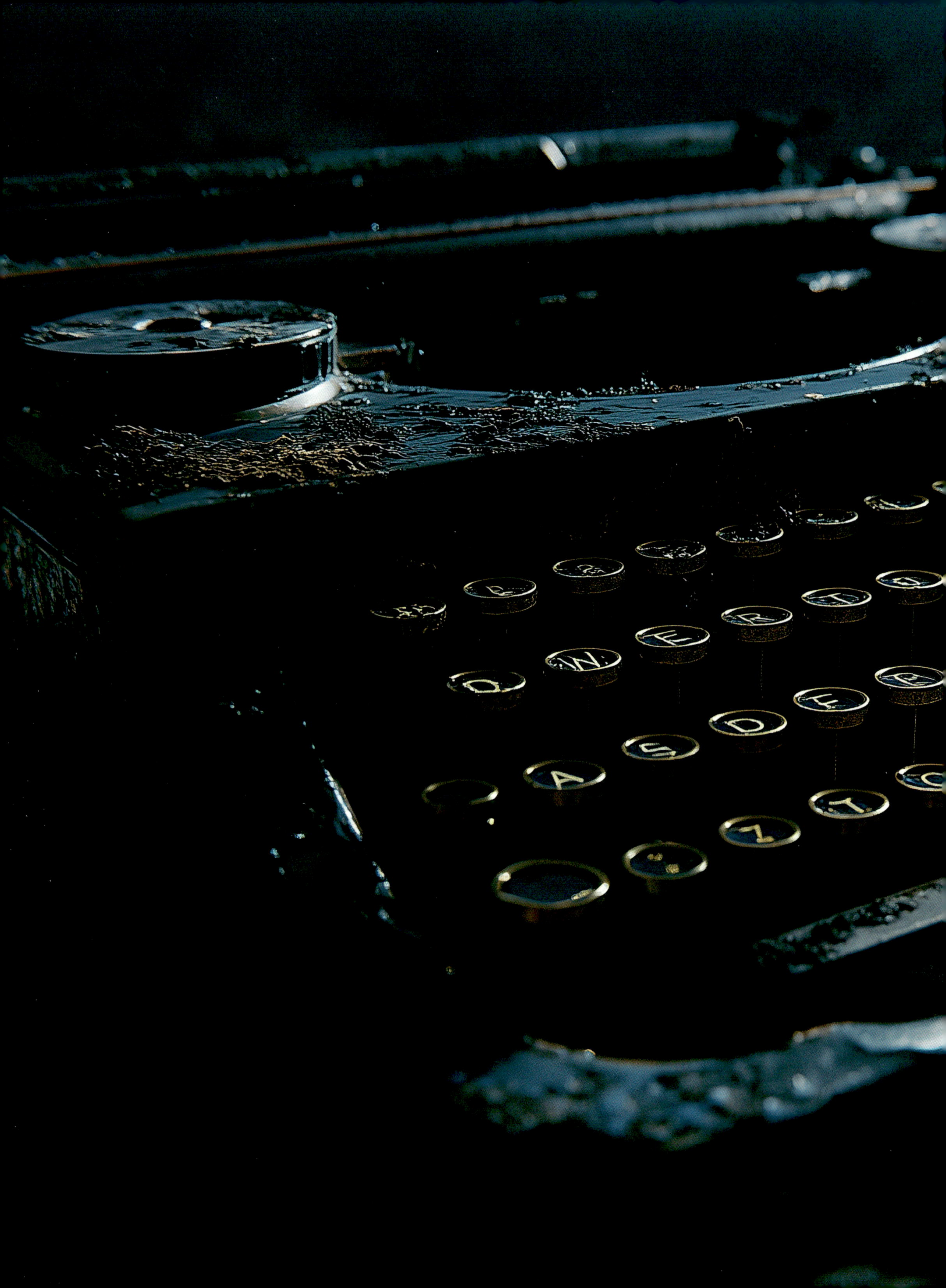

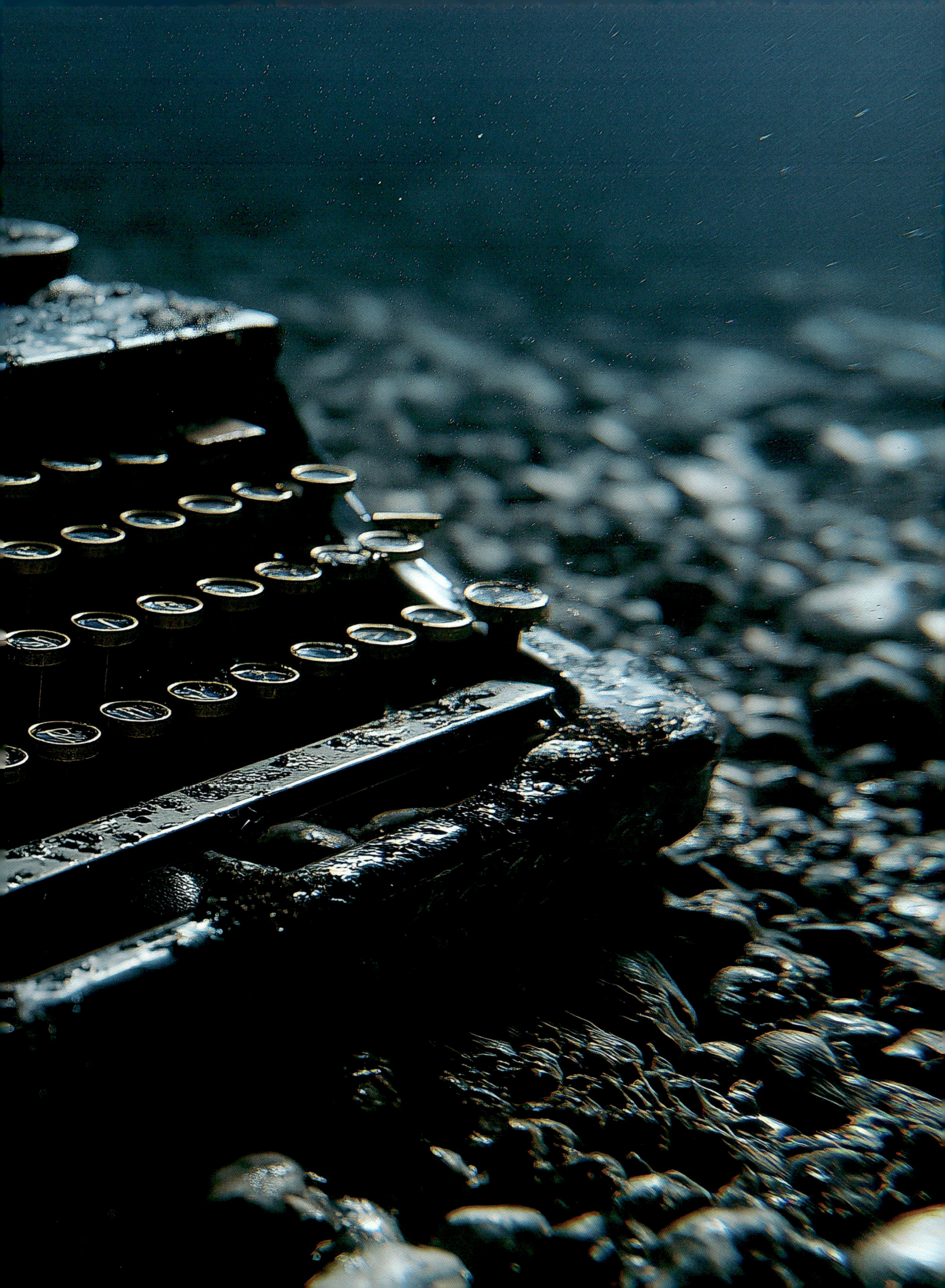

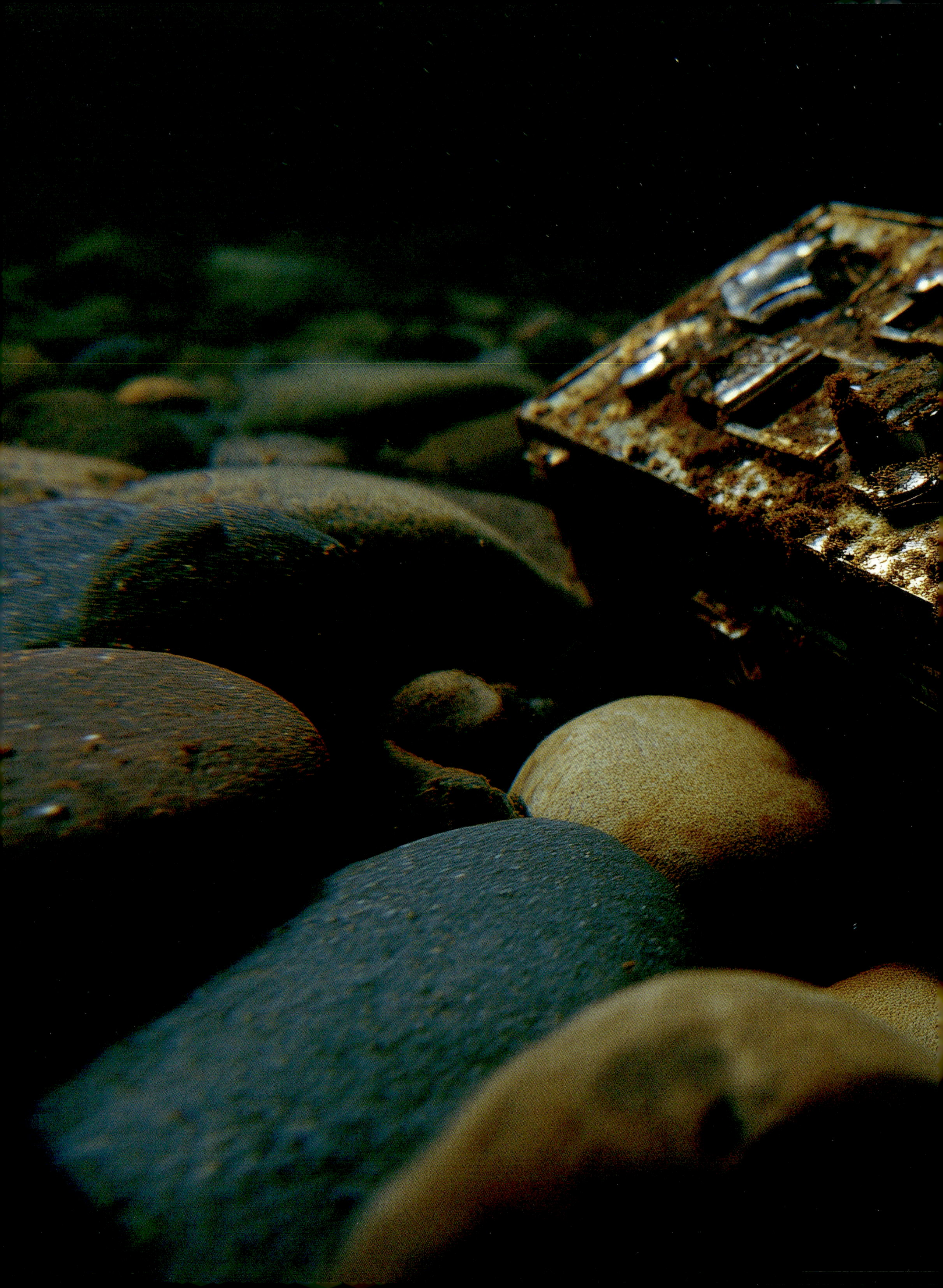

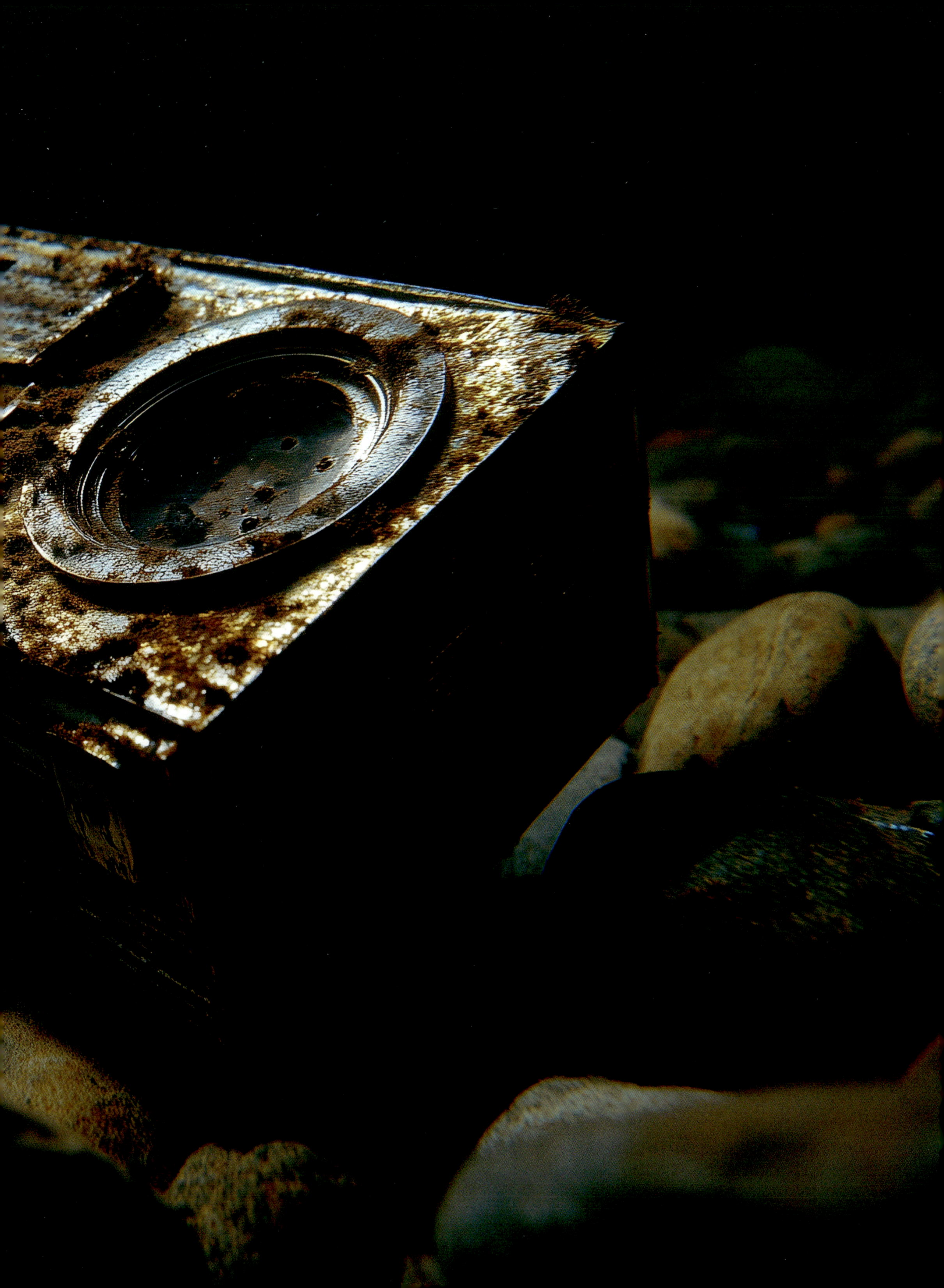

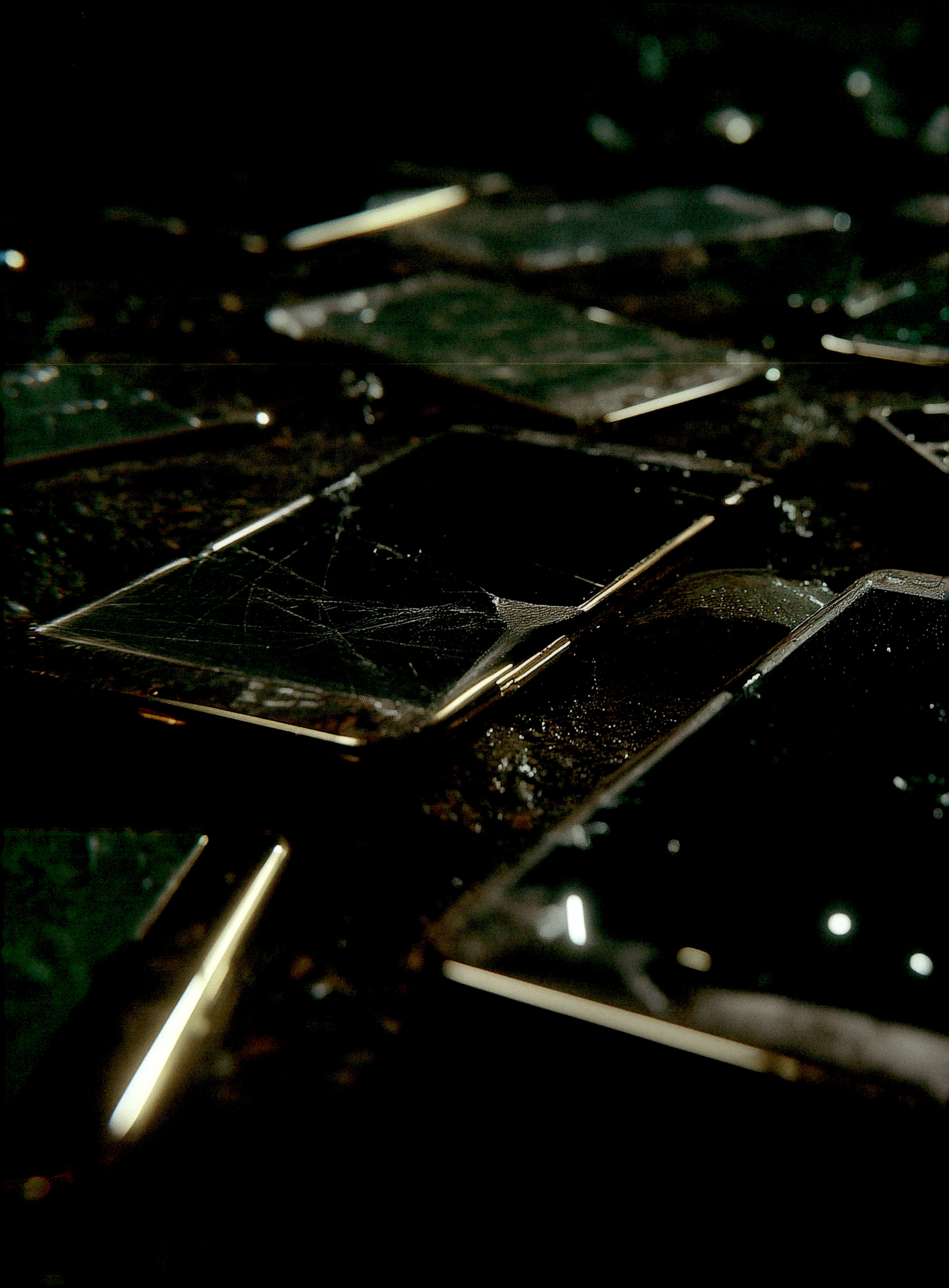

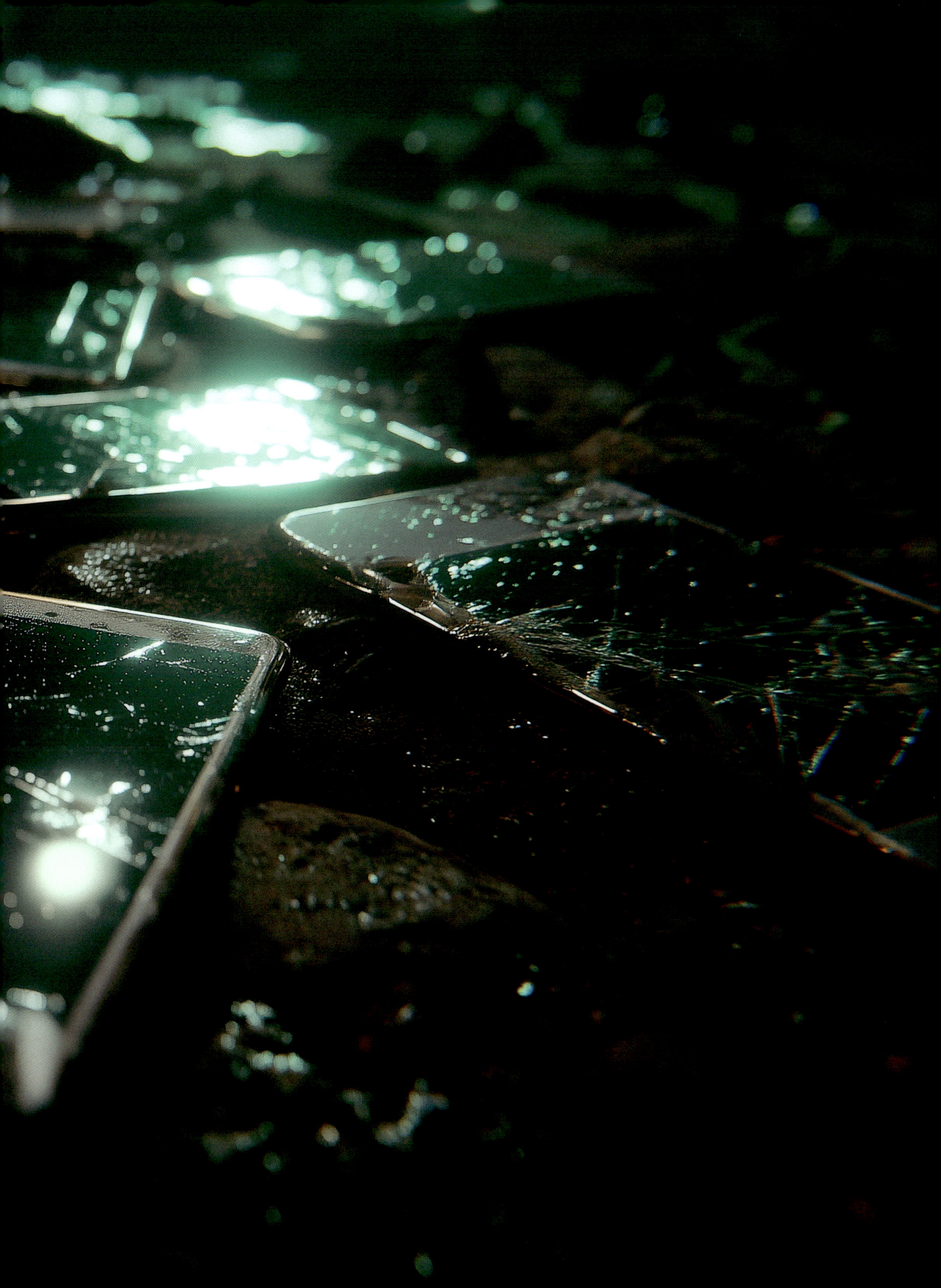

PROMPT_04 [medieval hammer underwater, heavy and rusted, buried partially in silt and gravel, surrounded by broken wood fragments, cinematic light piercing the water, detailed textures of decay and age. --chaos 15 --ar 16:9 --raw --stylize 50]

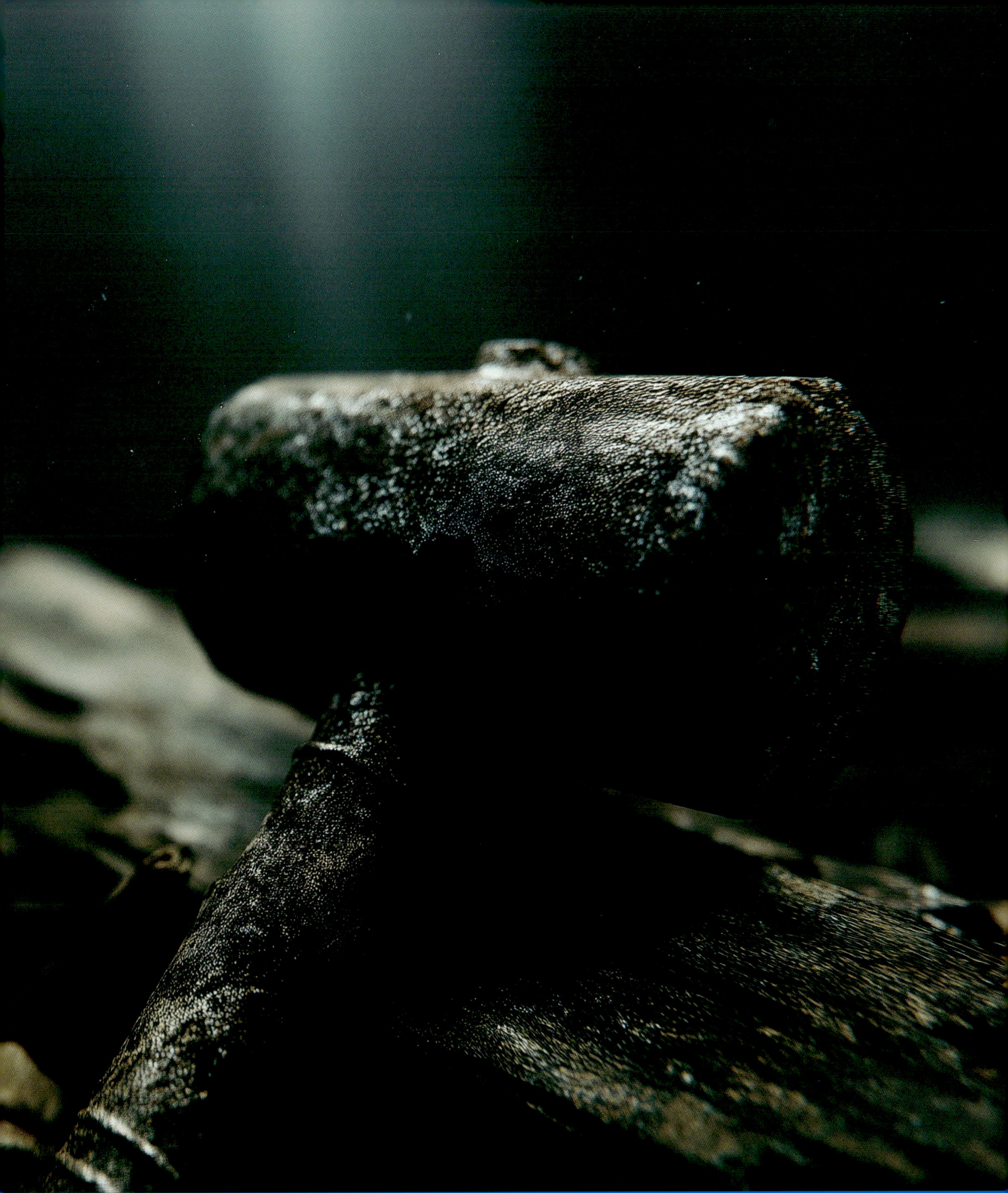

IMG_04

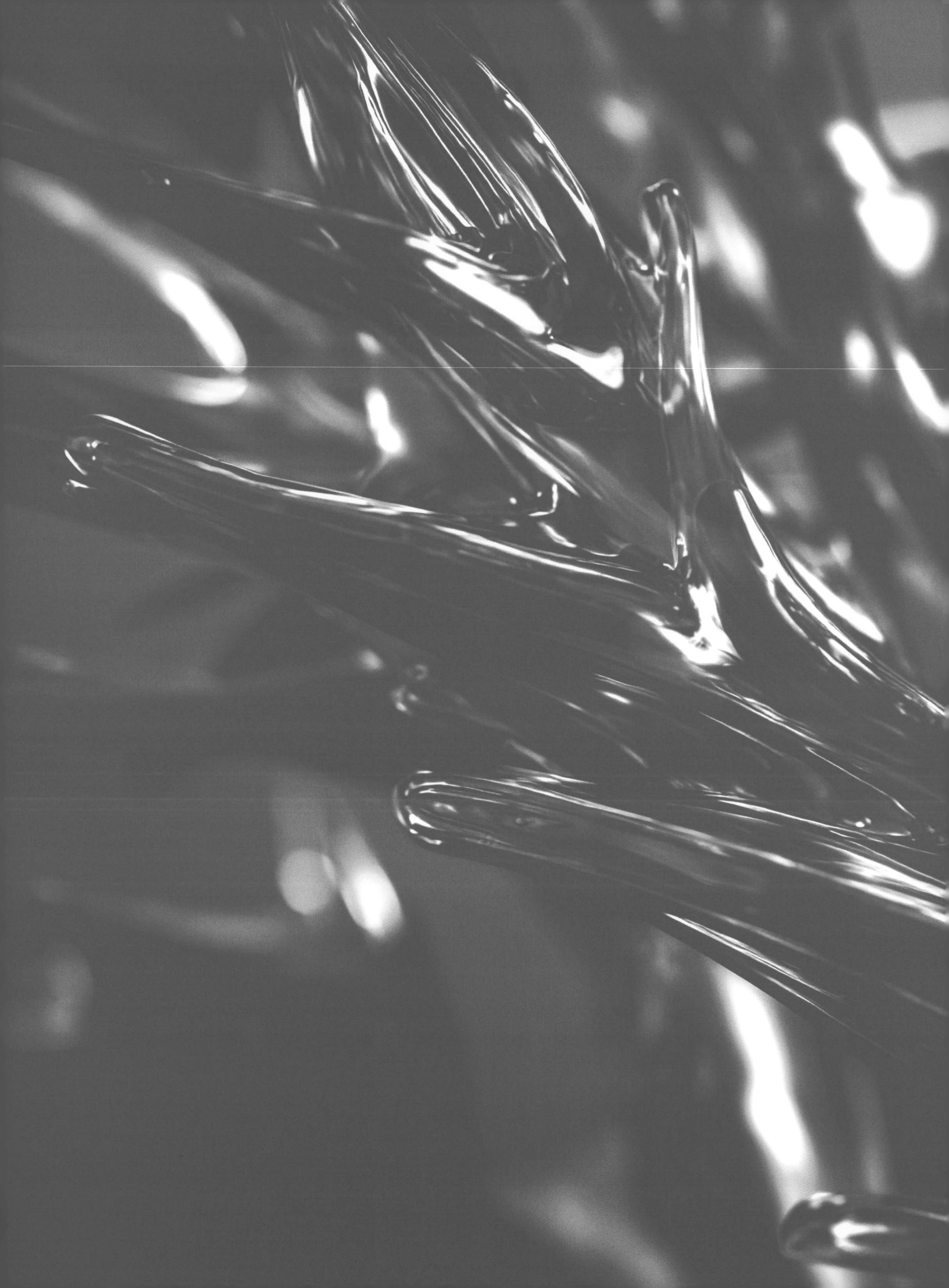

2.5

Life: Fluvial Ecosystems

The river is alive, inhabited by silent shapes that move and grow below the surface, where human eyes seldom observe them. A still camera slowly pans, guiding the vision of this underwater microcosm, revealing a fragile, dynamic ecosystem that pulses in the dark. Among the creatures that populate this habitat, two aquatic vegetable species stand out, the: *Ceratophyllum demersum*, or hornwort, and the *Potamogeton*, or pondweed. Their life cycle – from germination to full maturity – develops through a continuous metamorphosis. The plants bend and separate in a subtle balance between adaptation and resistance. The photographic and scientific realism of these images exalts the organic structure, and tangibility of their invisible lives. The camera goes even deeper, narrowing its focus, to where the water reveals a microscopic world teeming with planktonic species like *Bivalves*, *Water Fleas*, *Cyanobacteria*, *Diatoms*, *Nauplius*, *Nematodes*, *Rotifers*, *Vorticella* that move in suspension, each with its own distinctive geometry and motion. Life does not show itself on the surface here, but is perceptible in minutes details, minimal movements, slow processes. It is a presence that grows, breaths and alters the aquatic space from the inside.

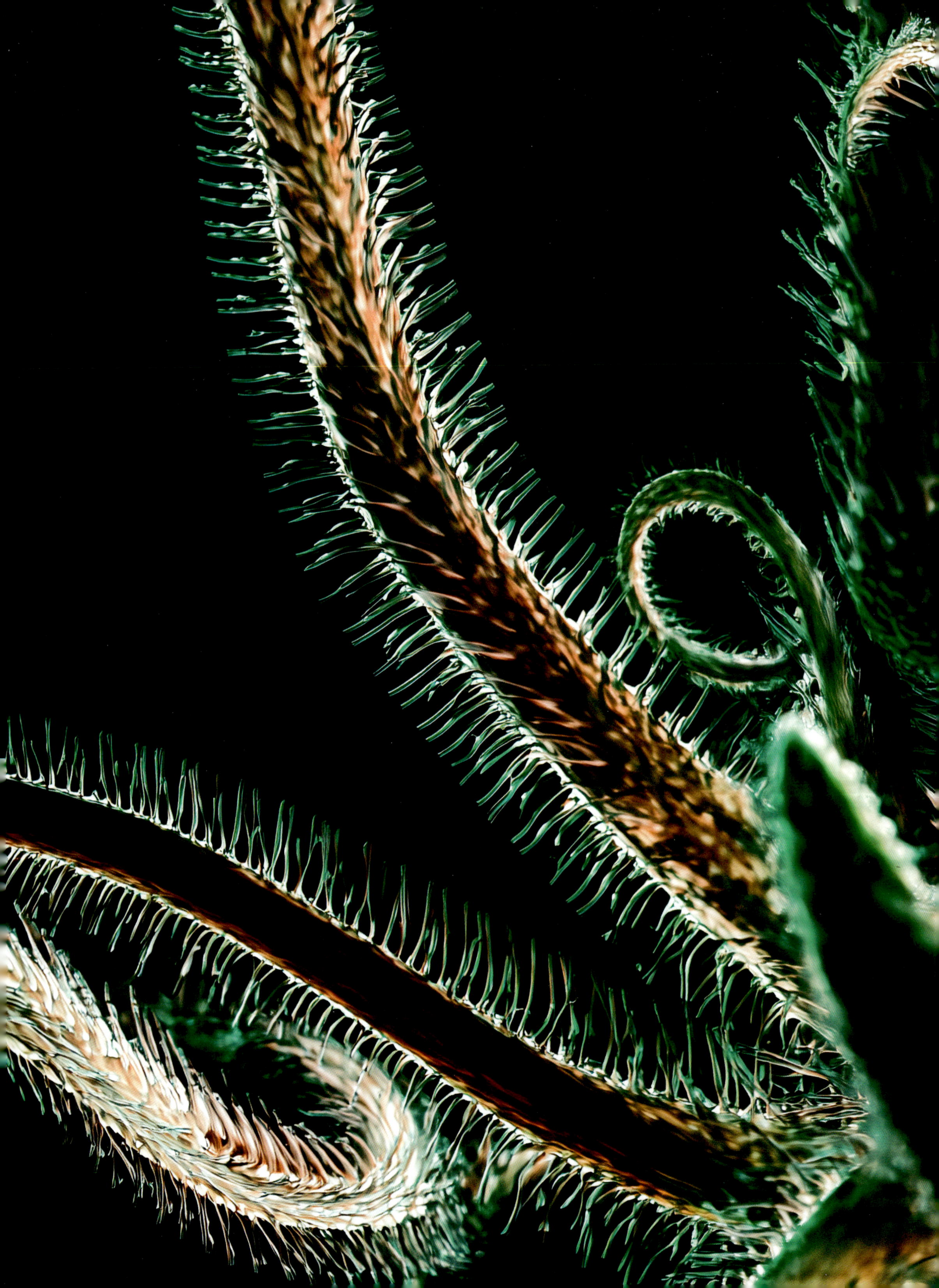

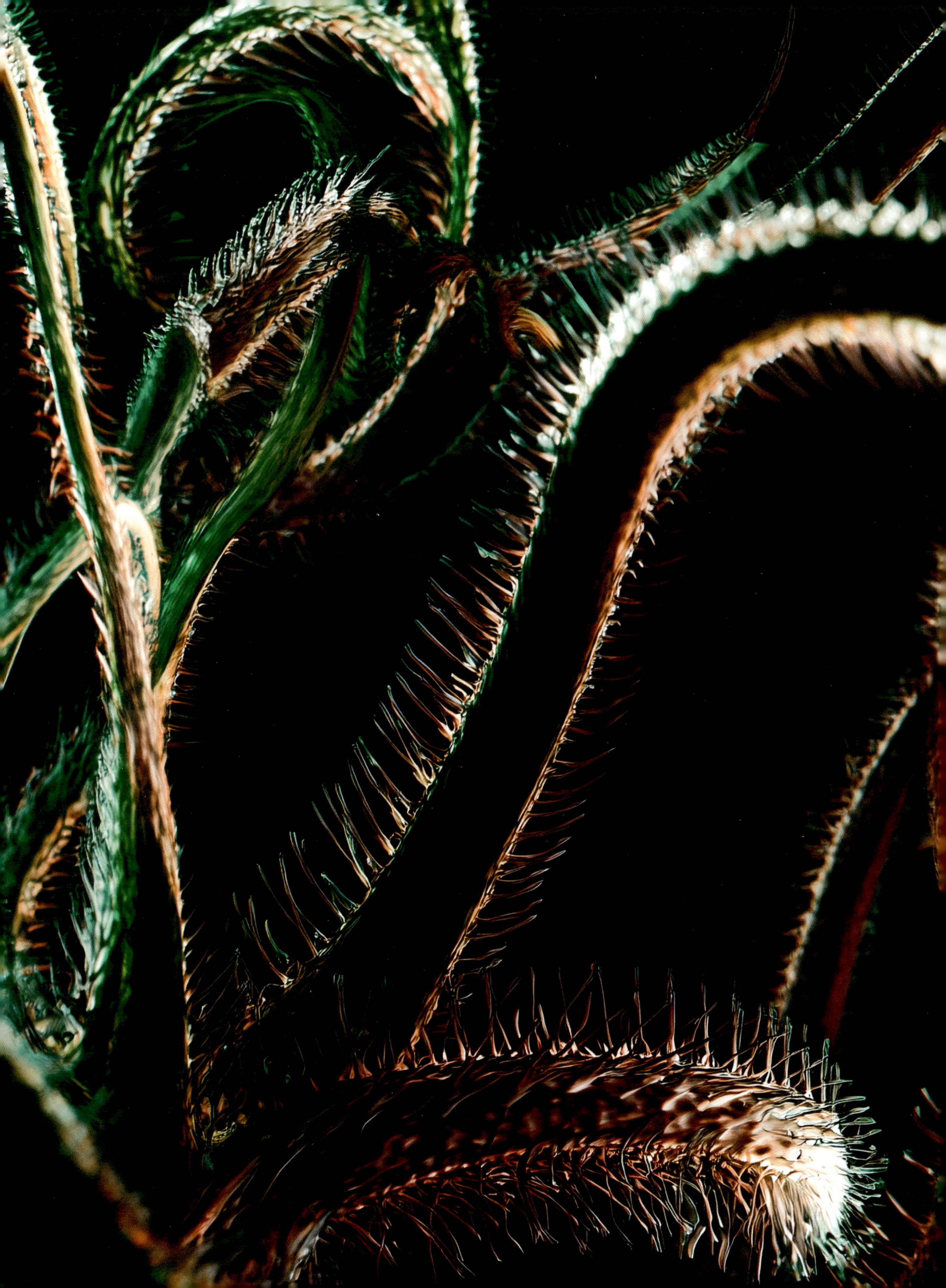

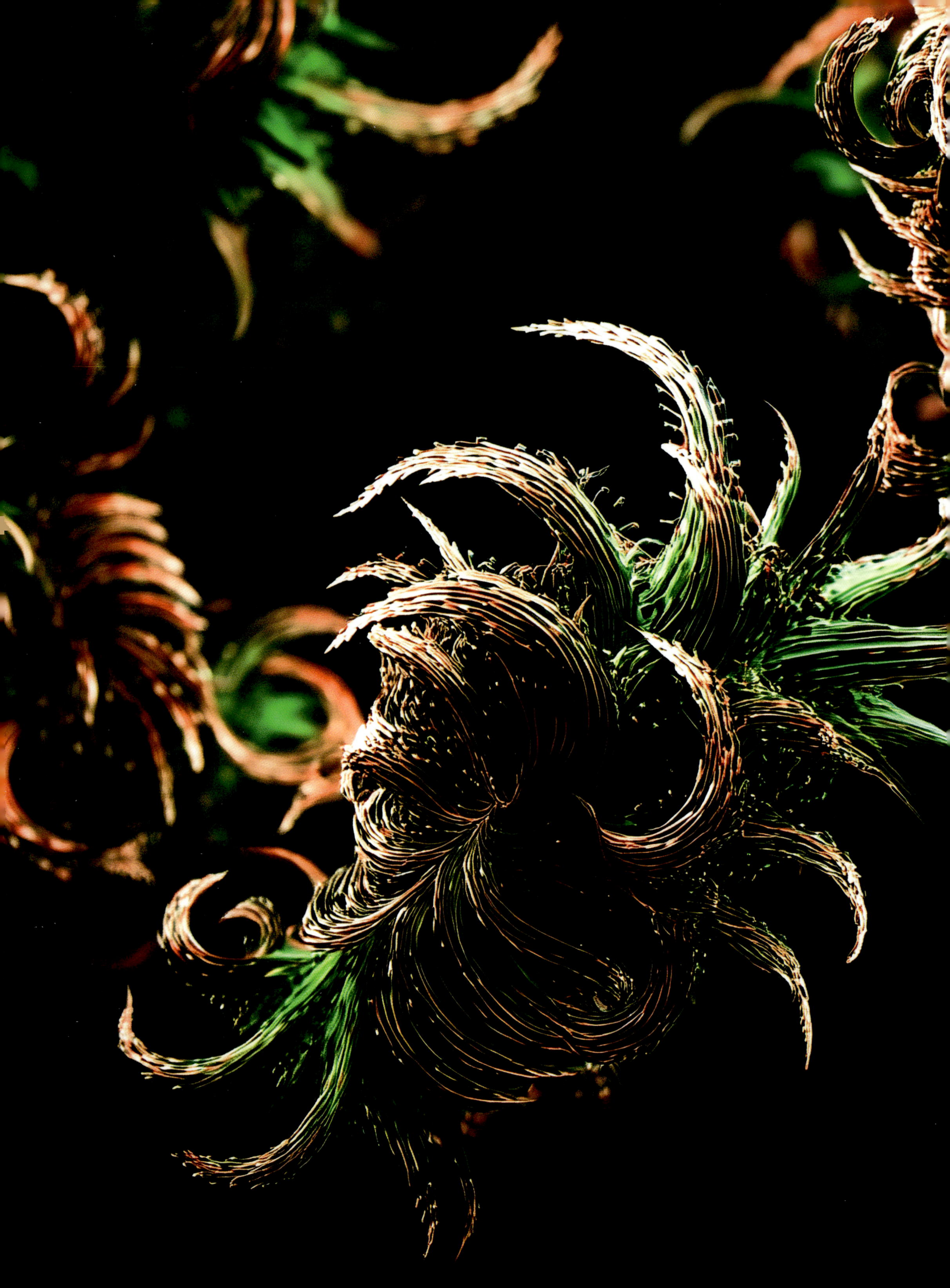

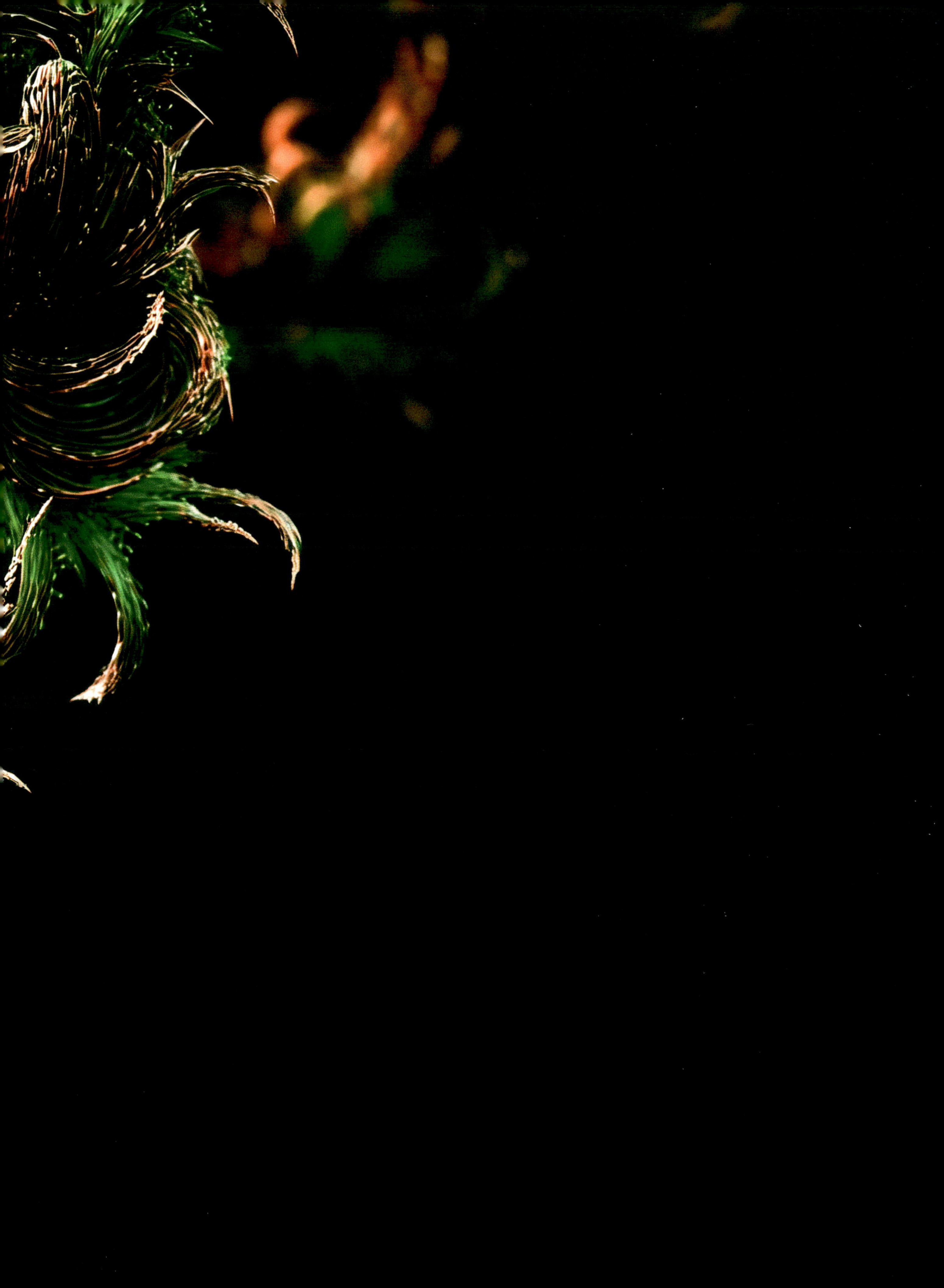

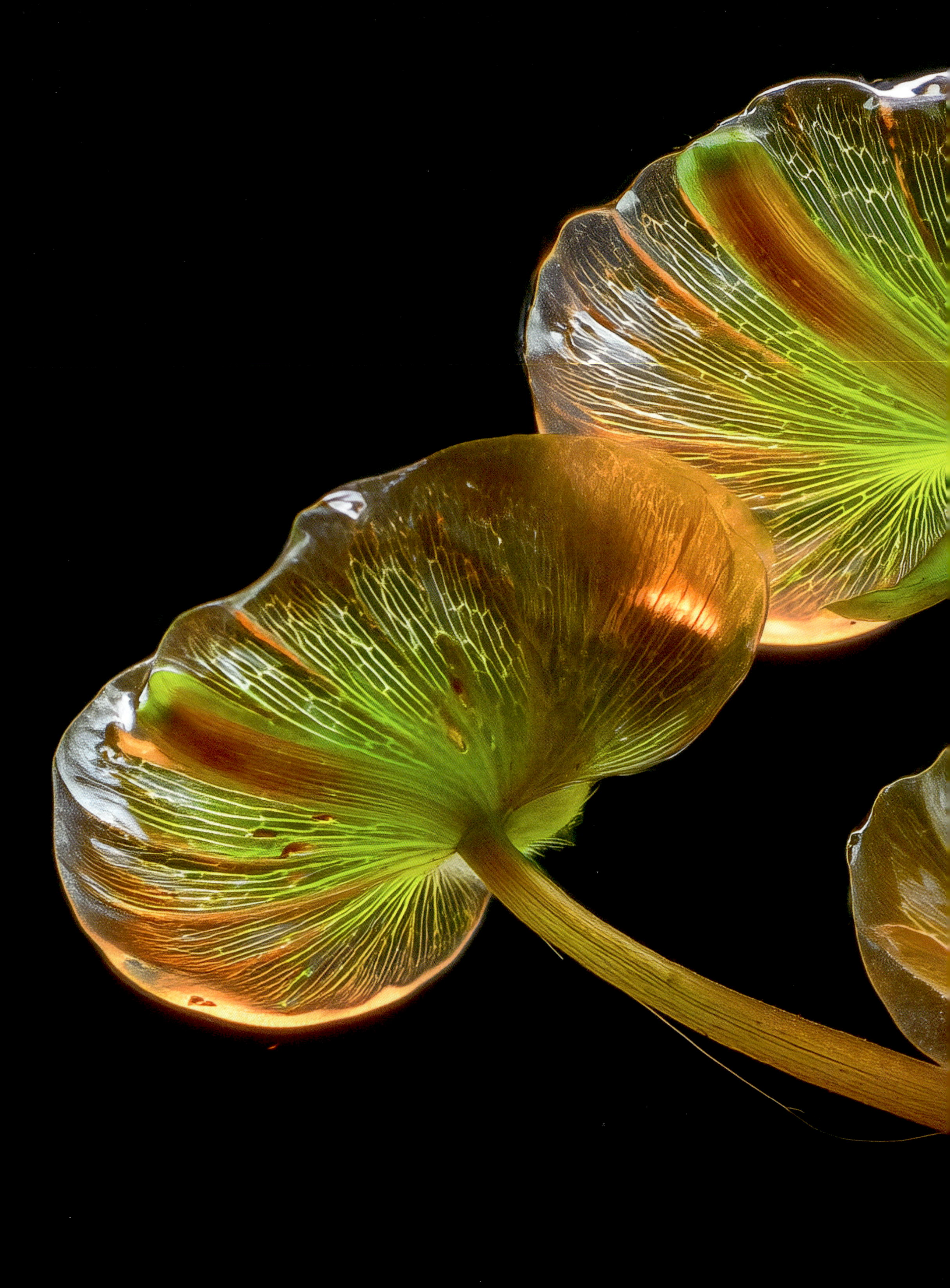

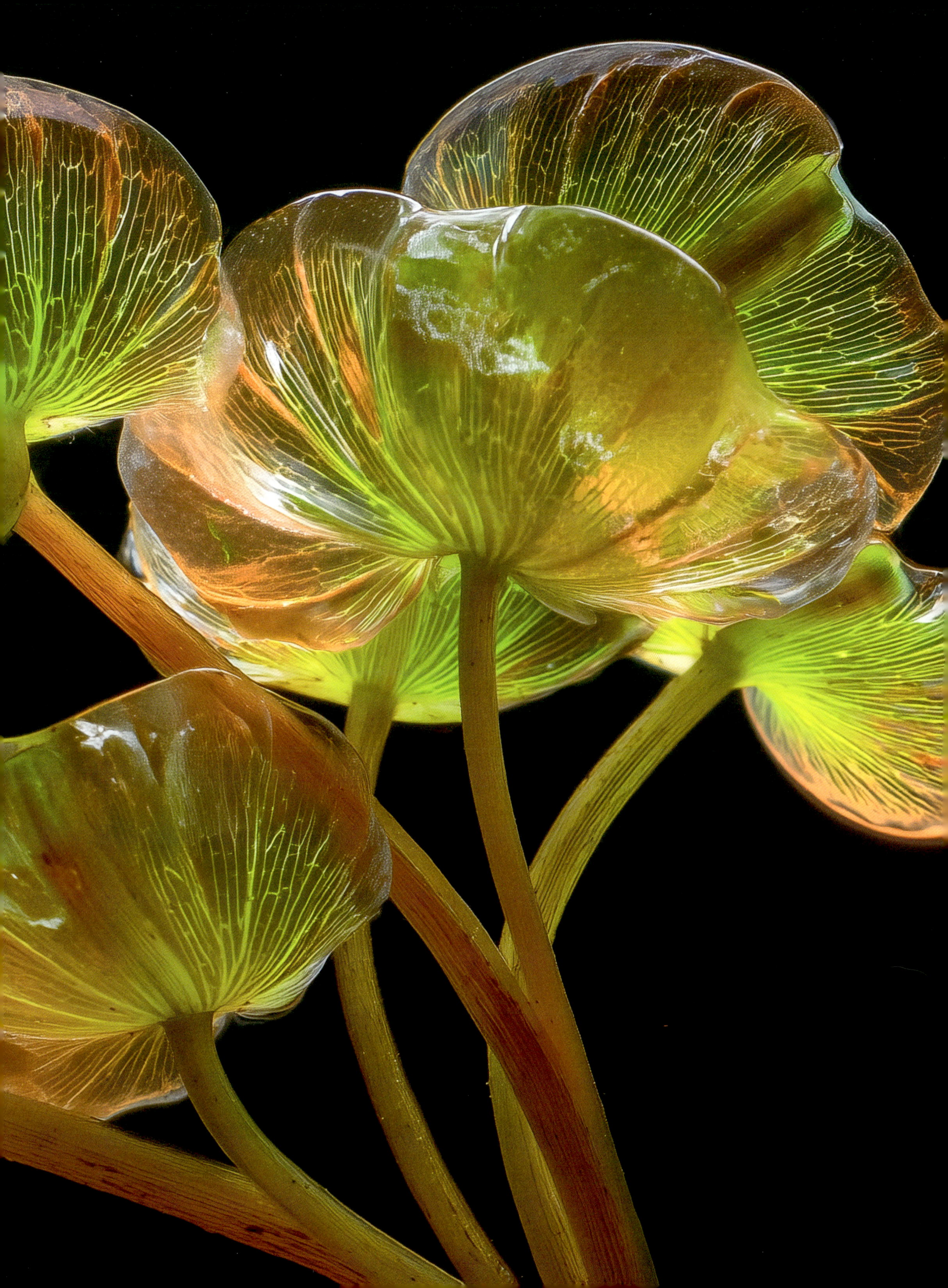

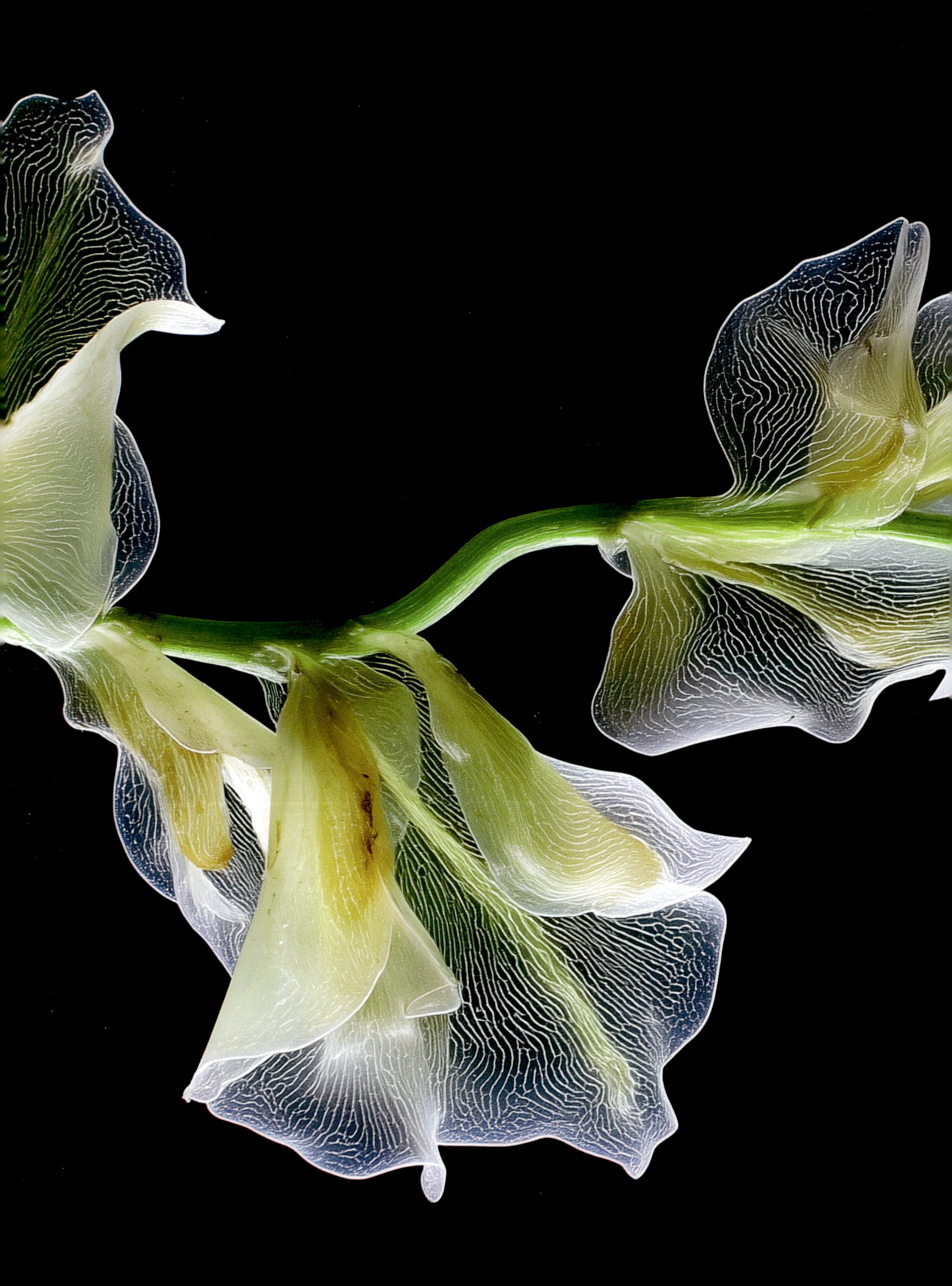

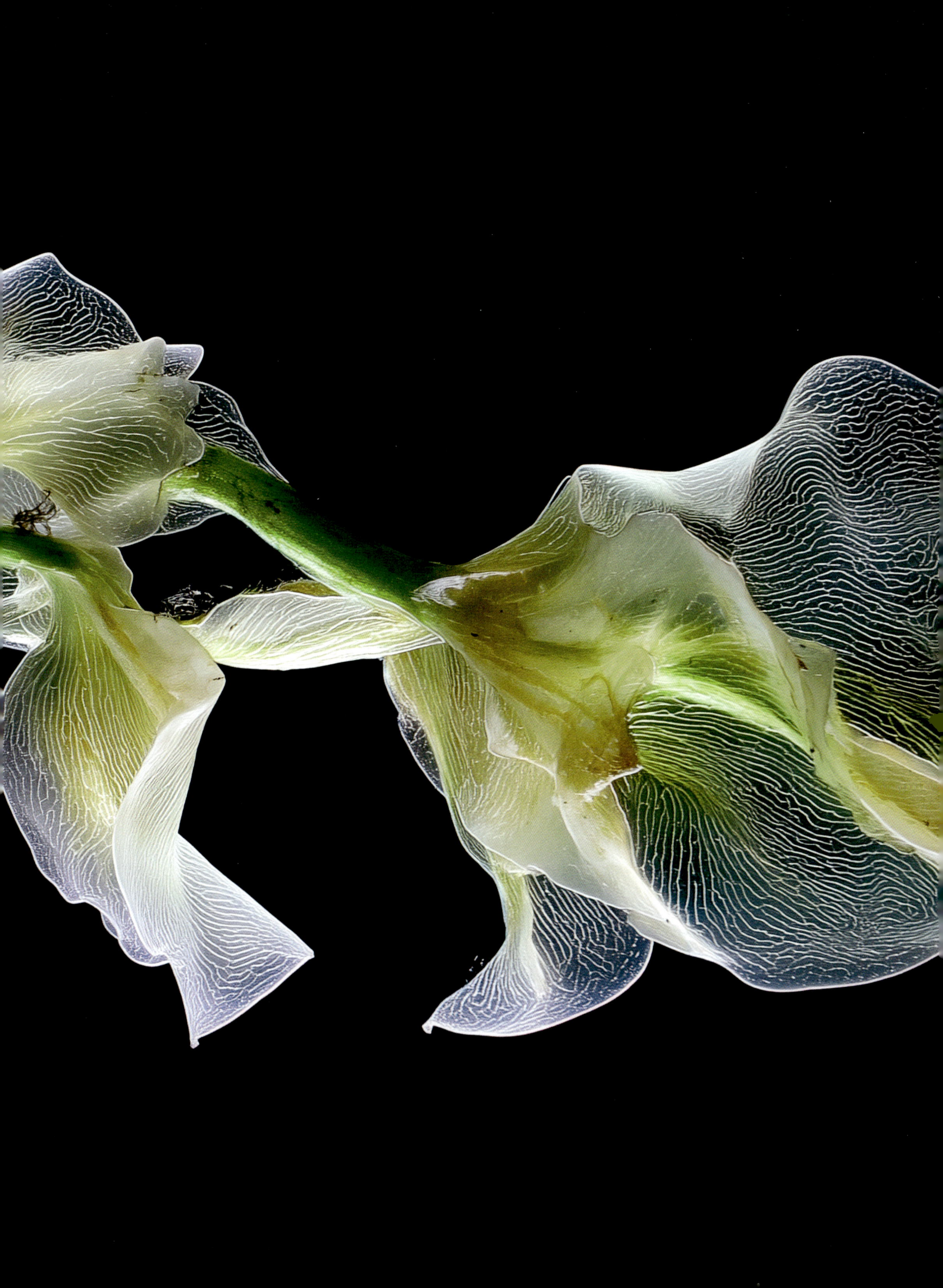

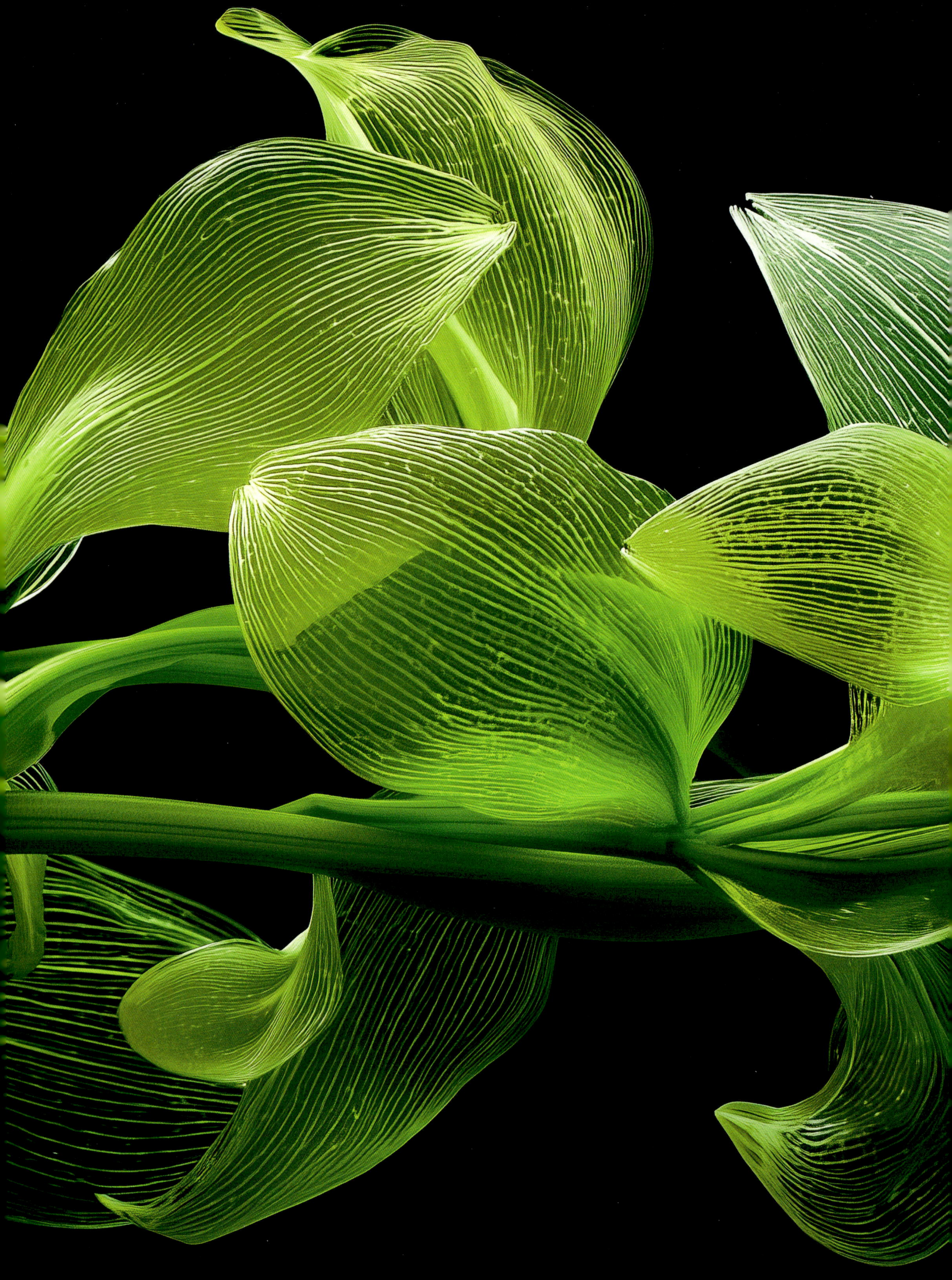

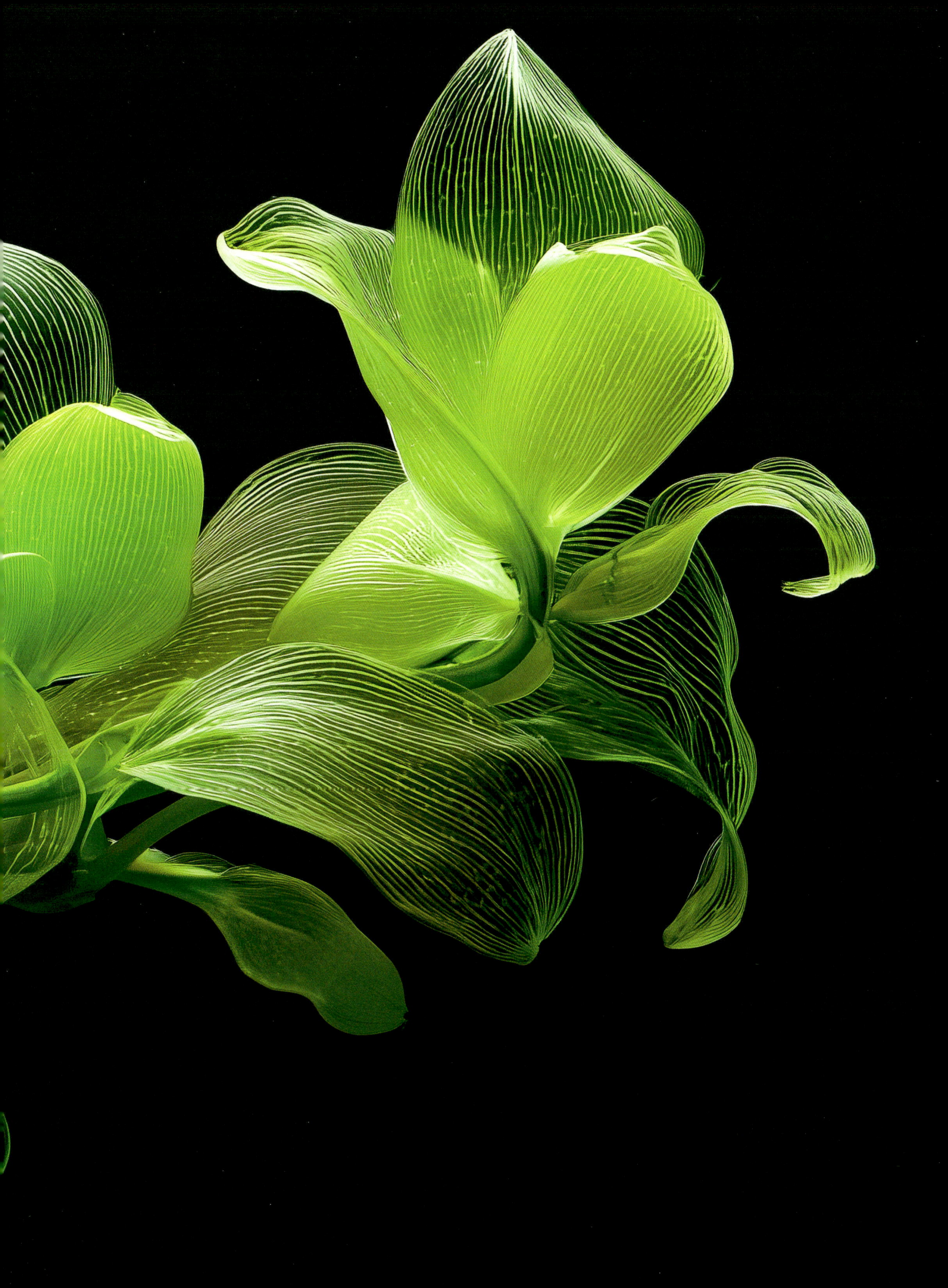

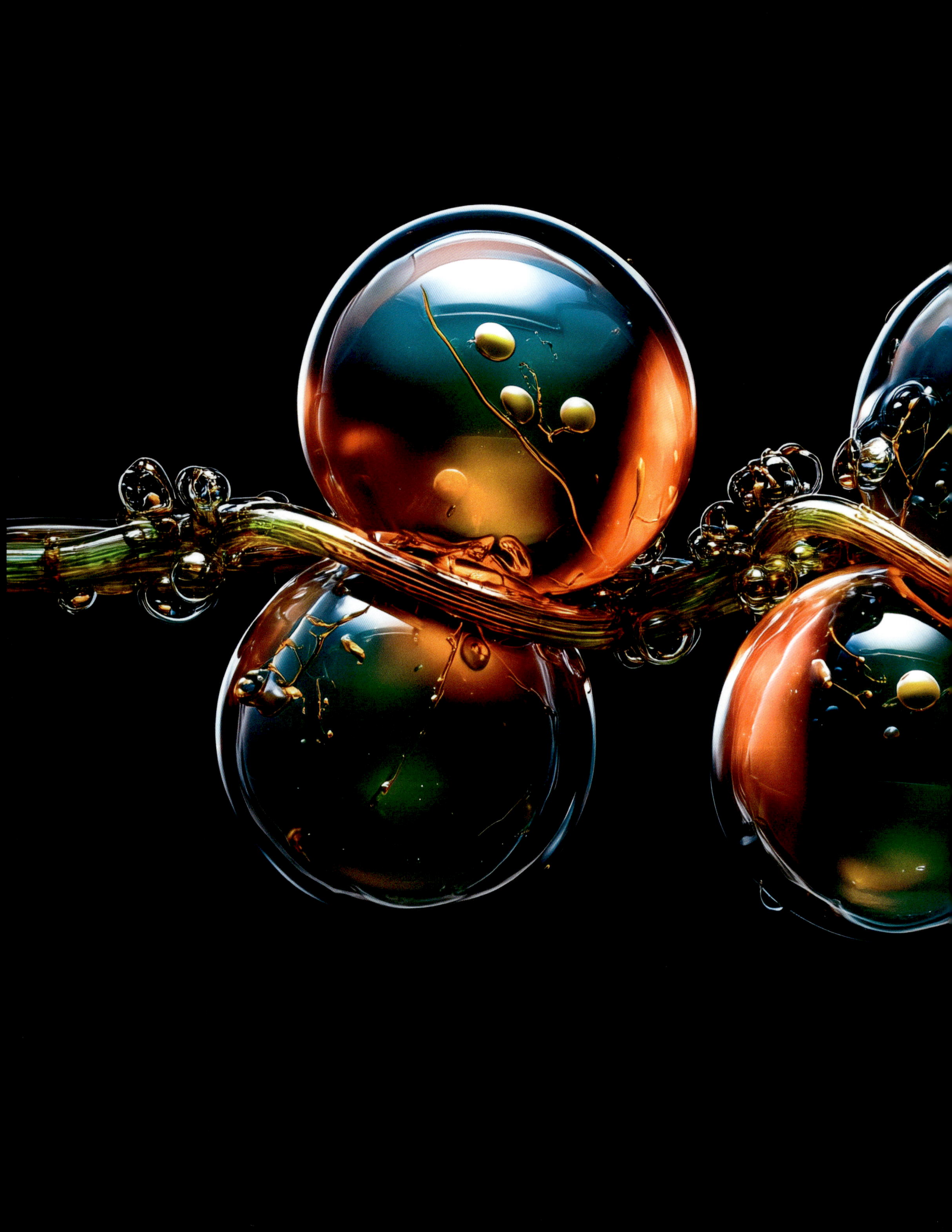

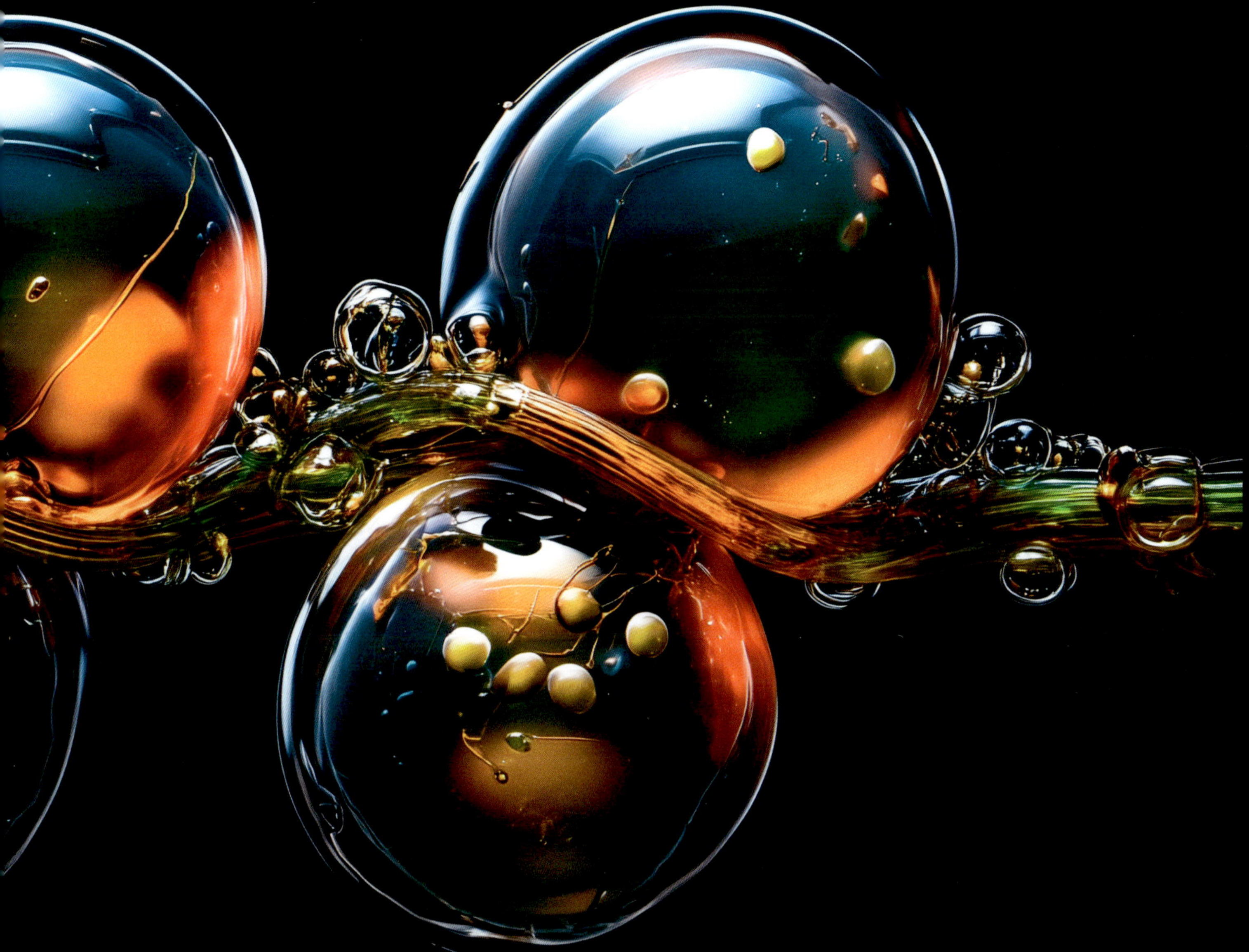

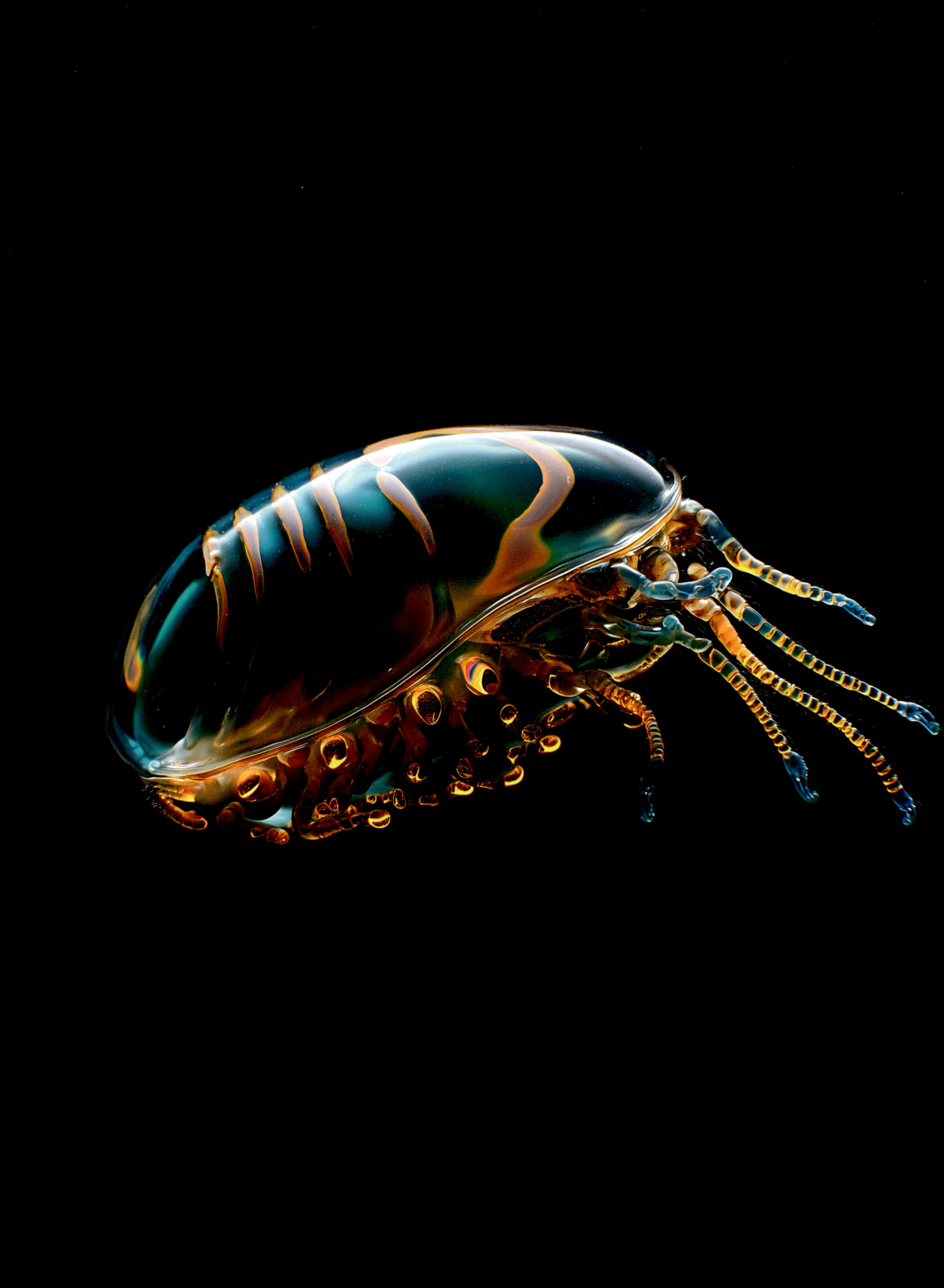

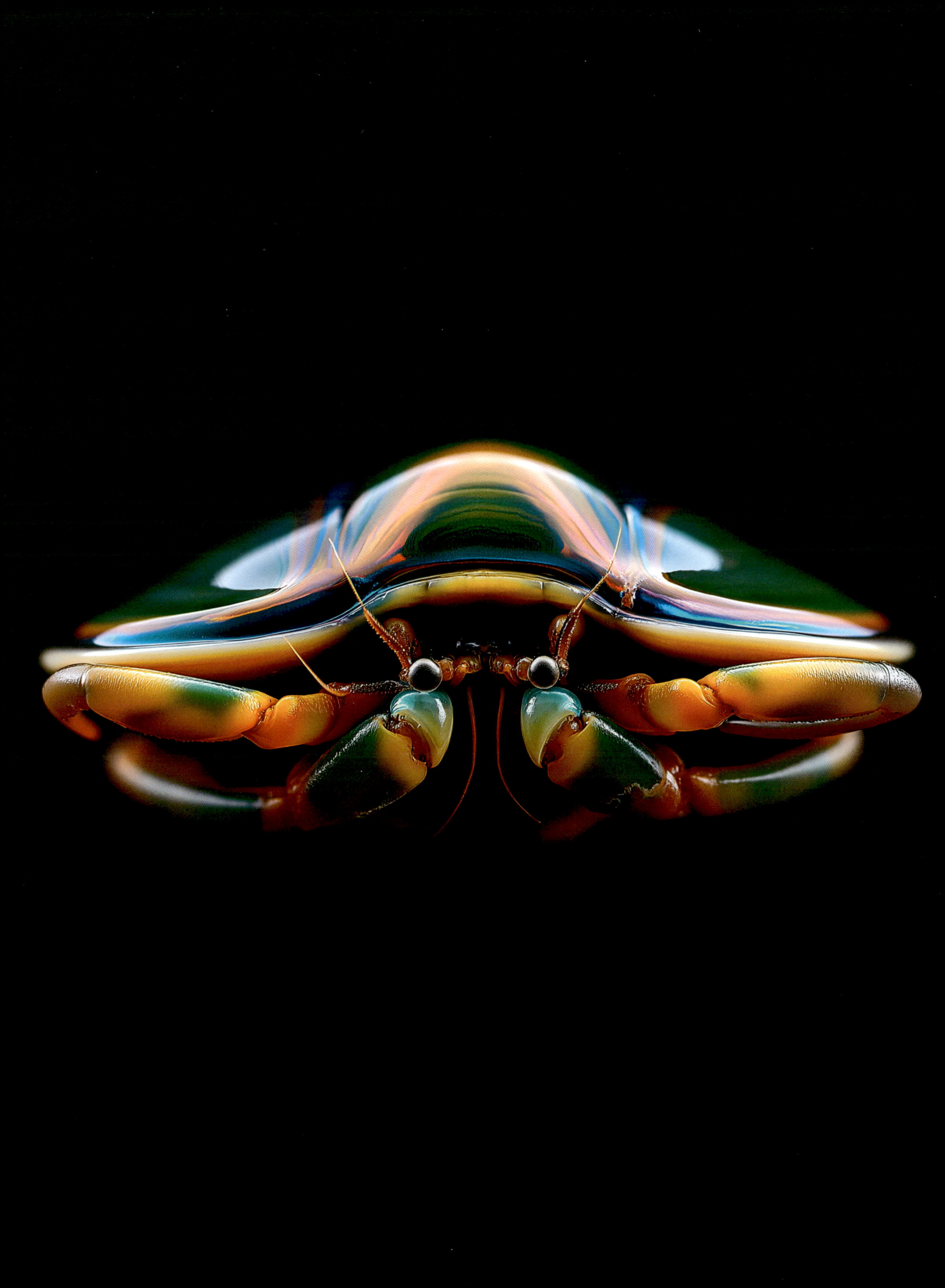

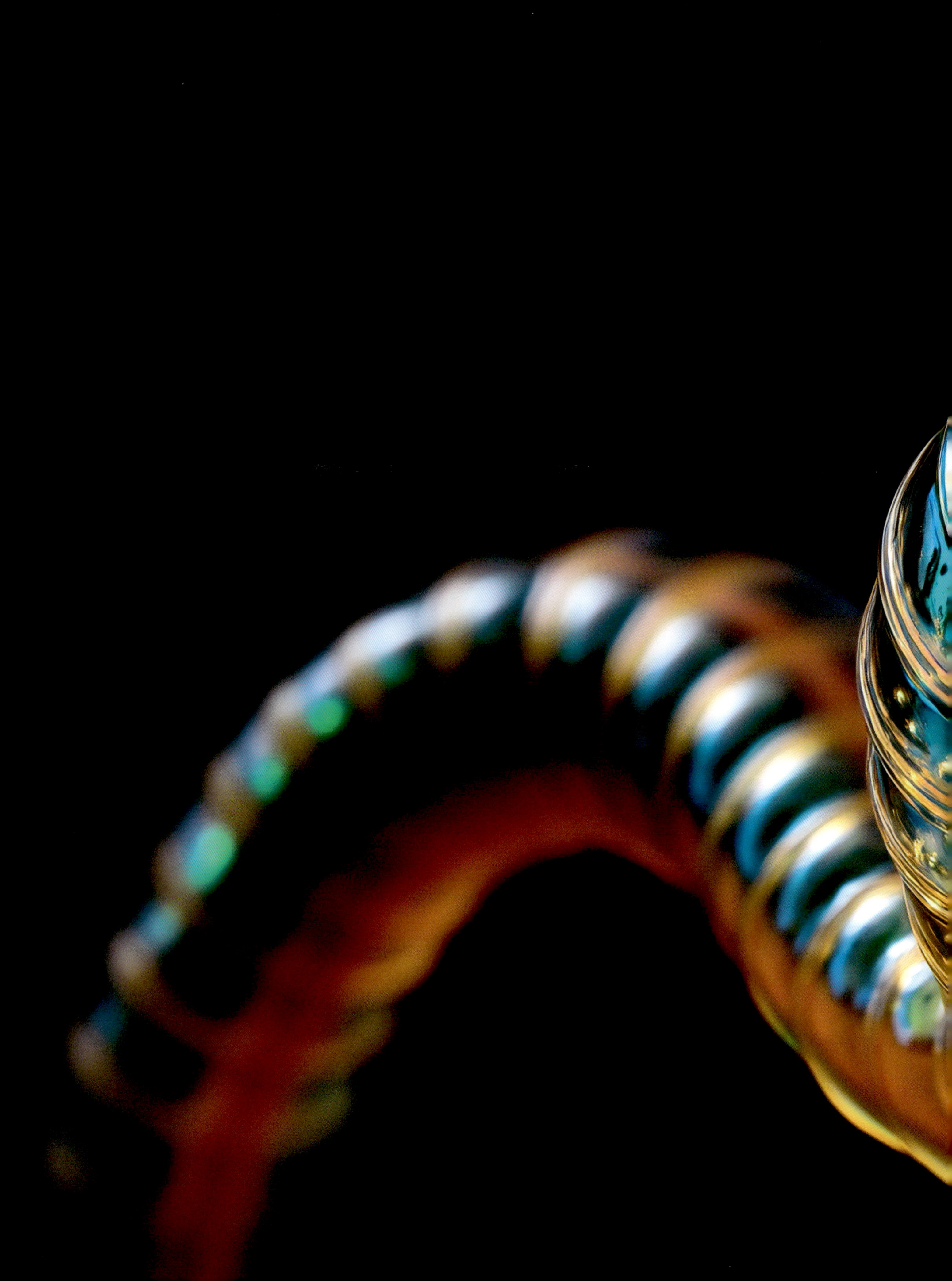

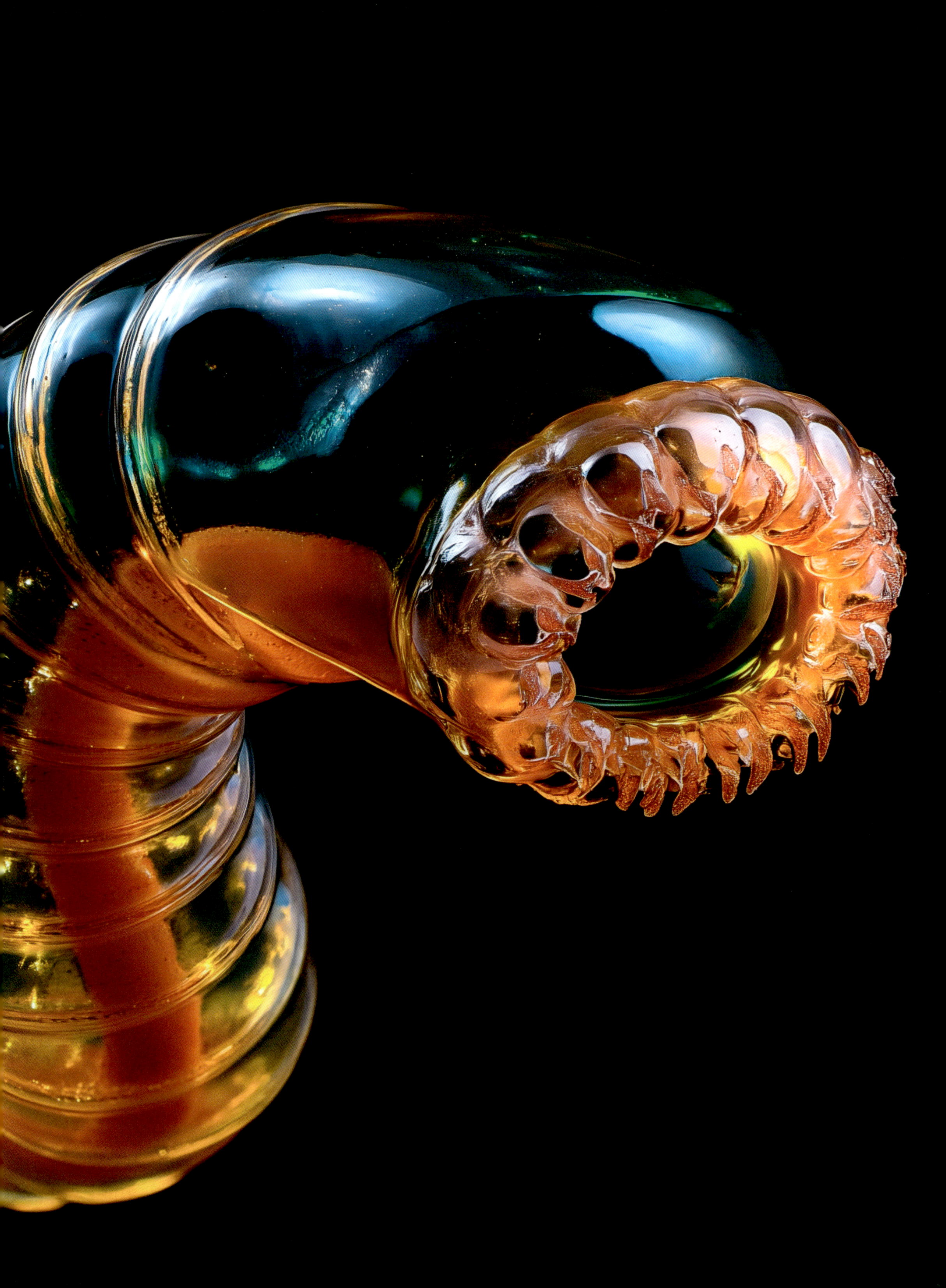

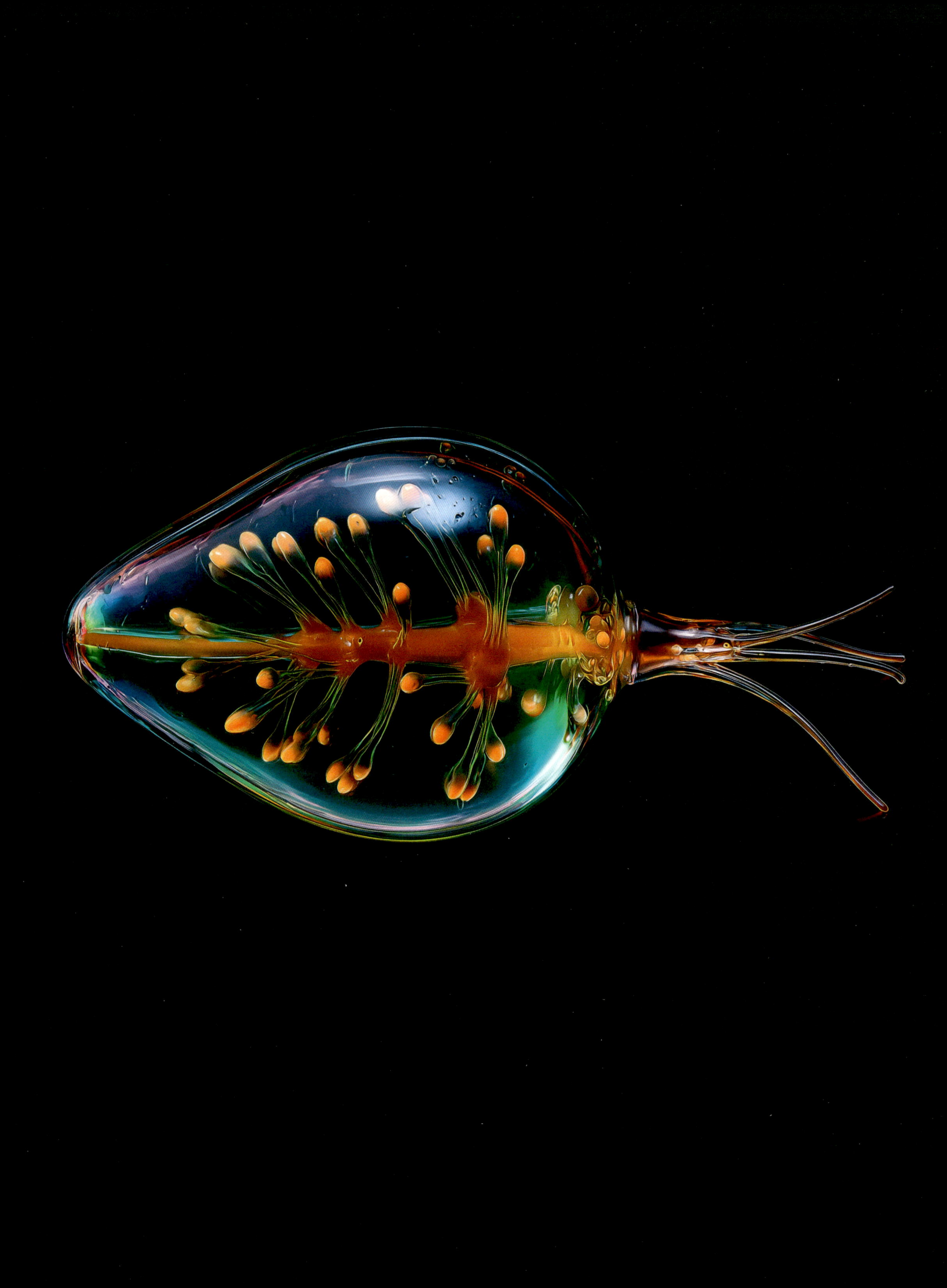

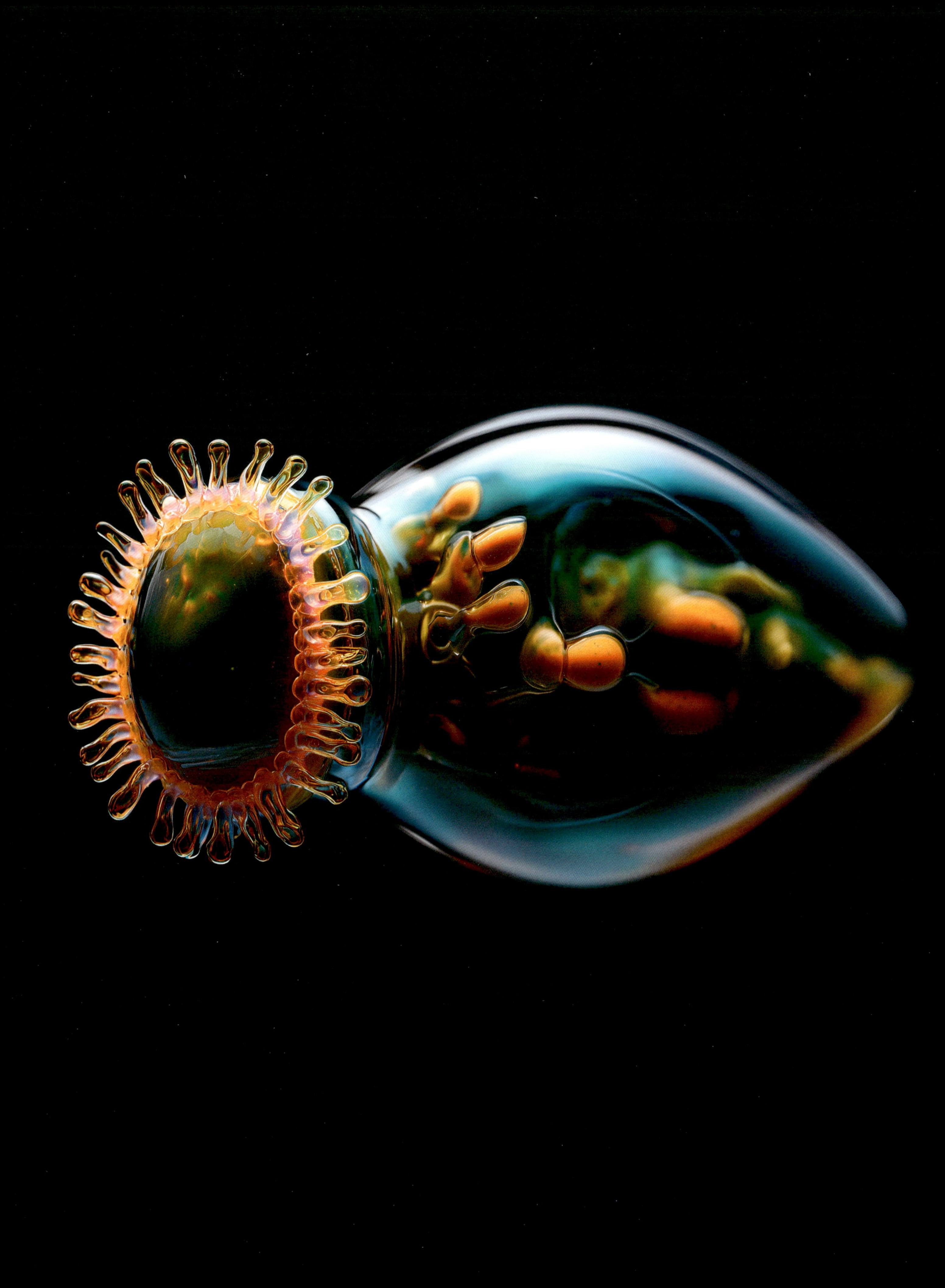

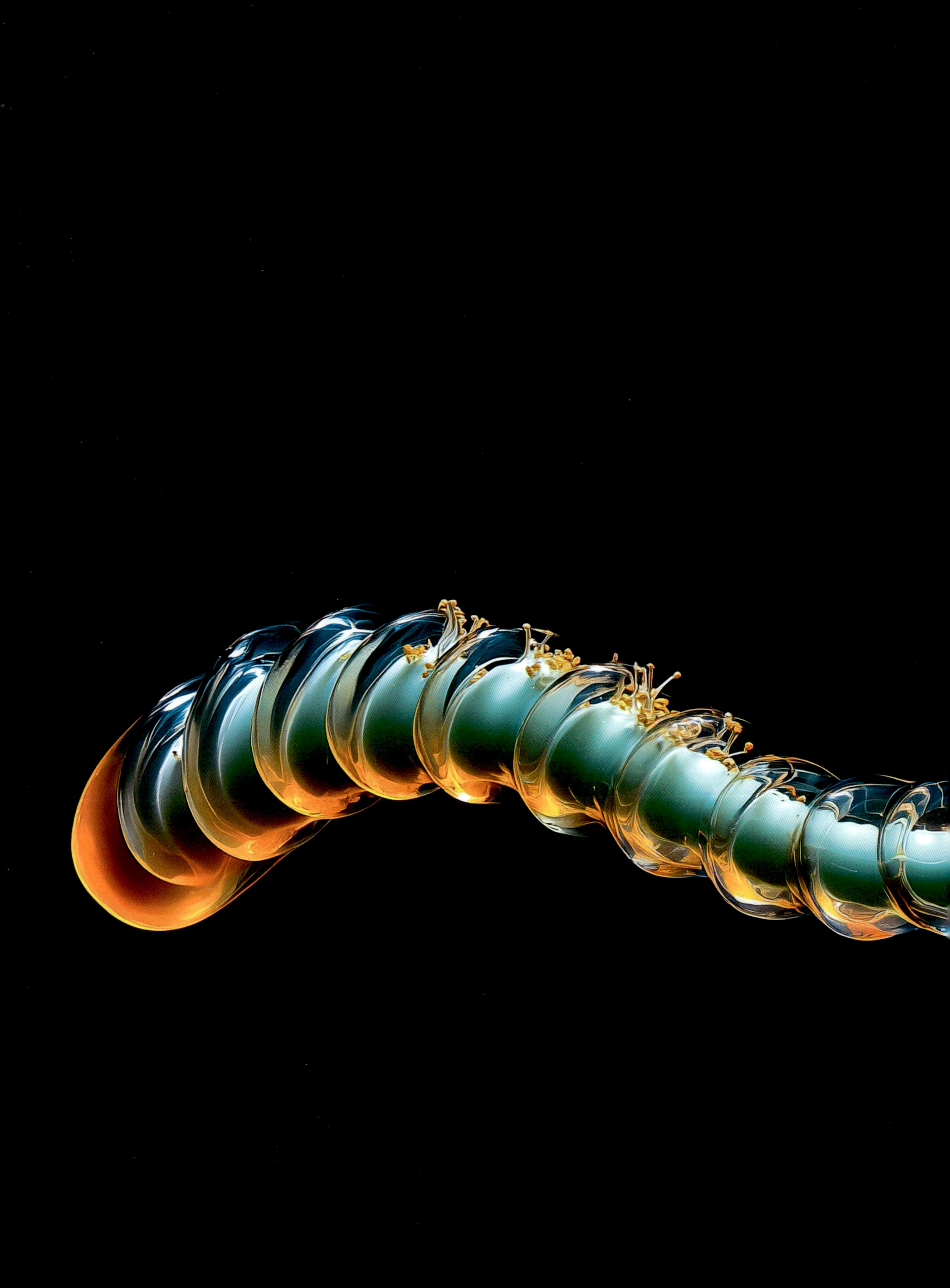

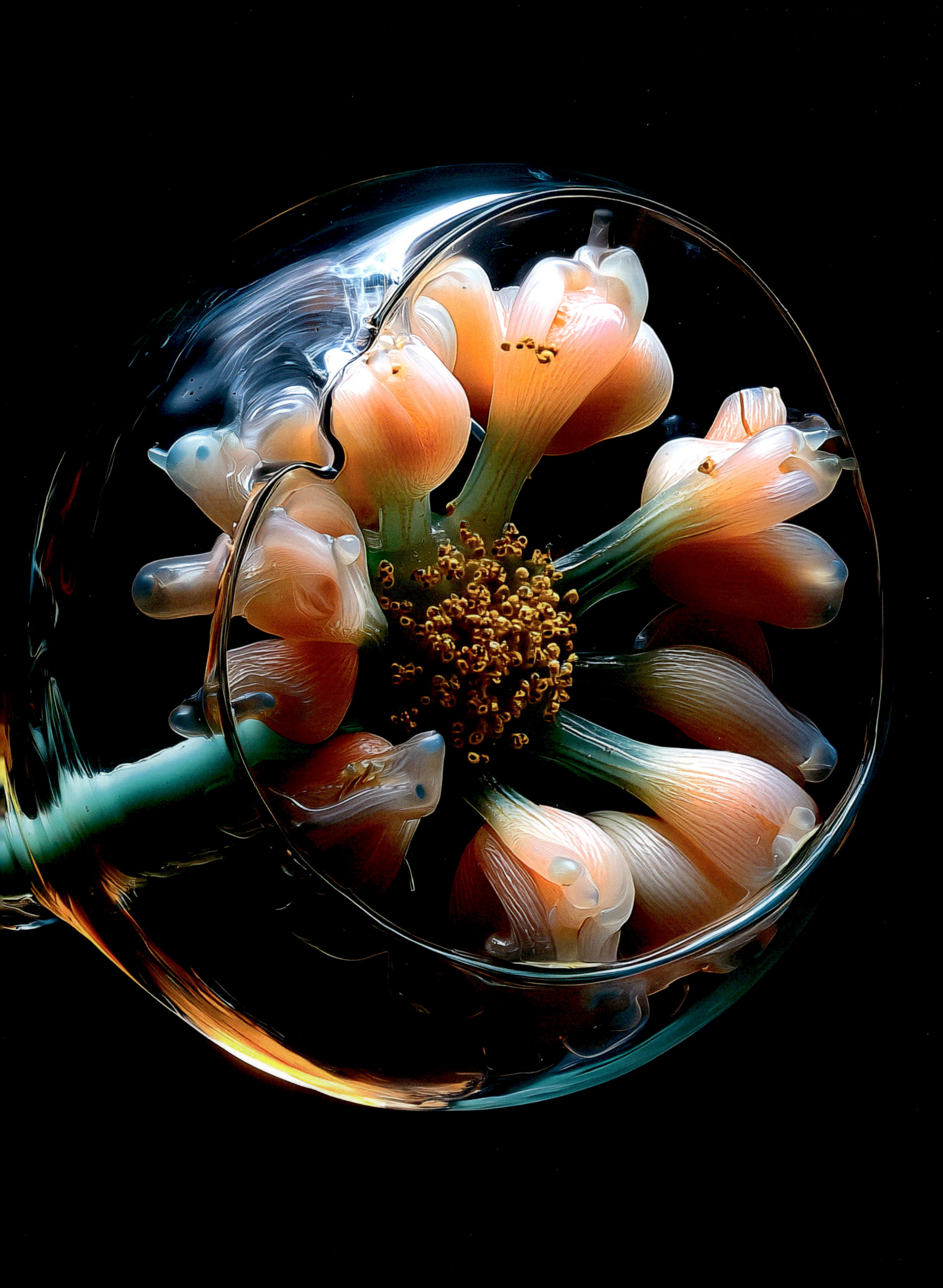

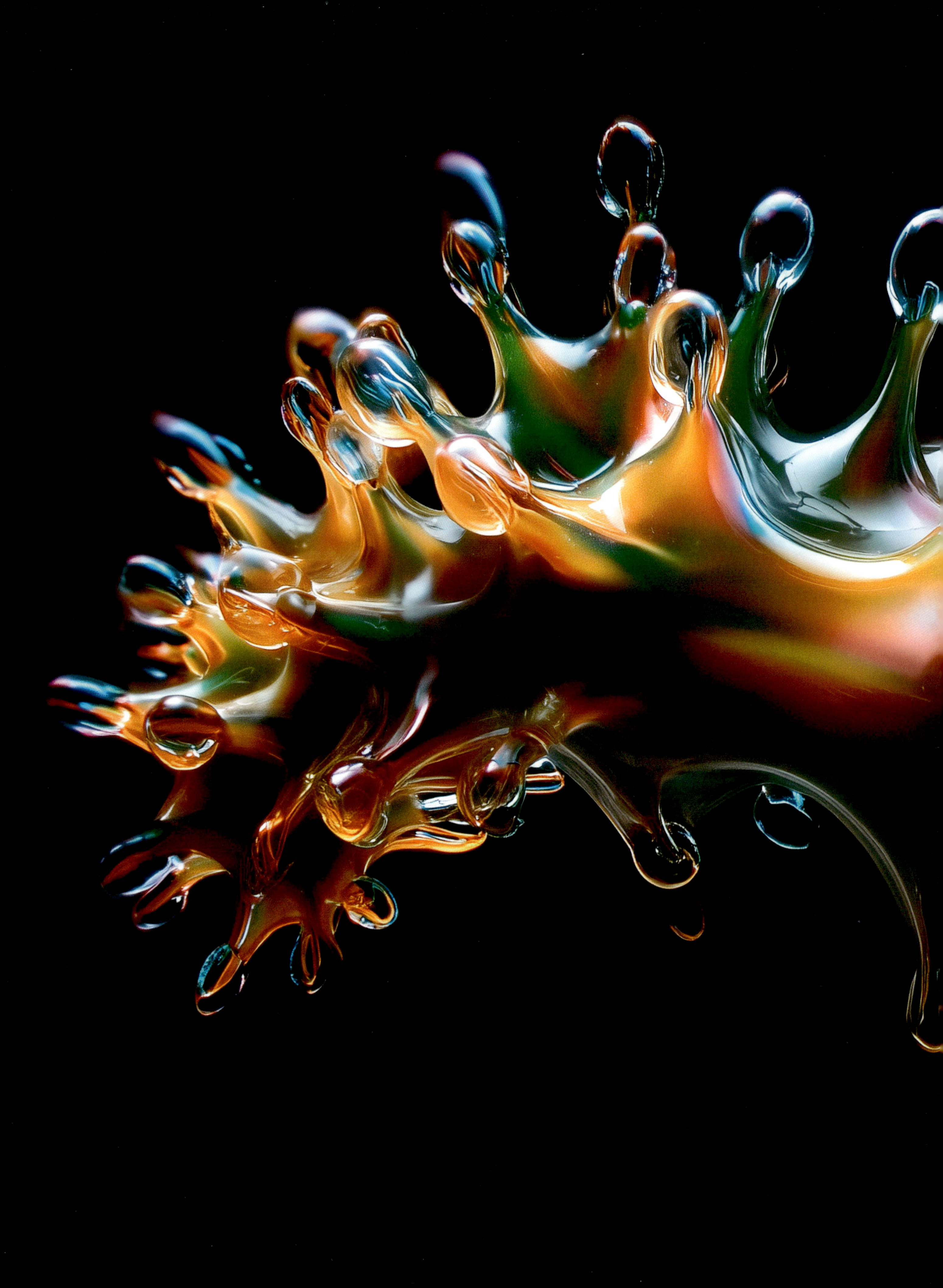

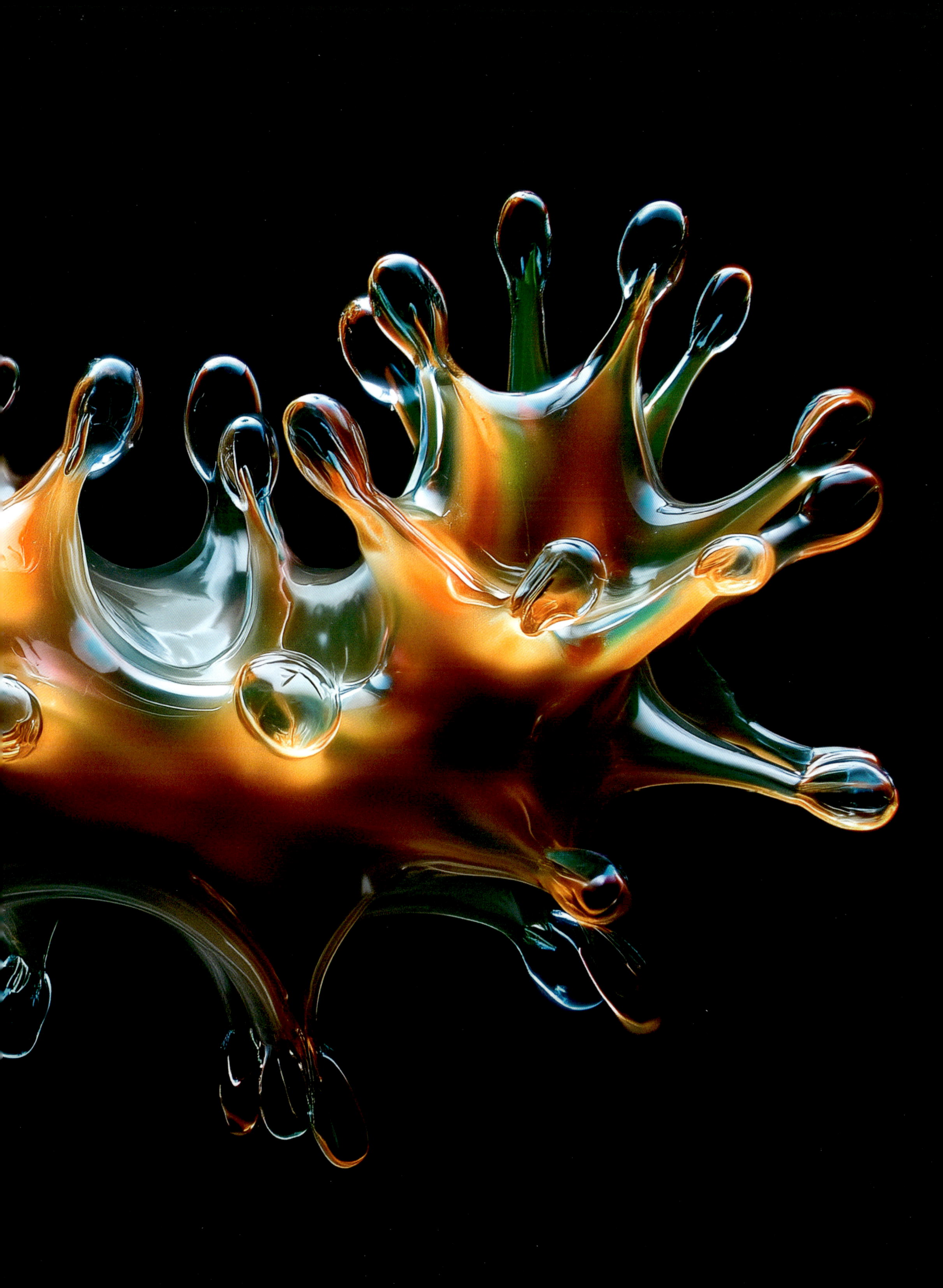

PROMPT_05

[A surreal photorealistic image of a single Vorticella-like protozoan, with a bell-shaped body and a long, spiraled stalk attaching it to an invisible surface. The bell surface is soft, membranous, slightly flared, and covered in fine, short cilia around its rim. The internal structure appears suspended and layered. The overall form floats in black like an alien flower. --chaos 15 --ar 16:9 --raw]

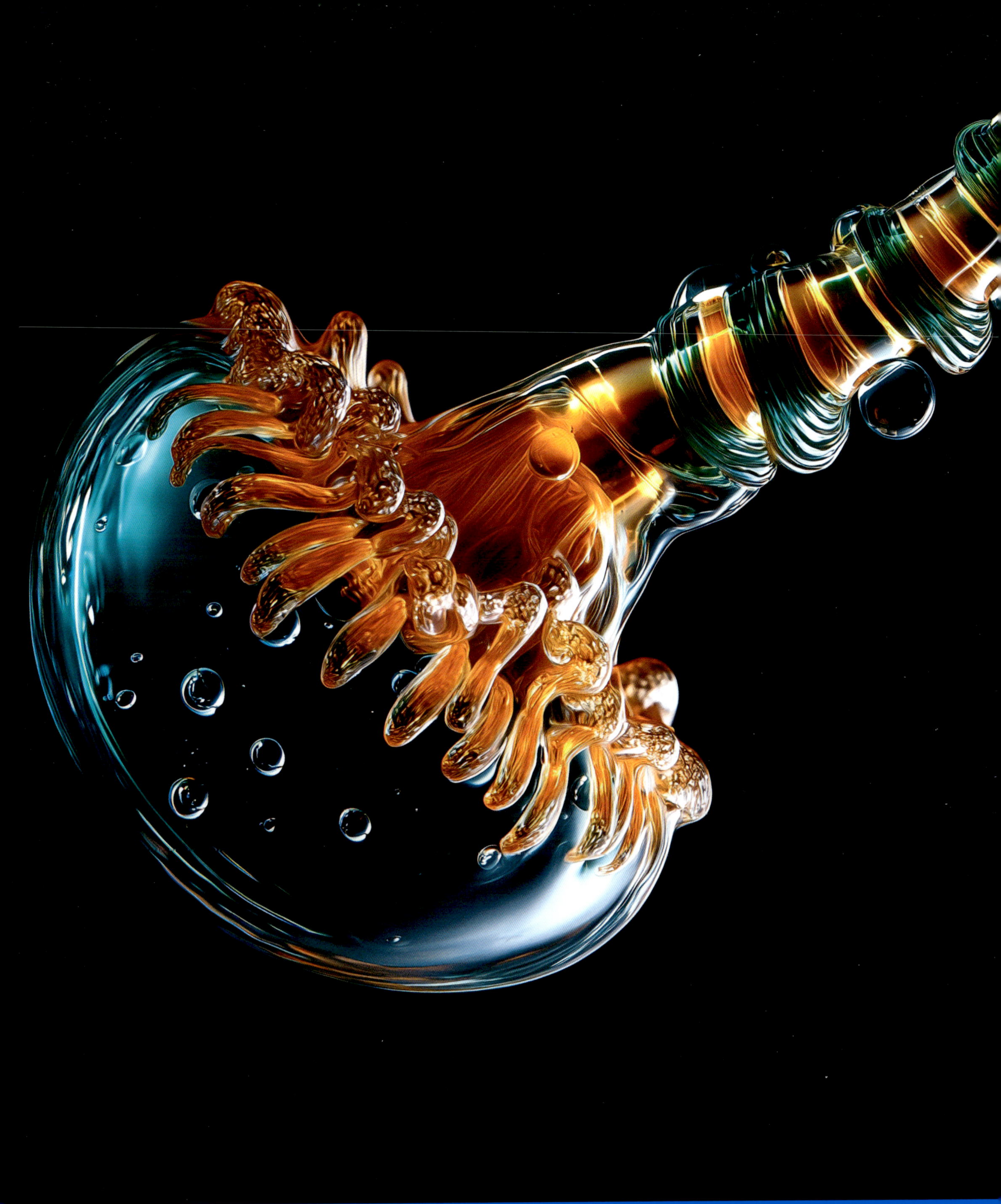

IMG_05

First printed in September 2025
by ABC Tipografia, Calenzano, Italy